STORY AND DISCOURSE

Narrative Structure in Fiction and Film

by SEYMOUR CHATMAN

Cornell University Press

ITHACA AND LONDON

First published 1978 by Cornell University Press.
Published in the United Kingdom by Cornell University Press Ltd., 2-4 Brook Street, London W1Y 1AA.

Second printing 1980
First printing, Cornell Paperbacks, 1980

Printed in the United States of America

Acknowledgment is made for:

Excerpts from *Nausea* by Jean-Paul Sartre, translated by Lloyd Alexander, copyright © 1964 by New Directions Publishing Corporation. All rights reserved. First published in Great Britain in 1962 by Hamish Hamilton Ltd. Reprinted by permission of New Directions Publishing Corporation and Hamish Hamilton Ltd.

Excerpts from *Lolita* by Vladimir Nabokov, copyright © 1955 by Vladimir Nabokov; reprinted by permission of G. P. Putnam's Sons and Weidenfeld & Nicolson.

A selection from *The Seance and Other Stories* by Isaac Bashevis Singer, copyright © 1965, 1968 by Isaac Bashevis Singer; reprinted with the permission of Farrar, Straus & Giroux, Inc., and Jonathan Cape Ltd.

Excerpts from *Mrs. Dalloway* by Virginia Woolf, copyright 1925 by Harcourt Brace Jovanovich, Inc.; renewed 1953 by Leonard Woolf. First published 1925 by The Hogarth Press. Reprinted by permission of the publishers.

Excerpts from "The Garden of Forking Paths" from *Fictions* by Jorge Luis Borges, translated by Anthony Kerrigan; copyright © 1962 by Grove Press, Inc.; © 1956 by Emece Editores, S.A., Buenos Aires; reprinted by permission of Grove Press, Inc., and Weidenfeld & Nicolson.

Excerpts from *Two Novels: Jealousy* by Alain Robbe-Grillet, translated by Richard Howard; copyright © 1959 by Grove Press, Inc.; reprinted by permission of Grove Press, Inc., and John Calder Ltd.

Excerpt from *The Four Gated City* by Doris Lessing, copyright © 1969 by Doris Lessing Productions Ltd; reprinted by permission of Alfred A. Knopf, Inc., and James Brown Associates.

Excerpt from "The Idol of the Cyclades" from *End of the Game and Other Stories* by Julio Cortàzar, translated by Paul Blackburn; copyright © 1967 by Random House, Inc.; reprinted by permission of Pantheon Books, a division of Random House, Inc.

Library of Congress Cataloging in Publication Data
(For library cataloging purposes only)

Chatman, Seymour Benjamin, 1928–
    Story and discourse.

    Includes bibliographical references and index.
    1. Arts.   2. Narration (Rhetoric)   I. Title.
NX650.N37C45   700'.1   78-9329
ISBN 0-8014-1131-9 (cloth)
ISBN 0-8014-9186-X (pbk.)

Burgess

NX
650
. N37
C 45

copy 3

For Elaine

CONTENTS

PREFACE

The French—with their new-found etymological enthusiasm —have coined the word *narratologie*, the study of narrative structure. The Anglo-American intellectual community is suspicious of free-swinging uses of *-ology*, perhaps with justification. The questionability of the name, however, should not be confused with the legitimacy of the topic. There are few books in English on the subject of narrative in general, though libraries bulge with studies of specific genres—novels, epics, short stories, tales, fabliaux, and so on. Beyond the analysis of generic differences there lies the determination of what narrative is *in itself*. Literary critics tend to think too exclusively of the verbal medium, even though they consume stories daily through films, comic strips, paintings, sculptures, dance movements, and music. Common to these artifacts must be some substratum; otherwise we could not explain the transformation of "Sleeping Beauty" into a movie, a ballet, a mime show.

To me the most exciting approach to these questions is dualist and structuralist, in the Aristotelian tradition. Following such French structuralists as Roland Barthes, Tzvetan Todorov, and Gérard Genette, I posit a *what* and a *way*. The what of narrative I call its "story"; the way I call its "discourse." Chapter 1 contains a brief statement of my argument and its presuppositions. Chapters 2 and 3 focus on the components of "story," events and existents (character and setting); Chapters 4 and 5 deal with "discourse," the means through which the story is transmitted. My arrangement is arbitrary only to the extent that I could reverse the two major groups, starting with discourse and ending with story. I prefer the present arrangement because it seems better to reflect the history of theorizing about narratives. (Not that I wish to engage that topic in any direct way; I shall introduce historical considerations only minimally, as background to the argument.) But much as I might like to, I cannot offer the reader the popular option of choosing his chapters, reading

backward, or whatever. The theory—for what it is worth—must be read as a whole for any of the parts to be meaningful.

Theory is difficult to read, as it is to write; it is exacting, obdurate, yawn-inducing. I have done my best to make it lively, to keep the distinctions provocative and not fussy, and above all, to validate and demonstrate its practicality by quoting examples wherever possible. Sometimes in the genesis of the book, the example came first and crystallized the distinction. Art has saved me (if it saves me) by gracing as well as documenting the pronouncements that the theory of theory suggests. It is pleasanter to read about the ins and outs of indirect free style when academic prose is mixed with dollops of Joseph Conrad. Indeed, I have had to eliminate many delightful and hard-sought examples to keep the book within buyable and readable limits.

The questions of balance and scope have been paramount, and I must justify presenting just this much theory and no more. My primary concern has been to work out, as clearly as I could, the ramifications of the story-discourse dichotomy and to explain those insights, by myself and others, which it has prompted. So I have excluded many narrative topics that have interested literary scholars—invention, mimesis, the historical development of genres, the relations of narratives to other aspects of literature, to anthropology, philosophy, linguistics, and psychology. One cannot include in a single volume every interesting issue that impinges upon narrative, and it is perhaps better not even to mention them than to mention them only, without integrating them into the central discussion. I propose a reasonable and modern answer to the question "What is a narrative?" That is, "Which are its necessary and which its ancillary components, and how do they interrelate?" But I do not wish (nor am I able) to account for everything that can be found in narratives. In particular I am concerned with form, rather than content, or with content when it is expressible as a form. My primary object is *narrative* form rather than the form of the surface of narratives—verbal nuance, graphic design, balletic movements. "Style" in this sense, the properties of the tex-

ture of the medium, is fascinating, and those who have read my work know that I have spent many hours on it. Here, however, I am concerned with stylistic details only insofar as they participate in or reveal the broader, more abstract narrative movements.

I have focused particularly on issues in narrative structure that seem to me salient, controversial, or difficult. Terms like "point of view," "stream of consciousness," "narrative voice," "third person narration" are frequently abused in critical discussion. In clarifying terminology, in making critical concepts as viable yet as consistent as possible, I hope to account for troublesome cases, avant-garde stories, *cas limites*. I am more concerned to achieve a theory accommodating a wide range of narrative texts than to garner a compendium of accepted opinions. I welcome counterexamples from engaged readers. I touch on many questions but dwell on those that are problematic, especially where redefinition seems called for. These are contributions to a theory of the narrative, not the theory itself.

Since theory is metacriticism, I unashamedly quote from the writings of critics and theorists, hence the sizable blocks from Wayne Booth, Mikhail Bakhtin, Barthes, Genette, Todorov. My purpose is not to polemicize, but to synthesize the most powerful insights—Anglo-American, Russian, and French. I argue for no particular school. It is the practice—I am tempted to say the behavior—of theorists and critics that interests me, as much as that of makers and audiences.

A final remark about one particular story so frequently cited as to suggest that I have some vested interest in it, James Joyce's "Eveline." I have, indeed, something of a love affair with the story: it was the object of my first venture into narrative theory, an overly detailed application of Roland Barthes's 1966 techniques. But my continued interest in "Eveline" is more than sentimental. By following the history of my encounters with the story, I have uncovered some analytical layers of theoretical interest that probably would not have occurred to me with fresh material. Furthermore, by comparing that original article with the present book the nonreader of French will find a reason-

able parallel to similar developments among the *narratologistes*. In all cases the translations are my own, unless otherwise indicated.

I should like to acknowledge the kind criticism and advice of Zelda and Julian Boyd, Eric Rabkin, Jonathan Culler, Bernhard Kendler, Barbara Herrnstein Smith, Susan Suleiman, and Thomas Sloane. Although they have not read the present manuscript, I've learned much from Robert Alter, Robert Bell, Christine Brooke-Rose, Alain Cohen, Umberto Eco, Paolo Fabbri, Marilyn Fabe, Stanley Fish, Gérard Genette, Stephen Heath, Brian Henderson, Frederic Jameson, Ronald Levaco, Samuel Levin, Louis Marin, Christian Metz, Bruce Morrissette, Ralph Rader, Alain Robbe-Grillet, Robert Scholes, Tzvetan Todorov, and the participants in the 1977 Summer Institute in Aesthetics, Boulder, Colorado, and the 1977 School of Criticism, Irvine, California. The work of Roland Barthes has been a special inspiration to me.

I am grateful to the Committee on Research of the University of California, Berkeley, for financial support during the writing of this book. Judith Bloch and Margaret Ganahl helped me in invaluable ways in the preparation of the manuscript.

My thanks to the editors and publishers who have granted me permission to use previously published material. Portions of Chapter 2 appeared as "Genette's Analysis of Time Relations" in *L'Esprit Créateur*, 14 (1974); of Chapter 1 as "Towards a Theory of Narrative" in *New Literary History*, 6 (1975); of Chapter 4 as "Narration and Point of View in Fiction and the Cinema," in *Poetica*, 1 (1974). Portions of Chapter 5 are reprinted from "The Structure of Narrative Transmission" in Roger Fowler, editor, *Style and Structure in Literature: Essays in the New Stylistics*, copyright © Basil Blackwell 1975, used by permission of Cornell University Press and Basil Blackwell.

SEYMOUR CHATMAN

Berkeley, California

STORY AND DISCOURSE

Narrative Structure
in Fiction and Film

1 INTRODUCTION

'Begin at the beginning,' the King said,
gravely, 'and go on till you come to
the end: then stop.'

Lewis Carroll,
Alice in Wonderland

When you coin a term, it ought to mark
a real species, and a specific difference;
otherwise you get empty, frivolous
verbiage.

Aristotle,
The Rhetoric

Among the many pressing needs of literary theory—poetics in the broad sense—is a reasoned account of the structure of narrative, the elements of storytelling, their combination and articulation. The task is delineated by Aristotle, but delineated only; the *Poetics* opens more questions than it answers. There is a distinguished tradition of Anglo-American studies on narrative: Henry James, Percy Lubbock, Wayne Booth. Less known in this country but of great importance is a flood of recent work from Russia and France.

The Russian formalist tradition, especially the work of Vladimir Propp, emphasized simple narratives: folk tales,[1] myths, *romans policiers*. But modern narrative fiction entails additional complexities of structure. The rigid homogeneity of plot and simplicity of characterization found in the Russian fairy tale are obviously not typical of many modern narratives. Still, much can be learned from these investigations, particularly about the theory of plot and the necessity of separating narrative structure

1. See *Morfologia Skazi* (Leningrad, 1928), translated by Laurence Scott as *The Morphology of the Folktale*, 2d ed. (Austin, 1970). A summary of Propp's analysis appears in the article "Les Transformations des contes fantastiques," *Théorie de la littérature*, ed. Tzvetan Todorov (Paris, 1966), pp. 234–262; and also Claude Bremond, "Le message narratif," *Communications*, 4 (1964), 4–10.

from any of its mere manifestations, linguistic or otherwise. Certain disadvantages must also be considered, particularly classificatory reductivism. On balance, what constitutes a viable and modern narrative theory?[2]

2. The largest selection of Russian Formalist writings is a recent German translation entitled *Texte der Russischen Formalisten*, ed. Juri Striedter (Munich, 1969), in two volumes. A French translation of a smaller selection has been made by Tzvetan Todorov, under the title *Théorie de la littérature* (Paris, 1966), which contains important articles by Eichenbaum, Shklovsky, Jakobson, Vinogradov, Tynianov, Brik, and Propp, as well as a reminiscent preface by Jakobson and introductory essay by Todorov. A still smaller selection is in *Russian Formalist Criticism*, ed. Lee Lemon and Marion Reis (Lincoln, Neb., 1965). See also L. Matejka and K. Pormorska, eds., *Readings in Russian Poetics* (Cambridge, Mass., 1971), and L. Matejka and I. Titunik, eds., *Semiotics of Art: Prague School Contributions* (Cambridge, Mass., 1976).

The relevant works of the French Structuralists are now numerous; the following is only a selection: Claude Lévi-Strauss, "La structure et la forme," in the Italian translation of Propp, *Morphologia della fiaba*, ed. Gian Bravo (Turin, 1966); Lévi-Strauss, *Anthropologie structurale* (Paris, 1958); Claude Bremond, "Le Message narratif," *Communications*, 4 (1964), 4–32, and "La Logique des possibles narratifs," *Communications*, 8 (1966), 60–76, both included in Bremond, *Logique du récit* (Paris, 1973); Roland Barthes, "Introduction à l'analyse structurale des récits," *Communications*, 8 (1966), 1–27, English translation by Lionel Duisit appeared in *New Literary History* (1975), 237–272; A.-J. Greimas, *Sémantique structurale* (Paris, 1966); Gérard Genette, "Frontières du récit," *Communications*, 7 (1966), 152–163, and in particular "Discours du récit," in *Figures* III (Paris, 1972), 67–282 (to be published in an English translation by Cornell University Press), which has had a great influence on my own work; Tzvetan Todorov, "Les Catégories du récit littéraire," *Communications*, 8 (1966), 125–151, included in *Littérature et signification* (Paris, 1967), "Poétique," in Oswald Ducrot, ed., *Qu'est-ce que le structuralisme?* (Paris, 1968), pp. 99–166, "Structural Analysis of Narrative," *Novel*, 3 (Fall 1969), 70–76, and *Grammaire du Décameron* (The Hague, 1970); Christian Metz, "Remarques pour une phénoménologie du narratif," in his *Essais sur la signification au cinéma*, I (Paris, 1968), 25–35, now in English, *Film Language*, trans. Michael Taylor (New York, 1974), pp. 16–30; and Roland Barthes, *S/Z*, now in English, trans. Richard Miller (New York, 1974).

In Germany and Holland a school of semiologists approaches narrative analysis from the point of view of "text grammar," attempting to extend the procedures of modern linguistics beyond the sentence to larger units of discourse. See Teun Van Dijk, *Some Aspects of Text Grammars* (The Hague, 1972), which contains an extremely rich bibliography, and his journal, *Poetics*.

In America, two books have appeared reviewing these developments, one by Robert Scholes, *Structuralism in Literature: An Introduction* (New Haven, 1974), and Jonathan Culler, *Structuralist Poetics* (Ithaca, N.Y., 1975). Gerald Prince has attempted a formalization of "stories" along Chomskian lines in *A Grammar of Stories* (The Hague, 1973). For my earlier thinking on the subject, see "New Ways of Narrative Analysis," *Language and Style*, 2 (1968), 3–36, and "The Structure of Fiction," *University Review*, 37 (1971), 199–214.

To begin, let me sketch the general conception of literature and of art in terms of which the present theory is conceived.

Narrative and Poetics

Formalists and structuralists argue that it is not the literary text itself that is the subject of poetics but rather—to use Roman Jakobson's phrase—its "literariness." The question for poetics (unlike literary criticism) is not "What makes *Macbeth* great?" but rather "What makes it a tragedy?" A statement by Tzvetan Todorov sums up the position very well:

> Literary theory [poetics, *poétique*] is . . . distinct, as is any science, from the description of literary works. For to describe is to try to obtain, on the basis of certain theoretical premises, a rationalized representation of the object of study, while to present a scientific work is to discuss and transform the theoretical premises themselves, after having experienced the object described. Description is, in literature, a reasoned resumé; it must be done in such a way that the principal traits of the object are not omitted and indeed emerge even more evidently. Description is paraphrase that exhibits (rather than conceals) the logical principle of its own organization. Any work is, in this sense, its own best possible description: entirely immanent and exhaustive. If we cannot satisfy ourselves with description it is because our principles differ too much.
>
> We have seen develop in our own time more and more perfected techniques for describing the literary work. All the constitutive and pertinent elements of a poem, for example, will be identified: then their relative disposition, and finally a new presentation of the same poem, a presentation that allows us to penetrate more deeply into its meaning. But description of a work can never lead us to modify our premises; it can only illustrate them.
>
> The procedure of the literary theorist ["poetician"] is quite different. If he analyzes a poem, it is not to illustrate his premises (or, if he does, he does so only once, and then for instructional reasons), but to draw from this analysis conclusions that complete or modify the underlying premises; in other words, the object of literary theory is not works but literary discourse, and literary theory will take its place beside the other sciences of discourse which will have to be established for each of the kinds. . . .
>
> Literary theory cannot avoid literature on the way to its own proper discursive goal; and at the same time it is only in going beyond the concrete work that it can reach that goal.[3]

3. *Littérature et signification*, p. 7.

On this view literary theory is the study of the nature of literature. It is not concerned with the evaluation or description of any particular literary work for its own sake. It is not literary criticism but the study of the *givens* of criticism, the nature of literary objects and their parts. It is, as René Wellek and Austin Warren point out, an "organon of methods."[4]

Like modern linguistics, literary theory might well consider a rationalist and deductive approach rather than the usual empiricist one. It should assume that definitions are to be made, not discovered, that the deduction of literary concepts is more testable and hence more persuasive than their induction. Poetics should construct "a theory of the structure and functioning of literary discourse, a theory which presents a set [*tableau*] of possible literary objects, such that existing literary works appear as particular realized cases."[5] Aristotle provides a precedent; the *Poetics* is nothing less than a theory of the properties of a certain type of literary discourse. Northrop Frye is outspokenly deductive in *Anatomy of Criticism*. We need not expect actual works to be pure examples of our categories. The categories plot the abstract network upon which individual works find their place. No individual work is a perfect specimen of a genre—novel or comic epic or whatever. All works are more or less mixed in generic character.

To put it another way, genres are constructs or composites of features. The novel and the drama, for example, require features like plot and character, which are not essential to the lyric poem; but all three may utilize the feature of figurative language. Further, works ordinarily mix features in different dosages: both *Pride and Prejudice* and *Mrs. Dalloway* contain examples of indirect free style, but the dosage in *Mrs. Dalloway* is much larger, making it a qualitatively different kind of novel. We should not be disconcerted by the fact that texts are inevitably mixed; in that respect they resemble most organic objects. It is their general tendencies that form the subject of rational inquiry.

Narrative theory has no critical axe to grind. Its objective

4. *Theory of Literature*, 3d ed. (Harmondsworth, England, 1963), p. 19.
5. Todorov, "Poétique," p. 103.

is a grid of possibilities, through the establishment of the minimal narrative constitutive features. It plots individual texts on the grid and asks whether their accommodation requires adjustments of the grid. It does not assert that authors should or should not do so-and-so. Rather, it poses a question: What can we say about the way structures like narrative organize themselves? That question raises subsidiary ones: What are the ways in which we recognize the presence or absence of a narrator? What is plot? Character? Setting? Point of view?

Elements of a Narrative Theory

Taking poetics as a rationalist discipline, we may ask, as does the linguist about language: What are the necessary components —and only those—of a narrative? Structuralist theory argues that each narrative has two parts: a story (*histoire*), the content or chain of events (actions, happenings), plus what may be called the existents (characters, items of setting); and a discourse (*discours*), that is, the expression, the means by which the content is communicated. In simple terms, the story is the *what* in a narrative that is depicted, discourse the *how*. The following diagram suggests itself:

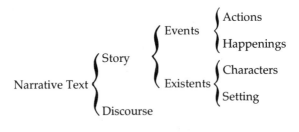

This kind of distinction has of course been recognized since the *Poetics*. For Aristotle, the imitation of actions in the real world, *praxis*, was seen as forming an argument, *logos*, from which were selected (and possibly rearranged) the units that formed the plot, *mythos*.

The Russian formalists, too, made the distinction, but used only two terms: the "fable" (*fabula*), or basic story stuff, the sum total of events to be related in the narrative, and, conversely,

the 'plot' (*sjužet*), the story as actually told by linking the events together.[6] To formalists, fable is "the set of events tied together which are communicated to us in the course of the work," or "what has in effect happened"; plot is "how the reader becomes aware of what happened," that is, basically, the "order of the appearance (of the events) in the work itself,"[7] whether normal (abc), flashed-back (acb), or begun *in medias res* (bc).

French structuralists also incorporate these distinctions. Claude Bremond argues that there exists a

. . . layer of autonomous significance, endowed with a structure that can be isolated from the whole of the message: the story [*récit*]. So any sort of narrative message (not only folk tales), regardless of the process of expression which it uses, manifests the same level in the same way. It is only independent of the techniques that bear it along. It may be transposed from one to another medium without losing its essential properties: the subject of a story may serve as argument for a ballet, that of a novel can be transposed to stage or screen, one can recount in words a film to someone who has not seen it. These are words we read, images we see, gestures we decipher, but through them, it is a story that we follow; and this can be the same story. That which is narrated [*raconté*] has its own proper significant elements, its story-elements [*racontants*]: these are neither words, nor images, nor gestures, but the events, situations, and behaviors signified by the words, images, and gestures.[8]

This transposability of the story is the strongest reason for arguing that narratives are indeed structures independent of any medium. But what *is* a structure, and why are we so ready to classify the narrative as being one? In the best short introduction to the subject, Jean Piaget shows how disciplines as various as mathematics, social anthropology, philosophy, linguistics, and physics have utilized the conception of structure, and how in each case, three key notions have been invoked: wholeness,

6. Victor Erlich, *Russian Formalism: History, Doctrine*, 2d ed. (The Hague, 1965), 240–241.

7. Boris Tomashevsky, *Teorija literatury (Poetika)* (Leningrad, 1925). The relevant section, "Thématique," appears in Todorov, ed., *Théorie de la littérature*, pp. 263–307 and in Lemon and Reis, eds., *Russian Formalist Criticism*, pp. 61–98. The quotations here translate the French text in Todorov, ed., p. 268. The distinction between *fabula* and *sjužet* appears on page 68 of Lemon and Reis.

8. "Le message narratif," p. 4.

transformation, and self-regulation. Any group of objects without these characteristic properties is merely an aggregate, not a structure. Let us examine narratives in terms of the three properties to see whether they are in fact structures.

Clearly a narrative is a whole because it is constituted of elements—events and existents—that differ from what they constitute. Events and existents are single and discrete, but the narrative is a sequential composite. Further, events in the narrative (as opposed to the chance compilation) tend to be related or mutually entailing. If we were to extract randomly from cocktail chatter a set of events that happened at different times and different places to different persons, we would clearly not have a narrative (unless we insisted upon inferring one—a possibility I will discuss below). The events in a true narrative, on the other hand, "come on the scene as already ordered," in Piaget's phrase. Unlike a random agglomerate of events, they manifest a discernible organization.

Second, narratives entail both transformation and self-regulation. Self-regulation means that the structure maintains and closes itself, in Piaget's words, that "transformations inherent in a structure never lead beyond the system but always engender elements that belong to it and preserve its laws. . . . In adding or subtracting any two whole numbers, another whole number is obtained, and one which satisfies the laws of the 'additive group' of whole numbers. It is in this sense that a structure is 'closed.'"[9] The process by which a narrative event is expressed is its "transformation" (as in linguistics an element in the "deep structure" must be "transformed" in order to occur in the surface representation). However this transformation takes place—whether, for example, the author elects to order the reporting of events according to their causal sequence or to reverse them in a flashback effect—only certain possibilities can occur. Further, the narrative will not admit events or other kinds of phenomena that do not "belong to it and preserve its laws." Of course certain events or existents that are not *immedi-*

9. Jean Piaget, *Structuralism*, trans. Chaninah Maschler (New York, 1970), p. 14.

ately relevant may be brought in. But at some point their relevance must emerge, otherwise we object that the narrative is "ill-formed."

So the evidence for calling narratives "structures" seems strong enough, even in the rigorous sense of the structuralists. So far we have spoken only of the story component of narratives. Narrative discourse, the "how," in turn divides into two subcomponents, the narrative form itself—the structure of narrative transmission—and its manifestation—its appearance in a specific materializing medium, verbal, cinematic, balletic, musical, pantomimic, or whatever. Narrative transmission concerns the relation of time of story to time of the recounting of story, the source or authority for the story: narrative voice, "point of view," and the like. Naturally, the medium influences the transmission, but it is important for theory to distinguish the two.

Is Narrative a Semiotic Structure?

Narrative is a structure: we may go on to ask if it is independently meaningful, that is, conveys a meaning in and of itself, separately from the story it tells. Linguistics and semiotics, the general science of signs, teach us that a simple distinction between expression and content is insufficient to capture all elements of the communicative situation. Crosscutting this distinction, there is that between substance and form. The following diagram is familiar to everyone who has read Ferdinand de Saussure and Louis Hjelmslev:

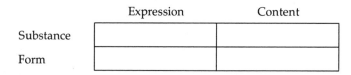

	Expression	Content
Substance		
Form		

Units of the expression plane convey meanings, that is, units of the content plane. In languages, the substance of expression is the material nature of the linguistic elements, for example, the actual sounds made by voices, or marks on paper. The sub-

stance of content (or "meaning") is, on the other hand, "the whole mass of thoughts and emotions common to mankind independently of the language they speak." [10] Now each language (reflecting its culture) divides up these mental experiences in different ways. Hence the *form* of the content is "the abstract structure of relationships which a particular language imposes . . . on the same underlying substance." [11] The vocal apparatus is capable of an immense variety of sounds, but each language selects a relatively small number through which to express its meanings. English, for example, makes a three-way distinction between high-front vowel sounds, as in *beat*, *bit*, and *bait*, whereas most other European languages have only two units within the same phonic range; in French, for instance, there are the vowels in *qui* and *quai*, but nothing between. So linguists distinguish the *substance* of (phonic) expression, the myriad audible sounds utilized by a given language, from the *form* of expression, the small set of discrete phonemes or range of phonic oppositions characteristic of it.

If narrative structure is indeed semiotic—that is, communicates meaning in its own right, over and above the paraphraseable contents of its story—it should be explicable in terms of the quadripartite array above. It should contain (1) a form and substance of expression, and (2) a form and substance of content.

What in narrative is the province of expression? Precisely the narrative discourse. Story is the content of the narrative expression, while discourse is the form of that expression. We must distinguish between the discourse and its material mani-

---

10. John Lyons, *Introduction to Theoretical Linguistics* (Cambridge, 1969), p. 56.
11. Ibid., p. 55. John Lyons' example: the English word "brother-in-law" can be translated into Russian as *zjatj*, *shurin*, *svojak*, or *deverj*; "and . . . *zjatj* must sometimes be translated as *son-in-law*. From this it should not be concluded, however, that the word *zjatj* has two meanings, and that in one of its meanings it is equivalent to the other three. All four words in Russian have a different meaning. It so happens that Russian brings together (under *zjatj*) both sister's husband and daughter's husband, but distinguishes wife's brother (*shurin*), wife's sister's husband (*svojak*) and husband's brother (*deverj*). So there is really no word which means 'brother-in-law' in Russian, just as there is no word which means 'zjatj' in English."

festation—in words, drawings, or whatever. The latter is clearly the *substance* of narrative expression, even where the manifestation is independently a semiotic code. But commonly codes serve other codes as substance; for instance, Barthes has shown that in the world of fashion, the codes of clothing "enjoy the status of systems only in so far as they pass through the relay of language, which extracts their signifieds (in the forms of usages or reasons)." He concludes that "it is . . . difficult to conceive a system of images and objects whose *signifieds* can exist independently of language." [12] In precisely the same way, narratives are *langues* conveyed through the *paroles* of concrete verbal or other means of communication.

As for narrative content, it too has a substance and a form. The substance of events and existents is the whole universe, or, better, the set of possible objects, events, abstractions, and so on that can be "imitated" by an author (film director, etc.). Thus:

	Expression	Content
Substance	Media insofar as they can communicate stories. (Some media are semiotic systems in their own right.)	Representations of objects & actions in real & imagined worlds that can be imitated in a narrative medium, as filtered through the codes of the author's society.
Form	Narrative discourse (the structure of narrative transmission) consisting of elements shared by narratives in any medium whatsoever.	Narrative story components: events, existents, and their connections.

But what does it mean practically to say that narrative is a meaningful structure in its own right? The question is not "What

12. Roland Barthes, *Elements of Semiology*, trans. Annette Lavers and Colin Smith (Boston, 1967), p. 10.

does any given story mean?" but rather "What does narrative itself (or narrativizing a text) mean?" The *signifiés* or signifieds are exactly three—event, character, and detail of setting; the *signifiants* or signifiers are those elements in the narrative statement (whatever the medium) that can stand for one of these three, thus any kind of physical or mental action for the first, any person (or, indeed, any entity that can be personalized) for the second, and any evocation of place for the third. We are justified, I believe, in arguing that narrative structure imparts meanings, of the three kinds listed above, precisely because it can endow an otherwise meaningless ur-text with eventhood, characterhood, and settinghood, in a normal one-to-one standing-for relationship. There are animated cartoons in which a completely contentless object is endowed with characterhood, that is, takes on the meaning "character" because it engages in a suitably anthropomorphic action (that is, a movement on the screen that is conceived as an instance of human movement). An example is the film by Chuck Jones called *The Dot and the Line*, whose plot runs roughly as follows: a line courts a dot, but the dot is going around with a squiggle, a sort of hip jokester. Whatever we think of the dot and the line as geometric familiars, the squiggle is surely without meaning until it moves. That is, as a drawn object projected on the screen, no one would identify it as anything but a random assemblage of swirling lines. In context, however, in its visible movement-relations with the dot and the line, it becomes a character. (It is true that a narrator tells the story through voice-over, but the story would be comprehensible even if seen without the sound track.)

This book is essentially about the form of narrative rather than its substance, but substance will be discussed where it seems to facilitate an understanding of narrative form. For instance it is clear that verbal narratives express narrative contents of time summary more easily than do cinematic narratives, while the latter more easily show spatial relations. A purely gratuitous visual link may tie together two shots (the line of the roof-support in Charles Foster Kane's childhood home in *Citizen Kane* "turns into" a string wrapping a Christmas package given him by his coldhearted guardian; the sweep of the curve of a Holly-

wood starlet's body on top of St. Peter's in *La Dolce Vita* "turns into" the sweep of a saxophone braying in an outdoor nightclub).

The above considerations prompt a redrawing of our first diagram:

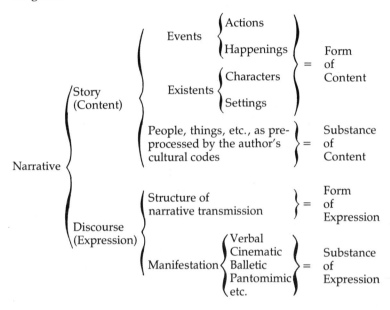

Manifestation and Physical Object

Story, discourse, and manifestation must further be distinguished from the mere physical disposition of narratives—the actual print in books, movements of actors or dancers or marionettes, lines on paper or canvas, or whatever.

This issue is resolved by phenomenological aesthetics, particularly by Roman Ingarden, who has established the fundamental difference between the "real object" presented to us in museums, libraries, the theater, and so on, and the "aesthetic object." [13] The real object is the thing in the outside world—the

13. Roman Ingarden, "Aesthetic Experience and Aesthetic Object," in Nathaniel Lawrence and Daniel O'Conner, eds., *Readings in Existential Phenomenology* (Englewood Cliffs, N.J., 1967), 304.

piece of marble, the canvas with pigment dried on it, the air-waves vibrating at certain frequencies, the pile of printed pages sewn together in a binding. The aesthetic object, on the other hand, is that which comes into existence when the observer experiences the real object aesthetically. Thus it is a construction (or reconstruction) in the observer's mind. Aesthetic objects may exist in the absence of a real object. One can have an aesthetic experience through purely fictitious objects; for example, we may "only imagine the 'letters' or the corresponding sound, e.g., when we are repeating a poem from memory." Thus the material book (or whatever) is not "a literary work, but only a means to 'fix' the work, or rather to make it accessible to the reader." To a certain point, the physical condition of a book (or other artifact) does not affect the nature of the aesthetic object fixed by it: *David Copperfield* remains *David Copperfield* whether it is read in an elegant library edition or a dirty, water-stained paperback version. Further, *mere* reading is not an aesthetic experience, just as merely looking at a statue is not one. They are simply preliminary to the aesthetic experience. The perceiver must at some point mentally construct the "field" or "world" of the aesthetic object.

The aesthetic object of a narrative is the story as articulated by the discourse, what Susanne Langer would call the "virtual" object of the narrative.[14] A medium—language, music, stone, paint and canvas, or whatever—actualizes the narrative, makes it into a real object, a book, a musical composition (vibrating sound waves in an auditorium or on a disc), a statue, a painting: but the reader must unearth the virtual narrative by penetrating its medial surface. (See the discussion below of "reading" versus "reading out.")

Narrative Inference, Selection, and Coherence

If discourse is the class of all expressions of story, in whatever medium possible to it (natural language, ballet, "program" music, comic strips, mime, and so on), it must be an abstract class, containing only those features that are common to all

14. Susanne Langer, *Feeling and Form* (New York, 1953), p. 48, and *passim*. The section on narrative is on pages 260–265.

actually manifested narratives. The principal features are order and selection. The first I have already spoken of; the second is the capacity of any discourse to choose which events and objects actually to state and which only to imply. For example, in the "complete" account, never given in all its detail, the "ultimate argument," or *logos*, each character obviously must first be born. But the discourse need not mention his birth, may elect to take up his history at the age of ten or twenty-five or fifty or whenever suits its purpose. Thus *story* in one sense is the continuum of events presupposing the total set of all conceivable details, that is, those that can be projected by the normal laws of the physical universe. In practice, of course, it is only that continuum and that set actually inferred by a reader, and there is room for difference in interpretation.

A narrative is a communication; hence, it presupposes two parties, a sender and a receiver. Each party entails three different personages. On the sending end are the real author, the implied author, and the narrator (if any); on the receiving end, the real audience (listener, reader, viewer), the implied audience, and the narratee. (These distinctions will be amplified in Chapter 4.)

The sense modality in which narrative operates may be either visual or auditory or both. In the visual category are nonverbal narratives (painting, sculpture, ballet, pure or "unbubbled" comic strips, mime, etc.), plus written texts. In the auditory category are bardic chants, musical narratives, radio plays, and other oral performances. But this distinction conceals an important commonality between written and oral texts. All written texts are realizable orally; they are not being performed but could be at any moment. That is, they are innately susceptible of performance.

Whether the narrative is experienced through a performance or through a text, the members of the audience must respond with an interpretation: they cannot avoid participating in the transaction. They must fill in gaps with essential or likely events, traits and objects which for various reasons have gone unmentioned. If in one sentence we are told that John got

dressed and in the next that he rushed to an airport ticket counter, we surmise that in the interval occurred a number of artistically inessential yet logically necessary events: grabbing his suitcase, walking from the bedroom to the living room and out the front door, then to his car or to the bus or to a taxi, opening the door of the car, getting in, and so on. The audience's capacity to supply plausible details is virtually limitless, as is a geometer's to conceive of an infinity of fractional spaces between two points. Not, of course, that we do so in normal reading. We are speaking only of a logical property of narratives: that they evoke a world of potential plot details, many of which go unmentioned but can be supplied. The same is true of character. We may project any number of additional details about characters on the basis of what is expressly said. If a girl is portrayed as "blue-eyed," "blonde," and "graceful," we assume further that her skin is fair and unblemished, that she speaks with a gentle voice, that her feet are relatively small, and so on. (The facts may be other, but we have to be told so, and our inferential capacity remains undaunted. Indeed, we go on to infer a variety of details to account for the "discrepancy.")

Thus there is a special sense in which narratives may be said to select. In nonnarrative paintings, selection means the separation of one portion from the rest of the universe. A painter or photographer will frame *this* much imitated nature, and the rest is left beyond the frame. Within that frame the number of details explicitly presented is a stylistic, rather than a general structural question. A Dutch still life painter may include an exact reproduction of minutiae in the set-up before him, down to the smallest dewdrop on a peach, while an Impressionist may dash off a distant pedestrian with a single brush stroke. But a narrative, as the product of a fixed number of statements, can never be totally "complete," in the way that a photographic reproduction is, since the number of plausible intermediate actions or properties is virtually infinite. In a highly realistic painting, what is shown is determined by what was visible to the painter, and that is a function of his distance from the depicted scene. Scale, then, controls the number of details. But narratives are not re-

stricted by spatial scale and undergo no such control: a visual narrative, a comic strip or movie, can move from close to long shot and return with no effort. And there is a virtually infinite continuum of imaginable details between the incidents, which will not ordinarily be expressed, but which *could* be. The author selects those events he feels are sufficient to elicit the necessary sense of continuum. Normally, the audience is content to accept the main lines and to fill in the interstices with knowledge it has acquired through ordinary living and art experience.

So far we have considered gaps common to all narratives regardless of medium. But there is also a class of indeterminacies—phenomenologists call them *Unbestimmtheiten*—that arise from the peculiar nature of the medium. The medium may specialize in certain narrative effects and not others. For instance, the cinema can easily—and does routinely—present characters without expressing the contents of their minds. It is usually necessary to infer their thinking from what they overtly say and do. Verbal narrative, on the other hand, finds such a restriction difficult—even Ernest Hemingway, at such pains to avoid directly stating his characters' thoughts and perceptions, sometimes "slips." Conversely, verbal narrative may elect not to present some visual aspect, say, a character's clothes. It remains totally *unbestimmt* about them, or describes them in a general way: "He was dressed in street clothes." The cinema, however, cannot avoid a rather precise representation of visual detail. It cannot "say," simply, "A man came into the room." He must be dressed in a certain way. In other words clothing, *unbestimmt* in verbal narrative, must be *bestimmt* in a film.

Another restriction on selection and inference is *coherence*. Narrative existents must remain the same from one event to the next. If they do not, some explanation (covert or overt) must occur. If we have a story like "Peter fell ill. Peter died. Peter was buried," we assume that it is the same Peter in each case. In E. M. Forster's example, "The king died, and then the queen died of grief," we assume that the queen was in fact the wife of that king. If not, there would have to be some explanation of the queen's death, for example, "Though she did not know him,

she died of the grief she felt for the decay of royal houses." Some principle of coherence must operate, some sense that the identity of existents is fixed and continuing. Whether or not the events must also be causally linked is not so clear.

The drawing of narrative inferences by the reader is a low-level kind of interpretation. Perhaps it doesn't even deserve the name, since "interpretation" is so well established as a synonym for "exegesis" in literary criticism. This narrative filling-in is all too easily forgotten or assumed to be of no interest, a mere reflex action of the reading mind. But to neglect it is a critical mistake, for this kind of inference-drawing differs radically from that required by lyric, expository, and other genres.

A Sketch of Narrative Structure

Narrative discourse consists of a connected sequence of narrative *statements*, where "statement" is quite independent of the particular expressive medium. It includes dance statement, linguistic statement, graphic statement, and so on. (The nature of the connection will be taken up in detail in Chapter 2.) "Narrative statement" and "to state narratively" are used here as technical terms for any expression of a narrative element viewed independently of its manifesting substance. The term has a broad discursive sense, not a grammatical one. For example, a narrative statement may be manifested by questions or commands as well as by declarative constructions in natural language.

Narratives are communications, thus easily envisaged as the movement of arrows from left to right, from author to audience. But we must distinguish between real and implied authors and audiences: only implied authors and audiences are immanent to the work, constructs of the narrative-transaction-as-text. The real author and audience of course communicate, but only through their implied counterparts. What is communicated is *story*, the formal content element of narrative; and it is communicated by *discourse*, the formal expression element. The discourse is said to "state" the story, and these statements are of two kinds—*process* and *stasis*—according to whether someone

did something or something happened; or whether something simply existed in the story. Process statements are in the mode of DO or HAPPEN, not as actual words in English or any natural language (these form the substance of the expression), but as more abstract expressional categories. Both the English sentence "He stabbed himself" and a mime's plunging an imaginary dagger into his heart manifest the same narrative process statement. Stasis statements are in the mode of IS. A text that consisted entirely of stasis statements, that is, stated only the existence of a set of things, could only imply a narrative. *Events* are either logically essential, or not ("kernels" versus "satellites"). Further, they are either *acts* or *actions*, in which an existent is the agent of the event, or *happenings*, where the existent is the patient. An existent, in turn, is either a *character* or an element of *setting*, a distinction based on whether or not it performs a plot-significant action. A stasis statement may communicate either or both of two aspects: the identity of an existent or one of its qualities, for example, traits (see Chapter 3).

A process statement may be said either to *recount* or to *enact* an event according to whether or not it is explicitly presented, that is, uttered as such by a narrator. These distinctions were already noted by the ancients. The difference between narration proper, the recounting of an event (the subject of Chapter 5), and enactment, its unmediated presentation (the subject of Chapter 4), corresponds to the classical distinction between *diegesis* and *mimesis* (in Plato's sense of the word), or, in modern terms, between *telling* and *showing*. Dialogue, of course, is the preeminent enactment. The contrast between narration proper and enactment is demonstrated in the two basic forms for depicting a character's speech—indirect versus direct: "John said that he was tired" versus "'I'm tired' [said John]." The first necessarily entails a person telling what John said, while the second simply has John saying something—in the audience's presence, so to speak.

Correspondingly, a stasis statement is either unmediated, that is, it *exposes*, or mediated, that is, it *presents*. This is the difference between "John was angry" and "Unfortunately, John was angry." Crosscutting this distinction is that of aspect: the

stasis statement may either *identify* ("John was a clerk") or *qualify* ("John was angry").

Further, events may imply or *index* existents; and, vice versa, existents may *project* events. For example, "John seduced Mary" indexes "there is a character named John" and "John is a seducer"; while "John is a loser" projects "John has lost many times and will continue to do so." Finally, one event may imply another, one existent another: "John murdered Mary" implies either "He was later caught" or "He escaped justice"; "John is a murderer" implies "He is not a very pleasant fellow."

"John left" or "John was tall" are as close as narrative can come to stage imitation, an actor walking into the wings or the choice of a tall rather than short actor. So it seems reasonable to call the narrative statements of such actions and presentations "unnarrated." But "John left, unfortunately" or "John was tall, unfortunately" necessarily presuppose a speaker who has taken it upon himself to judge what is and what is not unfortunate. They are clearly interpretive statements, and interpretation implies a narrator.

In the strict sense, of course, all statements are "mediated," since they are composed by someone. Even dialogue has to be invented by an author. But it is quite clear (well established in theory and criticism) that we must distinguish between the narrator, or speaker, the one currently "telling" the story, and the author, the ultimate designer of the fable, who also decides, for example, whether to have a narrator, and if so, how prominent he should be. It is a fundamental convention to ignore the author, but not the narrator. The narrator may be overt—a real character (Conrad's Marlow) or an intrusive outside party (the narrator of *Tom Jones*). Or he may be "absent," as in some of Hemingway's or Dorothy Parker's stories containing only dialogue and uncommented-upon action. The "narrator," when he appears, is a demonstrable, recognizable entity immanent to the narrative itself. Every narrative, even one wholly "shown" or unmediated, finally has an author, the one who devised it. But "narrator" should not be used in that sense. Rather it should mean only the someone—person or presence—actually telling the story to an audience, no matter how minimally evoked his

voice or the audience's listening ear. A narrative that does not give the sense of this presence, one that has gone to noticeable lengths to efface it, may reasonably be called "nonnarrated" or "unnarrated." (The seeming paradox is only terminological. It is merely short for "a narrative that is not explicitly told" or "that avoids the appearance of being told.") Thus there is no reason for positing some third category of narrative (like "dramatic" or "objective" or the like) since that is essentially "'nonnarrated' narrative."

It might seem that a discussion of existents is superfluous or at least secondary to a minimal narrative theory. But one cannot account for events without recognizing the existence of things causing or being affected by those events. At the level of discourse, no statement of an event can be made, in any medium, that does not include a subject. It is true, of course, that the narrative may have very little or even no overt description; but a narrative without an agent performing actions is impossible. A minimal kind of description is thereby entailed; for example, if we are told (or shown) absolutely nothing more about someone than that he loves a woman, we have at least the implicit description "He is a lover" (the character has been "indexed" by one process statement).

By way of example, let us consider a narrative in pictures, rather than words, partly to underline the generality of narrative components (they can occur in media other than natural language), and partly because the rest of this book will cite only verbal or cinematic examples. Picture narratives have, of course, been common for centuries, as the Bayeux Tapestry and paintings like Benozzo Gozzoli's *Dance of Salome and the Beheading of John the Baptist* attest. In its simplest form, the picture narrative represents the events in a clear sequence, say left to right, on the analogy of western alphabets. But the order might be different: in Gozzoli's painting, for example, Salome dances for Herod in the rightmost section of the painting, and a later event —a soldier holding the sword over John's head—occurs in the leftmost portion. It is in the middle that the final event occurs, Salome presenting the head to her mother.

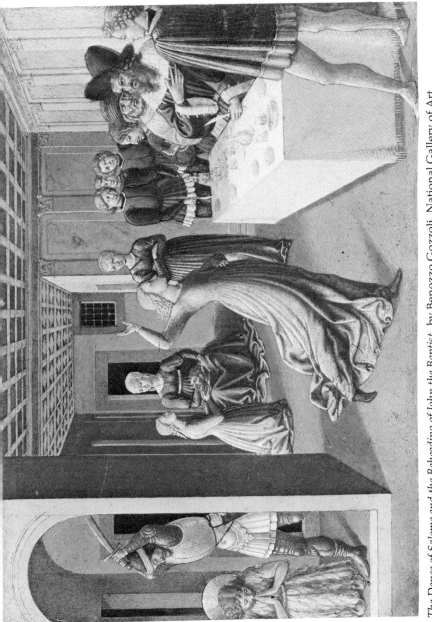

The Dance of Salome and the Beheading of John the Baptist, by Benozzo Gozzoli, National Gallery of Art, Washington, D.C., Samuel H. Kress Collection.

Short Ribs, by Frank O'Neal. Reprinted by permission of Newspaper Enterprise Association.

A Comic Strip Example

Picture narratives can be divided up into frames, the technique of the modern comic strip. Comic strips without dialogue, captions, or balloons are relatively pure (if banal) examples of narrative in picture form and as such conveniently illustrate my diagram of the narrative situation.

The comic strip I have chosen appeared in 1970 in the Sunday supplement of the San Francisco *Chronicle*. For convenience of discussion I have labeled the ten frames 0 through IX (0 containing introductory or "front" matter). With the exception of the bubble in I and the signs in IV, VI, and VII, there are no words in this narrative. Even those words could have been replaced by visual indications to distinguish the casino from the pawn shop. The traditional three balls could have been used for the one and perhaps a pair of dice for the other. But as it stands, the medium is mixed: we must distinguish (1) drawing, either representational or stylized-conventional, from two uses of words: (2) dialogue (in the comic-strip convention of the "bubble") and (3) legend (the signs identifying the two buildings).

The story might be verbalized as follows: *There once was a king. Standing on the tower of his castle, he saw something "that looked like fun" through his binoculars. He rushed downstairs and out of the castle and soon arrived at the Royal Casino. He played dice and lost. Leaving dejectedly, he happened upon the Royal Loan Company. A crafty thought came to him. He pawned his crown for a bundle of money so that he could go back to the Royal Casino to gamble some more.*

These are abstract narrative statements, hence I have italicized them. This English-language version is not at all the story per se; it is but one more (and poorer) manifestational representation of it. Story, in my technical sense of the word, exists only at an abstract level; any manifestation already entails the selection and arrangement performed by the discourse as actualized by a given medium. There is no privileged manifestation.

Further, though the above is, I think, a reasonably complete depiction of "what happens" in the story, it cites only some among an infinity of possible events. For example, the very existence of the king presupposes the event of his birth, his royalty

presupposes the existence of a father (or some ancestor) who was a king, the event of his coronation, and so on. These are essential (if trivial) to an understanding of the actual story. Even in this simple narrative, important events are left to the reader's inference. The crucial event—the loss at the dice table—occurs in the space between frame V and frame VI (just as the murder occurs in a "hole" in the plot of Robbe-Grillet's *Le Voyeur*). The cartoonist could have shown a croupier taking the money away from the king, but he elected not to, leaving the burden of inference to the reader. We infer the central event from existents, the dejected appearance of the king in frame VI, at odds with his animation in II and IV, his arms now hanging slackly down his body, and his mouth drawn downward. In other words, in terms of the diagram, the stasis statement *The king is dejected* has projected the event of his gambling loss.

Let us now consider a few of the abstract narrative statements in this story.

From frame 0, we conclude that *There is a king* (an unmediated stasis statement exposes (identifies) a character, manifested by a simple representational drawing, especially the pronged crown and the ermine collar and cuffs); *The king is excited* (stasis statement exposes a trait of the character, manifested by a conventional schema, the curved lines over the eyes to suggest movement); and *The king is looking through binoculars* (process statement enacts an action, manifested by representational drawing). These events are in the story. The discourse is primarily unmediated, that is, there is no audible or visible narrator. However, there is an important discursive feature communicated by the fact that what the king sees through binoculars has been intentionally deleted from this frame. Hence we are also unable to see it. It is clear that we are being invited to share the king's point of view or perspective, in what filmmakers would call an offscreen "eye-line match." (For "point of view," see Chapter 4.) Later, especially beginning with frame IV, we are looking objectively *at* the king, not *with* him; the point of view shifts.

From frame I we read out such narrative statements as *It is a sunny day; The king is on his tower; He thinks to himself* . . . (mani-

fested by conventional schema, namely, dialogue bubble with visual "thought" attachment, that is, disconnected bubbles of decreasing size); . . . *"that looks like fun"* (manifested by the king's thought, in printed words); and *There is a building below and to the right.*

Certain additional inferences can be made. We assume that it is a sunny day from the appearance of the elliptical (red) object. That it is not more perfectly round is a bit confusing until, putting it together with the anachronistic binoculars (and, later, the crazy tilt of the tower), we make some such inference as "These events are taking place in a zany world." That it is the king's tower is self-evident from common knowledge about kings, through what Barthes calls the Referential or Gnomic or Cultural Code.[15] The verbal statement "That looks like fun" explains the excited interest of the raised eyebrows of frame 0, and both are confirmed by the raised lines of the mouth in frame I to show a smile of eager interest. We are still associated with the king's point of view, but it is not yet clear what the object of his attention is. Since he is looking in the direction of the building, either the "fun" is there or it is still somewhere beyond the frame.

In frame II, we have *There is a bird sitting in a window of the tower; The king runs . . . down the stairs* (expressed as a moment when both feet are off the ground); . . . *rapidly* . . . (manifested by the conventional notation of a cloud of dust behind him and the curved "motion-lines" above his head).

Frame III has *The king runs towards the building that "looks like fun"* (using the conventional schema of puffs of dust again to mean "speed"). That it is the building associated with "fun" is inferred from the fact that no other building is visible and that it resembles the one in frame I. In frame IV, *The king is about to enter the Royal Casino* (natural-language used as legend on sign). We infer that the Royal Casino is the place that "looked like fun" since it is the goal (directionally) toward which the king has aspired since the first frame. *The king is eager to have fun* (from the smile on his face).

15. *S/Z*, trans. Richard Miller, p. 18: "made in a collective and anonymous voice originating in traditional human experience."

In frame V, *The king shoots crap* (conventional devices for showing two kinds of motion imparted to the dice). We infer that the king did in fact enter the Royal Casino between frames IV and V from cultural knowledge that throwing dice is customarily done in casinos. The act is shown in a visual synecdoche ("close-up" in cinematic language); only the royal hand and cuff are visible as they throw the dice.

Frame VI has *The king leaving slowly* (both feet are on the ground); *The king is dejected* (the downward cast of the mouth and the arms straight at the side). We infer, again "gnomically," that the king has lost all the money he had with him. A prior event is inferred from the stasis statement of an existent. In frame VII, *The king stumbles upon the Royal Loan Company* (curved lines to show the "double take"; legend in natural language to identify the loan company).

In frame VIII, *The king has a thought*, though strictly speaking, this is an inference drawn from a stasis statement like *The king looks pensive* (his pensiveness is read out of the hand placed over the mouth); *The king looks crafty* (conveyed by a gesture, the "devilish" angle of the eyebrows from which we infer, by metonymy, 'The king's thought is wicked'; thus, one stasis statement is inferred from another stasis statement). Frame IX shows *The king leaving the Royal Loan Company with a bag of money* (symbolic device as legend); . . . *without his crown* . . . (the absence of a previously represented prop), from which we infer that the king has pawned his crown; and *The king is on his way back to the casino*, from which we infer . . . *to gamble some more*.

Having read out the story, we are disposed to interpret the king's character, that he is silly or the like, at least that he holds his royalty in light regard. Thus we infer a character trait from the whole action, that is, the set of events has indexed the king's character. We need not end our interpretation there, of course. We might conclude that the whole of the king's performance is an exercise in futility, since, if "Royal" means what it says, he owns both the casino and the loan company. He is the only human figure in the entire narrative; the whole kingdom is his alone, and he seems its only inhabitant. He loses money to him-

self and then pawns his crown for more of his own money so that he can lose again. To himself. But then we were warned that his is a zany world. Those who feel prompted to search deeper interpretive mines—say Freudian or Marxist—are welcome to do so.[16]

"Reading" and "Reading Out"

Though this chapter has treated story as an object, I do not mean to suggest that it is a hypostatized object, separate from the process by which it emerges in the consciousness of a "reader" (using that term to include not only readers in their armchairs, but also audiences at movie houses, ballets, puppet shows, and so on). I have attempted to demonstrate the process by which one reads the relevant narrative features out of or through one sort of nonverbal manifestation, namely the comic strip. This kind of "reading out" is qualitatively different from ordinary reading, though so familiar as to seem totally "natural." But the conventions are there and are crucial, even if patently self-evident and self-instructional—the arbitrary figures, like the frame, the puffs of smoke to indicate speed, and the bubbles for dialogue or thinking are effortlessly learned by very small children. But that they are conventions is clear enough. From the surface or manifestation level of reading, one works through to the deeper narrative level. That is the process I call, technically, *reading out*. Reading out is thus an "interlevel" term, while mere "reading" is "intralevel." I am trying to avoid technical vocabulary wherever possible, but this seems a neces-

16. A learned reader comes to quite another interpretation of this comic strip. Noting that it makes "a big difference" that the *Royal* Casino is simply marked "Casino" in the sign in the final frame, he feels that despite the "Royal," the king does not own the casino or loan company at all. If he did, "a) he wouldn't need the loan company and b) they wouldn't require his crown as collateral. The world of *Short Ribs* is set initially by the king looking excitedly through his binoculars. It's a modern world, then, with advanced technology in which the king is isolated . . . in his tower. He hopes for an improvement in his state of affairs and descends to a world that *seems* to be his. But it isn't, we learn. The kernel of truth here applies to all of us and doesn't require (though it would support) a Marxian or other socioeconomic interpretation." The strip has elicited other profound interpretations from students and colleagues. Clearly hermeneutics has found a glorious new medium to munch on, along with Sunday pancakes.

sary distinction, and reading out a relatively transparent term for "decoding from surface to deep narrative structures." Narrative translation from one medium to another is possible because roughly the same set of events and existents can be read out.

Obviously this book is more concerned with reading narratives out than with simply reading their surfaces. I do not minimize the problems entailed in surface reading, itself a profoundly cultural and by no means "natural" process. Witness the reports of anthropologists that aborigines have difficulty in even seeing what are, to us, "self-evident" video and cinematic images. But it is at the "reading-out" level that occur the problems of the elementary literature class, where students understand the meaning of every sentence in isolation, but cannot make any sense (or any satisfying sense) out of the whole narrative text.

Let us now turn to a more detailed examination of story, considering first the event-dimension or plot.

2 STORY: CONTENT

Events

DISCOURSE

What the devil does the plot signify,
except to bring in fine things?
    The Duke of Buckingham,
        The Rehearsal

The events of a story are traditionally said to constitute an array called "plot." Aristotle defined plot (*mythos*) as the "arrangement of incidents." Structuralist narrative theory argues that the arrangement is precisely the operation performed by discourse. The events in a story are turned into a plot by its discourse, the modus of presentation. The discourse can be manifested in various media, but it has an internal structure qualitatively different from any one of its possible manifestations. That is, plot, story-as-discoursed, exists at a more general level than any particular objectification, any given movie, novel or whatever. Its order of presentation need not be the same as that of the natural logic of the story. Its function is to emphasize or de-emphasize certain story-events, to interpret some and to leave others to inference, to show or to tell, to comment or to remain silent, to focus on this or that aspect of an event or character. The author "can arrange the incidents in a story in a great many ways. He can treat some in detail and barely mention or even omit others, as Sophocles omits everything that happened to Oedipus before the plague in Thebes. He can observe chronological sequence, he can distort it, he can use messengers or flashbacks, and so forth. Each arrangement produces a different plot, and a great many plots can be made from the same story."[1]

Consider the following mini-plot: (1) Peter fell ill. (2) He died. (3) He had no friends or relatives. (4) Only one person came to his funeral. (These are not meant to represent actual English

---

1. O. B. Hardison, Jr., "A Commentary on Aristotle's Poetics," *Aristotle's Poetics* (Englewood Cliffs, 1968), p. 123.

sentences, but rather units at the abstract level of "story"; thus a silent movie might express unit one by showing Peter fainting in the street, or lying in bed tossing to and fro.) Statements one, two, and four clearly depict events; they are what I have called "process statements." We can display them as dots on a horizontal dimension representing time:

Notice, however, that statement (3) is not of this kind: it is not in the chronological or, better, "chrono-logical" sequence (the hyphen indicating that we are not merely talking about time, but about the *logic* of time). Indeed, it is not a process statement of an event at all, not something that Peter or someone else did or something that happened, but rather a citation of one of his aspects or qualities, that is, a stasis statement of description. Description must be overtly expressed by language in literary narrative; but in theater or cinema, we simply witness the physical appearance of the actor playing Peter.

But what is an event, in the narrative sense? Events are either *actions* (*acts*) or *happenings*. Both are changes of state. An action is a change of state brought about by an agent or one that affects a patient. If the action is plot-significant, the agent or patient is called a character.[2] Thus the character is narrative—though not necessarily grammatical—subject of the narrative predicate. Our discussion is still at the abstract level of story, quite separate from any particular kind of manifestation. In the linguistic manifestation, at the level of actual English sentence, for example, the character need not be grammatical subject: "The diamonds

2. "Event" is called *motif* in Russian Formalist writings: see Boris Tomashevsky, in Tzvetan Todorov, ed., *Théorie de la littérature* (Paris, 1966), p. 269: "The fable [*fabula*] appears as the set of motives in their chronological succession, and from cause to effect; the subject [*sjužet*] appears as the set of these same motives, but according to the order which they respect in the work." For an excellent account of the distinction between the notions of "state" and "event," and between "happening-events" and "action-events," see Zelda and Julian Boyd, "To Lose the Name of Action: The Semantics of Action and Motion in Tennyson's Poetry," *PTL*, 2 (1977), 21–32. They also distinguish "acts" from "actions." The first are punctual and the second durative.

were stolen by the thief" or "The police were informed that some diamonds had been stolen." In the latter case the character does not even appear in the manifestation; his presence must be inferred.

The principal kinds of actions that a character or other existent can perform are nonverbal physical acts ("John ran down the street"), speeches ("John said, 'I'm hungry,'" or "John said that he was hungry"), thoughts (mental verbal articulations, like "John thought 'I must go'" or "John thought that he must go"), and feelings, perceptions, and sensations (which are not articulated in words—"John felt uneasy," or "John saw the car looming ahead"). Narrative theory may use these as primitive terms without prior definition (though speeches can perhaps be usefully analyzed in terms of the "illocutionary" or speech act philosophy: see Chapter 4).

A happening entails a predication of which the character or other focused existent is narrative object: for example, *The storm cast Peter adrift.* Here again, what is important to a general theory of narrative is not the precise linguistic manifestation but rather the story logic. Thus in "Peter tried to pull down the sails, but felt the mast give way and the boat caught up by an enormous wave," Peter is the subject of a series of actions at the surface, manifestational level. At the deeper story level he is narrative object, the affected not the effector.

Sequence, Contingency, Causality

It has been argued, since Aristotle, that events in narratives are radically correlative, enchaining, entailing. Their sequence, runs the traditional argument, is not simply linear but causative. The causation may be overt, that is, explicit, or covert, implicit.

Consider again E. M. Forster's example (slightly altered for present purposes). Forster argues that "The king died and then the queen died" is only a "story" (in the sense of a "mere chronicle"); "The king died and then the queen died of grief" is a "plot," because it adds causation. But the interesting thing is that our minds inveterately seek structure, and they will provide it if necessary. Unless otherwise instructed, readers will tend to assume that even "The king died and the queen died" presents

a causal link, that the king's death has something to do with the queen's. We do so in the same spirit in which we seek coherence in the visual field, that is, we are inherently disposed to turn raw sensation into perception. So one may argue that pure "chronicle" is difficult to achieve. "The king died and then the queen died" and "The king died and then the queen died of grief" differ narratively only in degrees of explicitness at the surface level; at the deeper structural level the causal element is present in both. The reader "understands" or supplies it; he infers that the king's death is the cause of the queen's. "Because" is inferred through ordinary presumptions about the world, including the purposive character of speech.

In classical narratives, events occur in distributions: they are linked to each other as cause to effect, effects in turn causing other effects, until the final effect. And even if two events seem not obviously interrelated, we infer that they may be, on some larger principle that we will discover later.

Aristotle and Aristotelian theorists explain causation on a probabilistic model. Paul Goodman, for example: "The relationship of being after parts already presented and leading to other parts we call 'probability,' as there is a probability that Macbeth will seek out the Witches again after the incidents, character, speeches and atmosphere presented in Acts I-III." Mere "being after parts" and its converse "being before parts," however, are obviously not sufficient to characterize probability; the important word is "leading," which implies causation. Goodman's axiom would perhaps better begin "The relationship of following (or ensuing) from parts already presented and leading to other parts. . . ." He goes on to say: "The formal analysis of a poem is largely the demonstration of a probability through all the parts. Or better, in the beginning anything is possible; in the middle things become probable; in the ending everything is necessary."³ This is an important insight: the working out of plot (or at least some plots) is a process of declining or narrowing possibility. The choices become more and more limited, and the final choice seems not a choice at all, but an inevitability.

3. Paul Goodman, *The Structure of Literature* (Chicago, 1954), p. 14.

Aristotle's discussion of the terms "beginning," "middle," and "end" apply to the narrative, to story-events as imitated, rather than to real actions themselves, simply because such terms are meaningless in the real world. No end, in reality, is ever final in the way "The End" of a novel or film is. Even death is not an end—biologically, historically, or in any sense that one takes the word. Such a term marks out plot, the story-as-discoursed. It is strictly an artifact of composition, not a function of raw story-material (whatever its source, real or invented).

Is the relation between sequence and causality one of necessity or of probability? Can there be mere sequence, a depiction of events that simply succeed one another but in no sense owe their existence to each other?

Certainly modern authors claim to reject or modify the notion of strict causality. The change in modern taste has been described by many critics.[4] But then what does hold these texts together? Jean Pouillon has proposed the term "contingency," which may indeed cover extreme modern cases.[5] Not in the sense of "uncertainty" or "accident" but rather the stricter philosophical sense, "depending for its existence, occurrence, character, etc. on something not yet certain" (*The American College Dictionary*). The idea of contingency is attractively broad, for it can accommodate new organizing principles, like Robbe-Grillet's accumulative descriptive repetition.

But whether or not a single term like "contingency" can capture the principle of organization of any narrative whatsoever, theory must recognize our powerful tendency to connect the most divergent events. That narrative experiment in which the reader shuffles his own story from a box of loose printed pages[6] depends upon the disposition of our minds to hook things together; not even fortuitous circumstance—the random juxtaposition of pages—will deter us.

A narrative without a plot is a logical impossibility. It is not that there is no plot, but rather that the plot is not an intricate

4. For example, A. A. Mendilow, *Time and the Novel* (New York, 1965), p. 48.
5. Jean Pouillon, *Temps et roman* (Paris, 1946), 26–27.
6. Marc Saporta, *Composition N. 1* (Paris, 1962).

puzzle, that its events are "of no great importance," that "nothing changes." In the traditional narrative of resolution, there is a sense of problem-solving, of things being worked out in some way, of a kind of ratiocinative or emotional teleology. Roland Barthes uses the term "hermeneutic" to describe this function, which "articulate[s] in various ways a question, its response and the variety of chance events which can either formulate the question or delay its answer."[7] "What will happen?" is the basic question. In the modern plot of revelation, however, the emphasis is elsewhere; the function of the discourse is not to answer that question nor even to pose it. Early on we gather that things will stay pretty much the same. It is not that events are resolved (happily or tragically), but rather that a state of affairs is revealed. Thus a strong sense of temporal order is more significant in resolved than in revealed plots. Development in the first instance is an unraveling; in the second, a displaying. Revelatory plots tend to be strongly character-oriented, concerned with the infinite detailing of existents, as events are reduced to a relatively minor, illustrative role. Whether Elizabeth Bennet marries is a crucial matter, but not whether Clarissa Dalloway spends her time shopping or writing letters or daydreaming, since any one of these or other actions would correctly reveal her character and plight.

Verisimilitude and Motivation

We began this chapter with a look at how events seem to interconnect to form a narrative—whether we name the principle "causality," "contingency," or something else. Clearly the propensity is a conventional one, and fundamental to any theory of narrative is an understanding of the nature of convention as such. Convention is equally involved in all the other topics in this chapter (and the rest of the book), from the relative importance of events to the decisions of analysts about how to characterize plot macrostructures. The convention of "filling in" by verisimilitude is singled out first for discussion because it is so basic to narrative coherence. Its discussion may serve

7. See Roland Barthes, *S/Z,* p. 17.

as a suggestive prototype for later discussions of other narrative conventions.

Audiences come to recognize and interpret conventions by "naturalizing" them[8] ("nature" as one half of the anthropological dichotomy *nature/culture* established by Lévi-Strauss). To naturalize a narrative convention means not only to understand it, but to "forget" its conventional character, to absorb it into the reading-out process, to incorporate it into one's interpretive net, giving to it no more thought than to the manifestational medium, say the English language or the frame of the proscenium stage.[9]

The notion of "naturalization" is very close to that of verisimilitude, the ancient appeal to the probable, rather than the actual. Structuralists have recovered this concept with zest, for it explains the technique by which the reader "fills in" gaps in the text, adjusts events and existents to a coherent whole, even when ordinary life expectations are called into question.

I have broached the subject in Chapter 1, but there is more to be said about it in the special context of plot. Why should a theory of narrative structure require a discussion of the naturalization of narrative events to facts and to probabilities in the real world? Because the well-formedness of a narrative (that is, what makes it a narrative, good or bad, and not some other kind of text) depends on such questions. What constitutes "reality" or "likelihood" is a strictly cultural phenomenon, though authors of narrative fiction make it "natural." But of course the "natural" changes from one society to another, and from one era to another in the same society. Pre–World War I and even contemporary Anglo-Saxon readers of *The Secret Agent* under-

8. I am indebted to the excellent summary of these matters by Jonathan Culler in *Structuralist Poetics* (Ithaca, N.Y., 1975), Chapter 7, "Convention and Naturalization," as well as the special issue on *Vraisemblance* in *Communications*, 11 (1968), edited by Todorov.

9. Some of the synonyms collected by Culler to explain the process: "to recuperate" (recover, put to use), "to motivate," in the Russian Formalist sense —"to justify by showing that the element is not arbitrary or incoherent but comprehensible," "to bring within the reader's ken," "to restore [the oddity] to a communicative function," "to assimilate," "to reduce the strangeness of the text," "to bridge the distance (and the difference, Derrida's *différance*)," "to situate," "to give a framework to, in terms of appropriate expectations."

stand the following characterization of a "revolutionist," even if they disagree with it: "The majority of revolutionists are the enemies of discipline and fatigue." To citizens of the Soviet Union or China, however, the view is not simply objectionable, but probably incomprehensible. Or to quote an example offered by Jonathan Culler: "when Madame de Lafayette writes of the Comte de Tende that upon learning that his wife was pregnant by another man, '. . . he thought everything that it was natural to think in such circumstances . . .', she displays the immense confidence in her readers that this mode of writing implies."[10] To read out verisimilarly, as Culler argues, is "to take up or construct a reference." But clearly the modern European or American reader cannot construct a self-evident reference to suit this case. Modern sexual mores being what they are, readers will not agree upon an appropriate response, nor even that a single response is possible. The sentence has little meaning in the verisimilitude of present-day life. Even though the sentence "means" clearly enough at the surface level, it can only be read out at a deeper narrative level through familiarity with seventeenth-century mores.

What is the basis of the artistically probable, the verisimilar? In his seminal study, Genette shows the basis in public opinion, the ideology of common sense, the Aristotelian commonplaces or *topoi*.[11] The notion is ultimately Platonic. Verisimilitude concerns not the accidentally real, but the essentially ideal: "'not what things were but what they should have been'" (l'Abbé d'Aubignac).[12]

According to the structuralists, the norm for verisimilitude is established by previous texts—not only actual discourses, but the "texts" of appropriate behavior in the society at large. Verisimilitude is an "effect of corpus" or of "intertextuality" (hence intersubjectivity). It is a form of explication, pointing from effect

10. *Structuralist Poetics*, p. 134.
11. "What would be called today an ideology, that is, a body of maxims and presuppositions which constitute at once a vision of the world and a system of values," Gérard Genette, "Vraisemblance et motivation," *Communications*, 11 (1968), 6.
12. Ibid.

to cause, and even reducible to a maxim. Further, because maxims are public, that is, "tend to go without saying," they may be implicit or backgrounded. When Jonathan Wild proposes to Miss Laetitia, he utters a speech "which, as the reader may easily suggest it to himself, I shall not here set down." Fielding assumes that the reader can predict the speech, in the silent way of traditional verisimilitude. What *else* would an eighteenth-century man say than "Dear Madam . . ."?

In classical narratives, overt explanation only becomes urgent for acts that are improbable by prevailing (public and generic) standards of behavior, but then it is *de rigueur*. It takes the form of narrative commentary I call "generalization." Some "general truth" is expounded that would account for the apparently eccentric phenomenon. I put the phrase in quotation marks, because the "truth" in such cases is curiously variable, even reversible, according to the point to be "proved." While young Wild gambles with the crooked Count, "his hands made frequent visits to the Count's pocket." Public opinion would assume that the victim should feel rage. In an American Western an instant shootout would result. But that was not Fielding's plan; he wanted to keep the Count around as Wild's "friend" and occasional collaborator. Hence recourse to a generalized explanation:

So far was this detection from causing any quarrel between these two prigs [thieves] that in reality it recommended them to each other, for a wise man, that is to say a rogue, considers a trick in life as a gamester doth a trick at play. It sets him on his guard, but he admires the dexterity of him who plays it.

Fielding obviously felt that the implied reader might be unable to provide his own explanatory maxim or would forget whether it went "There's honor among thieves" or "There's *no* honor among thieves." Whether the generalization is "true" or not is beside the point; what counts is that it provides an "explanation." After all, the only requirement is plausibility. Improbable actions are permissible as long as they are accounted for or "motivated" in some way. Hence general commentary served to normalize difficult moments in classical fiction. No matter how

ludicrous or arbitrary the explanation itself, the fact that it was proffered was enough to satisfy the need for decorous plausibility.

Such overt explanation was only needed for extreme cases, however. The norm was *unmotivated* verisimilitude. Most events needed no explanation since "everyone" (that is, all respectable readers) would understand straight off how such things could happen or be. But history—the explosive political and social events of the late eighteenth and nineteenth centuries—was to change that basis of common understanding, especially in France. The most realistic novelists became enigmatic, since history was enigmatic. The brutally arbitrary narrative grew increasingly popular through the nineteenth century. Julien Sorel attacks Mme. Rênal, and no explanation is given. Roderick Hudson's behavior is mysterious even to his best friend. And think of Raskolnikov.[13]

Changing attitudes toward the verisimilitude of actions is extremely evident in the fast-changing world of film. For example, simple locomotion: movies made twenty years ago may strike us as excessively preoccupied with showing how characters get from one place to another. A sequence in a minor film of 1956, *Patterns* (directed by Fielder Cook), presents a business executive brooding in a bar over the death of a colleague. His wife finds him, and he tells her he has decided to fling his resignation in the face of the corporation president responsible for his colleague's death. His wife insists on accompanying him. The director's logistic problem was simply to get the executive and his wife from the bar to the president's executive suite. By modern standards he would cut straight from the bar to the latter setup. Instead he introduced no less than five shots of inter-

13. But explanation continued in the middle or Balzacian type of narrative—"too original (too 'true') to be transparent to the public [in the sense that its plausibilities could remain presupposed], but still too timid, or too complacent to assume [the] opacity" of Stendhal, Dostoevsky, or James. Hence Balzac's all-too-frequent "pedagogic clauses which introduce with potent weight the explicatory expositions in the *Human Comedy*: 'Voici pourquoi . . .' 'Ceci veut une explication,' etc." (Genette, "Vraisemblance et motivation," p. 13).

vening events: (1) the executive and his wife exiting through the bar door; (2) the two of them getting into a station wagon, followed by what contemporary editors would consider a gratuitous fade-out to underline the lapse of time that it took to arrive at; (3) the skyscrapers of the financial district; (4) the executive suite; and (5) the hero bursting through the office door to encounter the president. Even accepting the suitability of a shot to underline the oppressive atmosphere of skyscraper and corporation decor of shots (3) and (4), shots (1) and (2) seem superfluous. They slow the action down unnecessarily and "insult our intelligence" by showing what we could easily figure out for ourselves. The director, however, in 1956, clearly thought that such a cutaway would have been "too extreme," "confusing," and so on—a common complaint of studio management since the days, forty years before, when D. W. Griffith began evolving the whole apparatus of screen punctuation.

Kernels and Satellites

Narrative events have not only a logic of connection, but a logic of *hierarchy*. Some are more important than others. In the classical narrative, only major events are part of the chain or armature of contingency. Minor events have a different structure. According to Barthes, each such major event—which I call *kernel*, translating his *noyau*—is part of the hermeneutic code; it advances the plot by raising and satisfying questions. Kernels are narrative moments that give rise to cruxes in the direction taken by events. They are nodes or hinges in the structure, branching points which force a movement into one of two (or more) possible paths. Achilles can give up his girl or refuse; Huck Finn can remain at home or set off down the river; Lambert Strether can advise Chad to remain in Paris or to return; Miss Emily can pay the taxes or send the collector packing; and so on. Kernels cannot be deleted without destroying the narrative logic. In the classical narrative text, proper interpretation of events at any given point is a function of the ability to follow these ongoing selections, to see later kernels as consequences of earlier.

A minor plot event—a *satellite*[14]—is not crucial in this sense. It can be deleted without disturbing the logic of the plot, though its omission will, of course, impoverish the narrative aesthetically. Satellites entail no choice, but are solely the workings-out of the choices made at the kernels. They necessarily imply the existence of kernels, but not vice versa. Their function is that of filling in, elaborating, completing the kernel; they form the flesh on the skeleton. The kernel-skeleton theoretically allows limitless elaboration. Any action can be subdivided into a myriad of parts, and those parts into subparts. Satellites need not occur in the immediate proximity of kernels, again because discourse is not equivalent to story. They may precede or follow the kernels, even at a distance. But since events and existents, story and discourse, operate at a deep structural level and independent of medium, one does not look for their precincts in the actual words (or images or whatever) of a given text. They can only be discussed in the analyst's metalanguage, which is a paraphrase (another manifestation) of the narrative.

A convenient diagram to illustrate the relations of kernels and satellites is the following:

begin

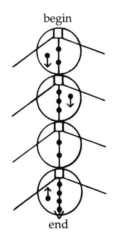

end

<hr />

14. This term translates the French structuralist *catalyse*. The English equivalent "catalyst" would suggest that the cause-and-effect enchainment could not occur *without* its supervention, but the satellite is always logically expendable.

The kernels are the squares at the top of each circle. The circle is the complete narrative block. Kernels are connected by a vertical line to indicate the main direction of the story-logic; oblique lines indicate possible but unfollowed narrative paths. Dots are satellites: those on the vertical lines follow the normal sequencing of the story; those outside the lines, with arrows attached, are anticipatory or retrospective of later or earlier kernels (depending upon which way the arrow points).

Such distinctions in structural narrative theory have been criticized as merely terminological and mechanical: it is said that they "add nothing, enhance no reading," at best "merely provide a cumbersome way of explaining what we all do, in the act of normal reading, with unconscious felicity."[15] But theory is not criticism. Its purpose is not to offer new or enhanced readings of works, but precisely to "explain what we all do in the act of normal reading, with unconscious felicity." Such an explanation is not to be despised. If it really *were* an explanation, it would be an important contribution to our understanding of narrative forms, and of texts in general. Noam Chomsky and other modern thinkers have shown us the vital importance of specifying what we "already know" at an intuitive level. Everyone "already knows" how to walk, but that does not embarrass the science of physiology. The distinction between the major hinge events and the minor supplementary ones in a narrative is a psychological reality that anyone can prove to himself. He can see how easily consensus is reached about which are the

---

Todorov's translation of Tomashevsky's term for kernel is *motif associé*, and for satellite *motif libre* (*Théorie de la littérature*, p. 270). I find the latter misleading since it is precisely the case that satellites depend upon kernels and are tied to them in important ways. Barthes abandons without explanation the *noyau-catalyse* distinction in *S/Z*, though such a distinction seems implicit in his manner of listing the events of "Sarrasine."

15. Frank Kermode, "Literature and Linguistics," *The Listener*, December 2, 1971, pp. 769–770. An answer is provided by Jonathan Culler, "The Linguistic Basis of Structuralism," in David Robey, ed., *Structuralism: An Introduction; Wolfson College Lectures 1972* (Oxford, 1973), who cites Barthes: "Distinguishing between a criticism which attempts to assign meanings to works, and a 'science' of literature or 'poetics,' he [Barthes] argues that the latter must be a study of the conditions of meaning" (p. 31). These conditions do not give an interpretation but describe the logic according to which interpretations are reached.

kernels and which the satellites of a given story. Whether these particular terms are cumbersome is beside the point; what is important is that the narrative elements exist, indeed are crucial to narrative theory. [16]

Stories and Antistories

One of the most interesting things about the above diagram of kernels is the way it highlights the difference between classical and one kind of modernist narrative. If the classical narrative is a network (or "enchainment") of kernels affording avenues of choice only one of which is possible, the *antistory* may be defined as an attack on this convention which treats all choices as equally valid.

Jorge Luis Borges has beautifully described and illustrated the logic of this kind of antistory in "The Garden of Forking Paths." The title refers to a novel of that name by a writer named Ts'ui Pên, whose method is described by a British sinologist to the narrator, a Chinese spy who is about to murder him. The sinologist says:

"My attention was caught by the sentence, 'I leave to various future times, but not to all, my garden of forking paths.' I had no sooner read this, than I understood. . . . The phrase 'to various future times, but

16. The question of how exactly one identifies and names the kernels, however, *is* a legitimate one. Some years ago, I tried to illustrate the process in an analysis of Joyce's "Eveline." Jonathan Culler, "Defining Narrative Units," in Roger Fowler, ed., *Style and Structure in Literature* (Ithaca, N.Y., 1975), p. 136, insightfully points out that my locating and labeling of kernels was not based on any identifiable procedure, and that my intuition could only have been (a) retrospective, and (b) based on cultural models that I had absorbed and brought to bear on the interpretation of texts. He observes: "it is when the reader begins to place actions in sequences, when he perceives teleologically organized structures, that he begins to grasp the plot. In the case of 'Eveline' we can say that the plot comes to take shape only when one retrospectively identifies the action of sitting by the window, reported in the opening sentence, as part of the process of musing or reflection that is [in turn] an essential component of the next sequence 'making a decision'. This constitutes the move from action to plot." In other words, I can only isolate and determine the appropriate name or *mot-clef* for the first kernel after I finish the entire narrative. Eveline's sitting at the window could have an entirely different function in another story. Until I *name* the sequence, I have not properly identified the kernel nor the boundaries of the sequence in which it is contained.

not to all' suggested the image of bifurcating in time, not in space. Re-reading the whole work confirmed this theory. In all fiction, when a man is faced with alternatives he chooses one at the expense of the others. In the almost unfathomable Ts'ui Pên, he chooses—simultaneously—all of them. He thus *creates* various futures, various times which start others that will in their turn branch out and bifurcate in other times. This is the cause of the contradictions in the novel.

Fang, let us say, has a secret. A stranger knocks at his door. Fang makes up his mind to kill him. Naturally there are various possible outcomes. Fang can kill the intruder, the intruder can kill Fang, both can be saved, both can die and so on and so on. In Ts'ui Pên's work, all the possible solutions occur, each one being the point of departure for other bifurcations. Sometimes the pathways of this labyrinth converge. For example, you come to this house; but in other possible pasts you are my enemy; in others my friend."[17]

In a genuine sense such texts may be called "antinarratives," since what they call into question is, precisely, narrative logic, that one thing leads to one and only one other, the second to a third and so on to the finale. But it is incorrect to say that they are without plot, for clearly they depend for their effect on the presupposition of the traditional narrative line of choice.[18]

The spectacular novels of Alain Robbe-Grillet exemplify another kind of antistory—or at least story-*manqué*. He does not deal in infinite options but has invented the intentional "failure" to mention crucial events. In *La Jalousie*, for example, the presence, indeed, the very existence of the narrator-character, the unnamed husband, is never stated. The syntax throughout is impersonal; the narrator is a *je-néant*, and his existence only dawns on us by surmise. But he *is* there: the narrative would be quite meaningless without him. Yet any reference to him, by noun or pronoun, is interdicted; so how to convey his actions, his simplest physical movements? They can only be projected

17. Translated by Anthony Kerrigan.
18. A reader observes: "'The Garden of the Forking Paths' refers not only to Ts'ui Pên's novel but *also* to itself and to the story it labels and to the landscape in the region of Yu Tsun's home and to Yu's private garden—and of course to Borges' story by that name." This is true: I only introduce this particular quotation because it so perfectly articulates the *theory* of infinite bifurcation, because Borges' story at this point itself offers so explicit a narrative-theoretical pronouncement.

by the naming of other existents. As long as he is in the presence of A . . . and Franck, his actions are relatively easy to guess. But when he leaves their sides, we can only infer what he does from stasis statements about the objects that he passes. For instance,

> One mouthful is enough to tell that this drink is not cold enough. Franck has still not answered one way or the other, though he has taken two already. Besides, only one bottle comes from the refrigerator: the soda whose greenish sides are coated with a faint film of dew where a hand with tapering fingers has left its print.
>
> The cognac is always kept in the sideboard. A . . . , who brings out the ice bucket at the same time as the glasses every day, has not done so today.
>
> "It's not worth bothering about," Franck says.
>
> To get to the pantry, the easiest way is to cross the house. Once across the threshhold, a sensation of coolness accompanies the half darkness. To the right, the office door is ajar.
>
> The light, rubber-soled shoes make no sound on the hallway tiles. The door turns on its hinges without squeaking. The office floor is tiled too. The three windows are closed and their blinds are only half-open, to keep the noonday heat out of the room. . . .
>
> Although the office—like the bedrooms and the bathroom—opens onto the hallway, the hallway itself ends at the dining room, with no door between. The table is set for three . . . A . . . has probably just had the boy add Franck's place, since she was not supposed to be expecting any guest for lunch today. . . .
>
> In the pantry the boy is already taking the ice cubes out of their trays. A pitcher full of water, set on the floor, has been used to heat the backs of the metal trays. He looks up and smiles broadly.[19]

As we go along in *La Jalousie*, we learn to read the narrator-protagonist's actions out of the actions of the other characters, particularly where these would be inexplicable if they were not somehow directed toward him, and particularly out of existence statements that are essential but only derivable from a change in the implied protagonist's physical position. How do we know that the protagonist goes for ice? From the long description of the discrete stages on the way to the pantry—of the coolness of the hall, the soundlessness of shoes over the hallway tiles, the view from the doorway of the office onto the patio, the

19. Translated by Richard Howard.

dining room with the table set for three, the pantry where the boy looks up and smiles, and so on. The order in which these descriptions occur is crucial: they project (in my technical sense) the movement of the protagonist to the kitchen and back to the veranda.

Suspense and Surprise

The distinction has long been made between suspense and surprise, and these terms are clearly related to the concepts of plot kernels and satellites. In a current dictionary of literary terms, we read the following definition of suspense:

> Uncertainty, often characterized by anxiety. Suspense is usually a curious mixture of pain and pleasure. . . . Most great art relies more heavily on suspense than on *surprise*. One can rarely reread works depending on surprise; the surprise gone, the interest is gone. Suspense is usually achieved in part by foreshadowing—hints of what is to come. . . . Suspense is . . . related to tragic irony. The tragic character moves closer and closer to his doom, and though he may be surprised by it, we are not; we are held by suspense. If, in fact, he is suddenly and unexpectedly saved (as is a hero of a melodrama), we may feel cheated.[20]

If, indeed, we are not surprised by the character's doom, how can we speak of "uncertainty?" At best, it must be a partial uncertainty: the end is certain, all that is uncertain is the means. (A parallel with bullfighting: the bull must finally die, but how he dies is the question.) So anxiety is not a reflex of uncertainty about the conclusion, since that is already foregone. It is rather that we know what is going to happen, but we cannot communicate that information to the characters, with whom we have come to empathize. In the words of a film director who has based his entire career on this effect:

> I've never used the whodunit technique, since it is concerned altogether with mystification, which diffuses and unfocuses suspense. It is possible to build up almost unbearable tension in a play or film in which the audience knows who the murderer is all the time, and from the very start they want to scream out to all the other characters in the

20. Sylvan Barnet, Morton Berman, and William Burto, *A Dictionary of Literary Terms* (Boston, 1960), 83–84.

plot, "Watch out for So-and-So! He's a killer!" There you have real tenseness and an irresistible desire to know what happens, instead of a group of characters deployed in a human chess problem. For that reason I believe in giving the audience all the facts as early as possible.[21]

The relation between "foreshadowing"—the semination of anticipatory satellites—and "giving the audience all the facts as early as possible" is interesting. Foreshadowing can also take the form of inferences drawn from existents, the kind of "projection" discussed above. But though suspense always entails a lesser or greater degree of foreshadowing, the reverse need not occur. Narratives may foreshadow in an unsuspenseful way. If no threat looms for the hero, the anticipatory satellite may result in a more "normal" event, an event of "due course." It would be a mistake to argue that all narrative progression depends on the principle of suspense.[22] A narrative may conceal how a character will react without being suspenseful. There are, clearly, *un*suspenseful narratives.

Suspense and surprise are complementary, not contradictory terms. The two can work together in narratives in complex ways: a chain of events may start out as a surprise, work into a pattern of suspense, and then end with a "twist," that is, the frustration of the expected result—another surprise. *Great Expectations* provides classic examples; its plot is a veritable network of suspense-surprise complexes. To add to the complexity, these operate at both the story and discourse levels. Let us follow one thread for a bit. The initial surprise is the shock that Pip receives when Magwitch grabs him unawares in the graveyard; this leads to the crescendo of suspense entailed in stealing the food and the file ("every board upon the way, and every crack in every board, calling after me, 'Stop thief!' and 'Get up, Mrs. Joe!'"). The suspense is partly relieved by their delivery to Magwitch. Pip need no longer fear for his heart and liver. But we experience a double suspense, that of the story, Pip's

21. Alfred Hitchcock, quoted in "Pete Martin Calls on Hitchcock," in Harry Geduld, ed., *Film Makers on Film Making* (Bloomington, 1971), p. 128. Kenneth Burke speaks briefly but insightfully about suspense, surprise, and disclosure in "Lexicon Rhetoricae," *Counterstatement* (New York, 1931), p. 145.

22. As Eric Rabkin seems to do in *Narrative Suspense* (Ann Arbor, 1973).

own fears, and that of the discourse, for we foresee trouble that Pip is not aware of. Pip takes whatever comes to hand, "some bread, some rind of cheese, about half a jar of mince-meat . . . some brandy from a stone bottle." A pork pie is singled out for special attention. The pie is for Christmas dinner, and we fear that Pip will be discomfited on new grounds. Our hunch proves correct: after the pudding, as Pip feels that "for the time at least [he] was saved," his sister suddenly says to Joe, "Clean plates—cold." Our feeling of suspense is now justi-fied, but to Pip the effect is surprise—as cold as his sister's plates. Thus, suspense in the discourse, surprise in the story. Pip's surprise turns into a suspense that he cannot bear: "I re-leased the leg of the table, and ran for my life." Only to be stopped by a new (story) surprise: soldiers at the door. At which point the chapter ends. The soldiers surprise *us* too, but for different reasons: we know (as of course does the narrator, the adult Pip, who avoids comment) that even if young Pip's theft had been discovered, it would not take a detachment of soldiers to set right. But why, then, are they there?

Further complexities arise. The suspenseful delivery of the food and the file is interrupted by a surprise—the man that Pip had taken to be Magwitch was in fact another escaped convict. Suspense now attaches to Magwitch's curiosity about the other fellow. Pip assumes simply that he is the "comrade" who would have cut out his heart and liver if Pip had not brought the food. But Pip is only a gullible youngster. The main communication is between Magwitch's reaction (depicted by Pip as adult nar-rator), and the narratee. Unlike young Pip, we get the point of Magwitch's grim joke about the young man. And our suspense about his identity begins.

This is only one of many complexes of surprise and suspense that operate at a local level. There is also the major or global complex—the mystery of Pip's Great Expectations. Here the narratee is expressly misled by the narrator Pip into accepting what the character Pip believed, namely that Miss Havisham was his benefactor, despite her announced charge to Estelle to "break his heart" and her remark to Joe that Pip is to "expect no other and no more" than the twenty-five pounds she pays

Joe for his indentures. But from the first announcement by Jaggers of his good fortune until Magwitch's visit and revelation of the secret, twenty-one chapters later, young Pip is convinced that it is Miss Havisham who has given him his new property. Not only does the adult Pip-as-narrator not comment, but there is the coincidence of Jaggers' double employment by Miss Havisham and Magwitch. And even a stronger, verbal coincidence. No more than a few days elapse between the moment when Jaggers says, "You are to understand, first, that it is the request of the person from whom I take my instructions, that you always bear the name of Pip," and the moment when Miss Havisham says:

". . . So you go tomorrow?"
"Yes, Miss Havisham."
"And you are adopted by a rich person?"
"Yes, Miss Havisham."
"Not named?"
"No, Miss Havisham."
"And Mr. Jaggers is made your guardian?"
"Yes, Miss Havisham."
". . . Goodbye, Pip!—you will always keep the name of Pip, you know."
"Yes, Miss Havisham."

Miss Havisham is merely making an observation, but under the circumstances, we, like Pip, interpret it as the command of a benefactor.

Time and Plot

There is reading-time and there is plot-time, or, as I prefer to distinguish them, discourse-time—the time it takes to peruse the discourse—and story-time, the duration of the purported events of the narrative.[23]

Several interesting theoretical questions are raised by the relations between the two. For example, how is the story anchored

23. Mendilow calls the former "chronological" time and the latter "pseudo-chronological" or "fictional" time (pp. 65–71). The handy German distinction *Erzählzeit* and *erzählte Zeit* comes from Gunther Muller, "Erzählzeit und erzählte Zeit" in *Morphologische Poetik* (Tübingen, 1968). Christian Metz, *Film Language: A Semiotics of the Cinema*, trans. Michael Taylor (New York, 1974), p. 18, distinguishes "the time of the thing told and the time of the telling (the time of

to a contemporary moment? When is the beginning? How does the narrative provide information about events that have led up to the state of affairs at that moment? What are the relations between the natural order of the events of the story and the order of their presentation by the discourse? And between the duration of the discursive presentation and that of the actual story events? How are recurrent events depicted by the discourse?

Narratives establish a sense of a present moment, narrative NOW, so to speak.[24] If the narrative is overt, there are perforce two NOWs, that of the discourse, the moment occupied by the narrator in the present tense ("I'm going to tell you the following story"), and that of the story, the moment that the action began to transpire, usually in the preterite. If the narrator is totally absent or covert, only the story-NOW emerges clearly. The time of narration is then past, except for the present of dialogue and external and internal monologue.

Order, Duration, and Frequency

Gérard Genette's elegant analysis of the time-relations between story- and discourse-time must form the basis of any current discussion.[25] Genette distinguishes three categories of relations: those of order (ordre), duration (durée) and frequency (fréquence).

A. Order. The discourse can rearrange the events of the story as much as it pleases, provided the story-sequence remains discernible. If not, the classical plot fails in "unity." The problem is particularly real for the cinema, whose normal compositional technique is montage or cutting; sometimes it can be difficult to tell whether a given cut signals a flashback, a flashforward, or simply an ellipsis followed by the next (spatially removed) event in the story.

---

the significate and the time of the signifier)." Brooks and Warren refer to this relation as "scale."

24. Mendilow: "one point of time in the story which serves as a point of reference."

25. Summarized by G. Genette, "Time and Narrative in *A la recherche du temps perdu*," trans. Paul de Man, in J. Hillis Miller, ed., *Aspects of Narrative* (New York, 1970), pp. 93–118.

Genette distinguishes between normal sequence, where story and discourse have the same order (1 2 3 4), and "anachronous" sequences. And anachrony can be of two sorts: flashback (*analepse*), where the discourse breaks the story-flow to recall earlier events (2 1 3 4), and flashforward (*prolepse*) where the discourse leaps ahead, to events subsequent to intermediate events.[26] These intermediate events must themselves be recounted at some later point, for otherwise the leap would simply constitute an ellipsis. Flashforwards can only be recognized retrospectively. The flashforward differs from the anticipatory satellite or narrative "seed" (Chekhov's gun hanging on the wall), since it clearly entails kernels.

But the terms "flashback" and "flashforward" should probably be limited to the specifically cinematic medium. It was not mere ignorance of the literary tradition that led early filmmakers to introduce these colorful metaphors. In the cinema, "flashback" means a narrative passage that "goes back" but specifically visually, as a scene, in its own autonomy, that is, introduced by some overt mark of transition like a cut or a dissolve. It is not correct to refer to traditional summary passages as "flashbacks." Flashbacks and -forwards are only media-specific instances of the larger classes of analepsis and prolepsis.

Sound films can even introduce partial or split flashbacks, since one of the two information channels, visual or auditory, may be kept in the present and the other flashbacked. The more ordinary case is that of offscreen narration. The voice-over introduces or interprets or simply reproduces verbally what the screen is showing. The voice-over is contemporary but the images are back "then," in story-time. The reverse case—though more rarely used—is also possible: the visual image remains contemporary, as the sound flashes back. In Henning Carlsen's *The Cats*, a film about the false charge raised by a group of female laundry workers that the manageress has forced

26. A typical, if banal, example from the film *The Anderson Tapes*: A gang occupies a whole apartment building and loots each apartment systematically. As the robberies occur, during NOW, flashforwards move to the scene at the police station where the various tenants tell their stories. They must be flashforwards—rather than NOW's with the robbery in flashback—since we do not yet know what happens ultimately to the protagonists, the burglars.

one of the girls into a lesbian relationship, the girl, Rika, comes to work one morning, sick and weary after a night of debauchery; the manageress gives her a shower and wraps her in a warm blanket; the two sit for a time looking at each other, but without moving their lips. At the same time we hear their voices, over; but it is clear from what is being said that these are not soliloquies, thought rendered audible, but rather echoes of a previous conversation that the two had at an earlier stage of their friendship.

Genette distinguishes between the "distance" of an anachrony (*portée*) and its "amplitude" (*amplitude*). "Distance" is the span of time from NOW backward or forward to the inception of the anachrony; amplitude is the duration of the anachronous event itself. There are different means for joining the anachrony to the ongoing story: external, internal, or mixed. An external anachrony is one whose beginning and end occur before NOW; an internal anachrony begins after NOW; a mixed anachrony begins before and ends after NOW. Internal anachronies in turn can be subdivided into those that do not interfere with the interrupted story ("heterodiegetic") and those that do ("homeodiegetic"). In the latter case we can distinguish between completive (*complétives* or *renvois*) and repetitive (*répétitives* or *rappels*). Completive anachronies fill in lacunae—past or future. These may be either straightforward, "frontal" ellipses, or lateral ellipses, *paralipses*, where deletions are not intervening events but rather components of the very situation unfolding—for example, Marcel's systematic concealment of the existence of a member of his family. Repetitive anachronies, on the other hand, repeat what has been stated before—"the narrative going back, sometimes explicitly, over its own tracks"—though with a different slant on the original events. This device has been familiar to the cinema since Eisenstein.

Genette's third possibility, which he labels *achrony* (and the parallel figure *syllepsis*), allows no chrono-logical relation (even inverse) between story and discourse. The grouping is either random or based on principles of organization appropriate to other kinds of texts—spatial proximity, discursive logic, thematics, or the like. We could cite, for instance, such narratives

as *La Jalousie*, which mystify us about the order in which events occur, the mystification being a function of the unreliability of the narration.

These distinctions are based on the assumption of a single story-strand, which bears the temporal center of gravity (so to speak). It is against this central strand that anachronies and achronies can be recognized. But narratives from time immemorial have included two or more story-strands, and sometimes it is undesirable to assume this kind of priority. Each has its own center of gravity, its own NOW. A classic cinematic example is D. W. Griffith's *Intolerance*. There are four story-strands: (1) "Modern Story (the Mother and the Law)," in which a young man falsely accused of murder is saved in the nick of time; (2) "The Judean Story (The Nazarene)," about the conflict between Jesus and the Pharisees; (3) "The Medieval Story," about the massacre of some Huguenots upon their arrival in Paris on St. Bartholomew's Day in 1572; and (4) "The Fall of Babylon," about the invasion of Babylon by the Persians. The film ends with an epilogue prophesying the ultimate elimination of intolerance. There is constant crosscutting between these stories, Griffith typically leaving characters in momentarily desperate straits in one to take up the thread of another. None of the four can be said to have a temporal priority over the others (the early ones in no sense "lead up" to the modern story, but are theoretically parallel to it). Therefore, each has its own NOW, and each has its own set of temporal relations between story and discourse.

Whether the different story-strands are of equal priority, as in *Intolerance*, or one is simply background for the other, as in the Yonville fair sequence in *Madame Bovary*, two possible dispositions of events may be suggested. Either the two sequences of events temporally overlap, each strand continuing at the very next second as if it had never been interrupted (as in *Madame Bovary*);[27] or the two are cotemporal, time passing in story-

27. Joseph Frank, "Spatial Form in Modern Literature," *Sewanee Review*, 53 (1945) (in Mark Schorer, Josephine Miles, and Gordon McKenzie, eds., *Criticism* [New York, 1948], p. 384): "For the duration of the scene, at least, the time-flow of the narrative is halted."

strand B at the same rate as in the explicitly narrated strand A, so that intervening events are not recounted. The latter has been aptly called the convention of "unchronicled growth."[28]

How does the concept of "exposition" fit into the discussion of narrative order? Exposition is a function rather than a sub-class of analepsis or prolepsis. That function is to provide "necessary information concerning characters and events existing before the action proper of a story begins."[29] Its emphasis is strongly explanatory. Exposition is traditionally done in the summary mode. Nineteenth-century novels typically introduce such summaries in a lump at the very outset (characteristically in the perfect tense): "Emma Woodhouse, handsome, clever, and rich, with a comfortable home and happy disposition, seemed to unite some of the best blessings of existence; and had lived nearly twenty-one years in the world with very little to distress or vex her." Or, after an initial *in medias res* scene, putting us into the Court of Chancery on a particularly foggy day, *Bleak House* begins: "Jarndyce and Jarndyce drones on. This scarecrow of a suit has, in course of time, become so complicated, that no man alive knows what it means."

The convention of "lumped summary" has been questioned by recent novelists and theorists of the novel. Ford Madox Ford argued for what he called "chronological looping" as a way of revealing antecedent events. His advice was to "distribute" the exposition, "to get in the character first with a strong impression, and then work backwards and forwards over his past."[30] Flashbacks function more or less expositorily, though abruptness may make unclear which aspects of the main narrative are being illuminated.

B. *Duration.* Duration concerns the relation of the time it takes

28. By Carl Grabo, *Technique of the Novel* (New York, 1928), p. 215: "When the story shifts from one sub-plot to another, the characters abandoned pursue an unrecorded existence."

29. Cleanth Brooks and Robert Penn Warren, *Understanding Fiction* (New York, 1959), p. 684. Meir Sternberg's essay "What Is Exposition?" in John Halperin, ed., *The Theory of the Novel* (New York, 1974), pp. 25–70, offers firm criteria for this feature in terms of Tomashevsky's distinctions between *fabula* and *sjužet*.

30. As quoted in Mendilow, *Time and the Novel*, p. 104.

to read out the narrative to the time the story-events themselves lasted. Five possibilities suggest themselves: (1) summary: discourse-time is shorter than story-time; (2) ellipsis: the same as (1), except that discourse-time is zero; (3) scene: discourse-time and story-time are equal; (4) stretch: the discourse-time is longer than story-time;[31] (5) pause: the same as (4), except that story-time is zero.

1. *Summary*: the discourse is briefer than the events depicted. The narrative statement summarizes a group of events; in verbal narrative, this may entail some kind of durative verb or adverb ("John lived in New York for seven years"), including iterative forms ("The company tried time and time again to end the strike but without success").

Language provides a variety of grammatical and lexical features for indicating summary, the aspectual distinctions among verbs and verb forms, for example. Some verbs are by semantic nature punctual. They denote events that happen once, in a relatively brief span of time, and do not recur. For example, "he jumped," or "she decided," or "they married." These verbs can be made durative or iterated only by means of external devices, like continuous verb forms ("he was jumping"), modals ("he kept on jumping"), repetition ("he jumped and jumped"), and so on. There are, on the other hand, a class of innately durative verbs—"waited," "considered," "strolled." These in their very semantics refer to a span of time only limitable by temporal adverbials ("for an hour," "since Tuesday").

Examples of summary occur even where precise cotemporality between discourse and story would seem to be *de rigueur*, for example, dialogue. Summarized dialogue—the gist of what a character said, but punctuated as a single quotation—occurs in novelists as early as Jane Austen.

The novelist is permitted to conflate into a single speech what must probably be supposed to have been uttered as several separate

---

31. Genette allows of only four, though he acknowledges the asymmetry. He does conceive of a "slowed-down scene," and thinks of examples in Proust. But these, he claims, are elongated by "extranarrative elements" or "descriptive pauses." "The detailed narration of acts or events told more slowly than

speeches. The gain in speed and concentration of effect is considerable. . . .

[for example in *Northanger Abbey*:] Anxiously awaiting her friends, and hearing the clock strike twelve, Catherine Morland declares: "I do not quite despair yet. I shall not give it up till a quarter after twelve. This is just the time of day for it to clear up, and I do think it looks a little lighter. There, it is twenty minutes after twelve, and now I *shall* give it up entirely. . . ." Unblushingly, the novelist permits twenty minutes to elapse during the uttering of less than forty words.[32]

The cinema has trouble with summary, and directors often resort to gadgetry. The "montage-sequence" has long been popular: a collection of shots showing selected aspects of an event or sequence usually integrated by continuous music. There have also been many cruder solutions, like peeling calendars, dates written as legend on the screen, and voice-over narrators. Some directors have been very ingenious in solving the problem. *Citizen Kane*, for example, opens with a newsreel summarizing the life of the protagonist. In Clouzot's film *Wages of Fear*, the fact that a number of drifters have been caught in the doldrums of a Central American town and cannot get out is explained as the film opens by a running conversation between a newcomer and one of the old hands. But we know that we are getting a summary of what Mario told Joe in a conversation that spread over several days. This is achieved by coupling their continuous dialogue on the sound track with disjunctive visuals of the two men in various parts of town, under different weather conditions, strolling in opposite directions, and so on. What we hear must then be a conventionalized representation of the gist of their conversations over a period of several days.

Interestingly enough, the montage-sequence technique, invented to solve a problem in film, has also found its way into verbal fiction. In *Lolita*, a summary is presented in brief characteristic vignettes that illustrate rather than state what the

---

they were performed or undergone . . . are doubtless realizable as deliberate experiments, but they do not constitute a canonic form" ("Discours du récit," p. 130). "Canonic" or not, such forms are common in modern fiction and especially in film and should not be excluded from the list of theoretical possibilities.

32. Norman Page, *Speech in the English Novel* (London, 1973), pp. 29–30.

summed period was like. Humbert gives us his life at Beardsley College in short, representative scenes, as it might be evoked by intermittent camera shots:

As I lay on my narrow studio bed after a session of adoration and despair in Lolita's cold bedroom, I used to review the concluded day by checking my own image as it prowled rather than passed before the mind's red eye. I watched dark-and-handsome, not un-Celtic, probably high-church, possibly very high-church, Dr. Humbert see his daughter off to school. I watched him greet with his slow smile and pleasantly arched thick black eyebrows good Mrs. Holigan, who smelled of the plague (and would head, I knew, for master's gin at the first opportunity). With Mr. West, retired executioner or writer of religious tracts—who cared?—I saw neighbor what's his name, I think they are French or Swiss, meditate in his frank-windowed study over a typewriter, rather gaunt-profiled, an almost Hitlerian cowlick on his pale brow. Weekends, wearing a well-tailored overcoat and brown gloves, Profesesor H. might be seen with his daughter strolling to Walton Inn (famous for its violet-ribboned china bunnies and chocolate boxes among which you sit and wait for a 'table for two' still filthy with your predecessors' crumbs). Seen on weekdays, around one P.M., saluting with dignity Arguseyed East while maneuvering the car out of the garage and around the damned evergreens, and down onto the slippery road. . . . At dinner with Dolly in town, Mr. Edgar H. Humbert was seen eating his steak in the continental knife-and-fork manner. Enjoying, in duplicate, a concert, two marble-faced, becalmed Frenchmen sitting side by side, with Monsieur H. H.'s musical little girl on her father's right, and the musical little boy of Professor W. (father spending a hygienic evening in Providence) on Monsieur H. H.'s left. Opening the garage, a square of light that engulfs the car and is extinguished. Brightly pajamaed, jerking down the window shade in Dolly's bedroom. Saturday morning, unseen, solemnly weighing the winter-bleached lassie in the bathroom. . . .

The sentences are equivalent to separate movie shots showing how Humbert spent his time. Though his name is elegantly varied, the syntax is kept relatively constant, iterating the commonplaceness of his actions. Thus we see a technique developing in one narrative medium *faute de mieux*, and then taken up as an exciting new possibility by another which is not itself under the same formative restrictions.

2. *Ellipsis*: the discourse halts, though time continues to pass in the story. Jake Barnes has lunch with Robert Cohn at the end of Chapter 5 of *The Sun Also Rises*: then, "We talked about one

thing and another, and I left him to come to the office." Chapter 6 begins "At five o'clock I was in the Hotel Crillon waiting for Brett." Thus three or four hours are unaccounted for; we assume that Jake did his usual journalistic work at the office, then made his way to the hotel. No need to report the details.

Ellipsis is as old as *The Iliad*. But, as many critics have pointed out, ellipsis of a particularly broad and abrupt sort is characteristic of modern narratives. Genette shows that Proust's ellipses in the *Recherche* become increasingly abrupt, perhaps as compensation for the fact that the scenes between, though they cover shorter and shorter periods of story-time, are more and more detailed. The whole effect is of an ever-growing discontinuity between discourse-time and story-time. The same kind of discontinuity characterizes *Mrs. Dalloway*.

Ellipsis is sometimes identified with the "cut" between shots in the cinema, the transition between two shots linked together by a simple join, giving the impression during projection that the first shot is suddenly and instantaneously displaced by the second. ("Cut" is precisely what the editor does: he snips the film exactly at the edge of the appropriate frame of shot *A* and at the beginning of *B*, and glues them together.) But the terms "ellipsis" and "cut" should be carefully distinguished. The difference is one of level. Ellipsis refers to a narrative discontinuity, between story and discourse. "Cut," on the other hand, is the manifestation of ellipsis as a process in a specific medium, an actualization parallel to a blank space[33] or asterisks on the printed page.

Or more precisely, a cut *may* convey ellipsis, but it may simply represent a shift in space, that is, connecting two actions that are absolutely or virtually continuous, as when shot *A* shows a man with his hand turning a doorknob and drawing the door toward him, and then, after the cut, a reverse shot *B* from out in the hall shows the same door opening, now inwards, toward the camera, and the man emerging. The discourse is no less continuous than the story in this instance; the cut is simply

33. The "white space, [the] enormous white space, without the shadow of a transition" that Proust speaks of in *Contre Sainte-Beuve* (quoted by Genette, p. 132).

necessitated by the spatial problem of passing the camera through the wall. A cut may also be used to show that the next shot takes place in a character's mind, that it is imaginary, or whatever. And so with the other transitions or cinematic technology—the dissolve, the wipe, irising in and out, and so forth. These are all in the repertoire of cinematic manifestation, not parts of narrative discourse. In themselves they have no specific narrative meanings. Only the context can tell us whether a given dissolve means "several weeks later" or "several weeks earlier" or "meanwhile, in another part of town."

3. *Scene*: the scene is the incorporation of the dramatic principle into narrative. Story and discourse here are of relatively equal duration. The two usual components are dialogue and overt physical actions of relatively short duration, the kind that do not take much longer to perform than to relate. An example from John Dos Passos's *USA*:

> Fainy was sweeping out the office, when a man with a face like raw steak walked up the steps; he was smoking a thin black stogy of a sort Fainy had never seen before. He knocked on the groundglass door.
> "I want to speak to Mr. O'Hara, Timothy O'Hara."
> "He's not here yet, be here any minute now, sir. Will you wait?"
> "You bet I'll wait."

Let us turn now to cases where discourse-time is slower than story-time.

4. *Stretch*: here discourse-time is longer than story-time. By "overcranking"—that is, running the camera at a faster speed than its later projection—the cinema can manifest stretch in the well-known "slow motion." But there are other ways in which it can cause discourse-time to take longer; story-time can be stretched, for instance, by a kind of overlapping or repetitious editing.[34] A classic example occurs in Eisenstein's *October*, where the full poignancy of the initial defeats of the Bolsheviks

34. Called by Noël Burch, *Praxis du cinéma* (Paris, 1969), p. 17, *retour en arrière* (which is badly translated in the English version, *Theory of Film Practice* [New York, 1973], as "time-reversal"). Burch, in an interesting account clearly on the same track as current narrative theory, shows that the *retour en arrière* is one of five possible time relations that can occur between two spatially separated shots.

in Petrograd is associated with the opening of the bridges, blocking the proletariat from crossing the river and reaching the Winter Palace. By overlapping editing, the bridges seem to open interminably; defeated frustration is underlined by the recurrence of an image of a dead horse that had pulled a Bolshevik wagon hanging grotesquely from the center of the bridge raised on high. The same technique is used in the famous Odessa steps sequence in *Battleship Potemkin*, stretching out the viewer's experience of the soldiers' descent to the point of excruciation.

Obviously literary narratives do not have the resources of overlapping editing or slow motion, though words can be repeated or paraphrased and given events can be verbalized many times. In the *story* of Robbe-Grillet's *La Jalousie*, perhaps, A . . . cries out only once at the sight of the centipede. But the statement of this event by the discourse recurs and recurs.

Verbal expression may last longer (at least on an impressionist measure) than the events themselves. The case of mental events is especially interesting. It takes longer to say your thoughts than to think them, and still longer to write them down. So, in a sense, verbal discourse is always slower when it communicates what has transpired in a character's mind, especially sudden perceptions or insights. Many authors apologize for the disparity, for the delay caused by words.[35] A classic instance of stretch is Ambrose Bierce's "Occurrence at Owl Creek Bridge," in which a man being hung for espionage fantasizes an entire escape from his executioners—breaking his bonds, swimming down the river in a hail of bullets, crawling ashore, running for miles until he reaches his home. As he embraces his wife "a blinding white light blazes all about him with a sound like the shock of a cannon—then all is darkness and silence. Peyton Farquhar was dead; his body, with a broken neck, swung gently from side to side beneath the timbers of the Owl Creek bridge." A fantasy of several hundred words has depicted a split second of consciousness.

35. Joseph Conrad has his narrative spokesman Marlow (himself no mean theoretician) say about a scene he has just depicted to his cronies: "All this happened in much less time than it takes to tell, since I am trying to interpret for you into slow speech the instantaneous effect of visual impressions."

5. *Pause*: story-time stops though the discourse continues, as in descriptive passages. Since narrative is essentially a temporal art, another discourse form takes over. From *Lolita*:

> . . . there came from the upper landing the contralto voice of Mrs. Haze. . . .
> I think I had better describe her right away, to get it over with. The poor lady was in her middle thirties, she had a shiny forehead, plucked eyebrows, and quite simple but not unattractive features of a type that may be defined as a weak solution of Marlene Dietrich.

Modern narratives tend to avoid barefaced pauses of description (unless they self-consciously delight in them, as in the passage above), preferring a dramatic mode. Authors like Zola, as a recent article points out, developed regular formulas for the necessary transformation. Desiring to detail as much as possible of the surface of the fictive world, but refusing to put the words in a narrator's mouth, he made the characters do it for him. Typically, an inquisitive or knowledgeable person (painter, aesthete, spy, technician, explorer, or the like), finding himself with time on his hands (out for a stroll, waiting for an appointment, resting in the middle of his work), takes the opportunity, for whatever reason (distraction, pedantry, curiosity, aesthetic pleasure, volubility), to describe (instruct, point out, demonstrate) some complex object (a locomotive, a garden) to someone who does not know about it (for reasons of youth, ignorance, lack of expertise). In other words, a conversation, an interaction between characters, is created for the express purpose of describing something, relieving the narrator of the task.[36]

It is my impression that description per se is generally impossible in narrative films, that story-time keeps going as long as images are projected on the screen, as long as we feel that the camera continues to run. In the sequence in Stanley Kubrick's film version of *Lolita* that corresponds to the passage quoted above, Humbert simply watches Charlotte descend the stairs; the focus remains on the event. And in the sense that time is passing for the film Humbert, story-time continues to pass for us.

36. Philippe Hamon, "Qu'est-ce qu'une description?" *Poétique*, 12 (1972), 465–487.

The effect of pure description only seems to occur when the film actually "stops," in the so-called "freeze-frame" effect (the projector continues, but all the frames show exactly the same image). An example in Joseph Mankiewicz's *All About Eve*: at the moment that Eve (Anne Baxter) is offered a coveted theatrical award, the image freezes as her hand reaches out to receive it. Story-time stops, while the cynical drama critic (George Sanders), speaking as narrator off-screen, hints at the dark side of Eve's rise to fame and introduces the other principals seated around the banquet table.

It has been remarked by critics (for example Percy Lubbock) that classical novels exhibit a relative constancy of alternation between scene and summary. Contrarily, modernist novels, as Virginia Woolf observed in both theory and practice, tend to eschew summary, to present a series of scenes separated by ellipses that the reader must fill in. Thus, the modernist novel is more cinematic, although I do not argue that it changed under the influence of the cinema.

If we pick a chapter randomly from an early novel like *Pride and Prejudice*, say Chapter 6, we do seem to find the classical alternating rhythm, provided we define "scene" and "summary" broadly enough. It presents: an opening summary (about Jane's growing involvement with Bingley); a scene (Charlotte and Elizabeth talk); another summary (Darcy's growing interest in Elizabeth); a scene (a party at Sir William Lucas'). This final scene is divided into a number of different scenelets—Elizabeth's complaint and her teasing of Darcy, her performance at the piano (separated by a brief summary and descriptive excursus on Mary's musical penchant), Sir William's frustrated conversation with Darcy and attempt to match him as dancing partner with Elizabeth, Darcy's revery, and finally his briefly summarized talk with Miss Bingley.

But the "rhythm" is rough and approximate, and the scene mostly coheres in its spatial dimension. A kind of constant spatial framing (Sir William's house) guarantees the continuation of the scenic sense, even in moments when discourse-time is clearly shorter than story-time (the time-space of Darcy's revery or talk with Miss Bingley). Thus we can distinguish an-

other function of summary—to give the gist of attitudes and actions within scenes.

The reverse is also true. A brief isolated scene may do little more than illustrate or enliven the general summary in which it occurs. In *Pride and Prejudice* such scenes are often not spatial. They are scenes only in the pure temporal sense: the discourse-time slows down to the same pace as the story-time. For example:

Her tour to the Lakes was now the object of her happiest thoughts; it was her best consolation for all the uncomfortable hours, which the discontentedness of her mother and Kitty made inevitable; and could she have included Jane in the scheme, every part of it would have been perfect.

"But it is fortunate," thought she, "that I have something to wish for. Were the whole arrangement complete, my disappointment would be certain. But here, by carrying with me one ceaseless source of regret in my sister's absence, I may reasonably hope to have all my expectations of pleasure realized. A scheme of which every part promises delight, can never be successful; and general disappointment is only warded off by the defence of some little peculiar vexation."

When Lydia went away, she promised to write very often and very minutely to her mother and Kitty.

The middle paragraph represents the literal words passing through Elizabeth's mind; its discourse-time clearly equals its story-time, hence by definition, it must be a "scene." But it is clear that the exact place and the time-point at which these words occur is indefinite, that the passage does not enact an independent event but simply illustrates the kind of thinking going on in Elizabeth's mind during the summarized period.

The usual means of summarizing in contemporary fiction is to let the characters do it, whether in their own minds or externally in dialogue. But such passages are not "summaries" in the classical sense since the ratio is not between the duration of the events and of their depiction but between the duration of the characters' memories of those events and the time that it takes to read them, a ratio that is roughly equal, and hence "scenic." The summary aspect is secondary, a by-product of ratiocinative action.

Much of *Mrs. Dalloway* consists of the reminiscences of char-

acters, not only of major characters like Clarissa, Peter, and Lucrezia but also of those who make single, brief appearances and bear little or no relationship to the protagonists and the main action. This dipping into the consciousnesses of passers-by is one of the interesting innovations of the book. It collaborates with the modernist presentation of the sights and sounds of the city—the buses, Big Ben, the skywriting airplane, the lady on the bench in Regent's Park, and the inner lives of random passers-by, who, strangely and provocatively, bear names—Moll Pratt, Mr. Bowley, Mrs. Coates. The external and internal life of the city is communicated through the switchboard of the novel's discoursive technique. The elimination of summary contributes precisely to the abruptness and speed of the urban experience. The narrator need not summarize since the past so dominates the reminiscences of the major characters:

> She owed him words: "sentimental," "civilized"; they started up every day of her life as if he guarded her. A book was sentimental; an attitude to life was sentimental. "Sentimental" perhaps she was to be thinking of the past.

Clarissa, now over fifty, home from shopping, like a nun withdrawing to her narrow room, undresses, mulls over the past, her youth at Bourton and her later relationship with Peter. A long period is covered, but discourse-time equals story-time: story-time is not the thirty years or so of elapsed life, but rather the time of her thinking about them. Structurally, the summarized material is secondary to the principal narrative event upon which we focus, namely Clarissa's act of reminiscing.

A 1925 reviewer observed that "'Mrs. Woolf . . . makes great the little matter and leaves us with that sense of the inexhaustible richness of the fabric of life." The little matter is made great through the orchestration of rich reminiscence: "she could remember going cold with excitement and doing her hair in a kind of ecstasy (now the old feeling began to come back to her, as she took out her hairpins, laid them on the dressing table, began to do her hair), with the rooks flaunting up and down in the pink evening light, and dressing, and going downstairs, and feeling as she crossed the hall 'if it were now to die, 'twere now to be

most happy!'" In a way, the whole book is a celebration of reminiscence caught fleetingly among the hurly-burly of today, by characters with sufficient age and leisure to do so. Indeed, reminiscence is the principal narrative activity; the others convey mere outward facade.

In this kind of narrative and for these kinds of characters, exposition is no longer a problem. As in Proust, the past is no less vivid than the present—often more vivid. The status of NOW is no longer important; there is no need for information to "unravel" the plot, since the plot poses no problem, no ratiocinative path to be followed, no goal toward which we need orientation. The last lines of the novel overtly draw the picture of what in a sense has been there all along.

It is Clarissa, he said.
For there she was.

The modernist rhythm of *Mrs. Dalloway*, then, is not an oscillation between summary and scene, but a rhythm of scenes alone, a passing of the story's relay baton from one character to another, even when they do not know each other but simply "materialize" in each other's unconscious proximity.

C. *Frequency.* The third possible relationship between discourse-time and story-time is frequency. Genette distinguishes among: (1) singularly, a single discursive representation of a single story moment, as in "Yesterday, I went to bed early;" (2) multiple-singulary, several representations, each of one of several story moments, as in "Monday, I went to bed early; Tuesday, I went to bed early; Thursday, I went to bed early," etc; (3) repetitive, several discursive representations of the same story moment, as in "Yesterday I went to bed early; yesterday I went to bed early; yesterday I went to bed early," etc; (4) iterative, a single discursive representation of several story moments, as in "Every day of the week I went to bed early."

Little need be added to Genette's discussion of the first three categories. The singular form is of course basic and perhaps obligatory, at least in traditional narratives. Genette's second and third categories form *cas limites*, occurring relatively rarely,

for special effects. But living as we do in extreme times, the limits are sometimes approached. Recall, for example, the exhausting repetition of events in Robbe-Grillet's *La Jalousie*: the squashing of the centipede, A . . . 's serving drinks or brushing her hair, the native crouching over the surface of the river, and so on. We are perplexed: are they single discoursive representations of single different, if highly resemblant, story moments (1), or multiple discoursive representations of the same story moment (3)? For instance, how many times *does* A . . . serve drinks on the veranda to Franck and the narrator, and if more than once to which occasion does each statement correspond?

Genette's fourth category needs further comment. Iterative forms have certain terms in English as in other languages. They can be communicated by prepositions like "during," by nouns expressing periods of time, and particularly by special iterative modals like "would" or "kept" (plus the present participle). From the beginning of *Jude the Obscure*: "*During* the three or four succeeding *years* a quaint and singular vehicle *might have been discerned* moving along the lanes and by-roads near Marygreen, driven in a quaint and singular way." (My italics.) That the effect is iterative, and not simply durative, is a product of our understanding of the context: the vehicle's trips were around Marygreen and not in a straight line, cross-country; from that we attribute iteration. The route itself was regular: "in this turn-out it became Jude's business thrice a week to carry loaves of bread to the villagers and solitary cotters immediately around Marygreen." The function of "might have been observed" is of course to distance the perception, not only spatially (it is the literary equivalent to the cinematic "long shot") but also temporally—the randomness of the perception is emphasized. The implication is that if the perceiver did not see the cart, it was because he happened to be at the wrong time and place, for Jude's route itself was perfectly regular.

How Time Distinctions Are Manifested

Verbal narratives signal story time not only through a whole set of grammatical elements like verb tenses, moods (the speak-

er's "attitude toward the fulfillment of the predicate"), and aspects (the duration of the action, as a point in time, a span or whatever), as well as adverbs, but also through semantic means. The cinema, too, has its ways of indicating temporal changes in the story, although it is not clear whether these amount to anything like a "grammar." Christian Metz argues that it is more proper to consider them as a system of "punctuation."

The English tense system is not particularly rich, but it is capable of indicating without the aid of adverbs at least four temporal stages in a sequence of events: (1) an earliest, by the past perfect, (2) a subsequent period, by the preterite (or past progressive), (3) a still later period, by the present (or present progressive), and (4) a latest, by the future (or the simple present or present progressive functioning as future). Let us refer to the narrative periods as "anterior time," "past time," "present time," and "future time." We must also recognize the existence of a "timeless" reference, the "time"—or rather absence thereof—of statements that specify a general case, ordinarily through the simple present tense—"Life is wonderful," "Gold is precious," "Time marches on." (In narratives, this time may be expressed by the preterite.) Most narratives set their story-NOW at the second of these stages, "past time"; verbal narratives usually show it by the preterite. But a few narratives set story-NOW at the third. At least one novel puts it in the future.[37] Discourse-NOW is generally in the third stage, "present time" except in the case of "frame" narratives (for example, Marlow telling about what happened at an anterior time).

What may complicate things is the relation of temporal adverbs to verb forms. This is a matter of considerable interest to narrative analysis. It has long been recognized that adverbs of present reference can occur with verb forms in the preterite. Joyce's "The Sisters" begins (my italics): "There was no hope for him *this time*: it was the third stroke. . . . He had often said to me: 'I am not long for this world,' and I thought his words idle. *Now* I knew they were true." In ordinary circumstances

37. Michael Frayn's *A Very Private Life* (London, 1968), discussed by W. J. M. Bronzwaer, *Tense in the Novel* (Groningen, 1970), pp. 70ff.

one would of course use "that time" and "then" instead of the present adverbial forms. "This time" and "now" clearly serve to emphasize the NOW of the "I"-as-character, to animate his point of view as opposed to that of his later incarnation, the "I"-as-narrator looking back to his childhood feelings. We might call this a device for "character contemporization." One theorist takes it to be the central component of the indirect free style,[38] and another makes an even stronger claim—that by itself, it separates fiction from nonfiction, that preterites so used form a special "epic" tense.[39] The latter claim is clearly excessive; the mixture of preterite tense forms and present-time adverbials is a locution available to any speaker. By no stretch of the imagination can it be used to define that bristling theoretical entity we call "fictionality."[40]

The former question is more viable; but since it has to do with narrative transmission, that is, discourse, I shall discuss here only what relates to the question of time, reserving the definitions of "free" kinds of discourses for a later chapter.

I have repeatedly distinguished between story-time and discourse-time. A parallel distinction is that between the character-NOW—the moment of the character's present time—and narrator-NOW, the moment in the telling of the story that is contemporary for the narrator. What then is the relation between time and purely linguistic phenomena such as tense and aspect? Time is a matter of narrative, of story and discourse; tense, of the grammars of languages. Points and periods of time are *in* the story, and are expressed *by* the discourse. The discourse, in turn, is manifested by a medium. In verbal narrative,

38. Franz Stanzel, "Episches Praeteritum, Erlebte Rede, Historisches Praesens," *Deutsche Vierteljahrfeschrift für Literaturwissenschaft und Geistesgeschichte*, 33 (1959), 1–12. Bronzwaer supports this view.

39. Käte Hamburger, *Die Logik der Dichtung* (Stuttgart, 1968) *passim*. In his own conception, Stanzel argues that the "epic" effect occurs only when the reader's "center of orientation" lies "in the consciousness of a figure or in an imaginary observer on the scene of the fictional action."

40. There have been several critiques of Hamburger's theory, but the most detailed is that of Bronzwaer, who furnished persuasive examples from clearly nonfictive texts—an article on linguistics, a letter to a magazine, a popular history book—to show how widespread the practice is.

a given time element may be manifested by varying choices among verb forms, temporal adverbs, vocabulary, and so on. Often grammatical choices are absolutely minimal. In the second story in *The Dubliners*, "An Encounter," the simple preterite marks practically every temporal contingency. The story starts —with durative and iterative reference—"It was Joe Dillon who introduced the Wild West to us. He had a little library made up of old numbers of *The Union Jack, Pluck*, and *The Halfpenny Marvel*. Every evening after school we met in his back garden and arranged Indian battles." After a vivid description of Joe Dillon's cavorting as an Indian, ending with a direct quotation of his war-cry—"'Ya! yaka, yaka, yaka!'"—we read, "Everyone was incredulous when it was reported that he had a vocation for the priesthood. Nevertheless it was true." The report is of events taking place much later, in a future time period, yet the verb form is still the simple preterite. We do not even need an adverb ("later" or the like) to help us understand; the context is sufficient.

Indeed, the past perfect is relatively little used in English speech even among sophisticated speakers except when the anteriority of events must be underlined. In highbrow literary language, it is more frequent, and its use or nonuse can have stylistic implications of various sorts, including character-contemporization.

Another mark of character-contemporization is the use of the preterite in statements of general, timeless, or (as they have been called) "gnomic" purport. If we read in a narrative otherwise in the preterite a sentence like "War is hell," the generalization is thought to hold for the narrator, as well as (or even rather than) for the characters. But "War was hell," must mean that a character thinks so. (This is not always true of ironic generalizations. *Pride and Prejudice* begins: "It is a truth universally acknowledged, that a single man in possession of a good fortune, must be in want of a wife." For all the "universality" of this opinion, the narrator and the narratee know not to accept it. If the sentence read "It *was* a truth universally acknowledged . . ." the irony would also hold, but only for the characters.)

Verbal narratives in English are occasionally written in the present tense. But story-time is still usually the past. Hence the tense is referred to as the "historical present." But it is a mere surrogate of the preterite: the distinction between story-NOW and discourse-NOW remains perfectly clear, for the narrator knows the outcome of the story, and it is evident that his present remains posterior to that of the characters. An interesting example is Truman Capote's "A Christmas Memory." Discourse-NOW, the present time of the narrator, a college or prep-school student "walking across [an unnamed] school campus," is established in the final paragraph of the text as a "particular December morning" ten or fifteen years after the main events of the story, which occurred when he was seven. Those events—elaborate preparations for Christmas, lovingly shared with his "sixty-something" spinster cousin—are depicted in seven story-NOWs, separated by ellipses ranging from three hours to several weeks. The first NOW occurs in that last paragraph—the message to the young man about the death of his cousin. Thus an eighth story-NOW coincides with the moment of discourse-NOW. Capote uses the present progressive to emphasize the punctual aspect, that is, the exact moment in story-time, because the simple present, unlike the preterite, implies repetition, habitualness, and the like. In this story the simple present is saved for reminiscences of acts seasonally performed. Thus a double effect: the events are of "this" particular Christmas season, but they are identical with events of past Christmas seasons. "But before these purchases can be made, there is the question of money. Neither of us has any." That means not only "at that particular moment," but "ever." As for the simple present ("Our reflections mingle with the rising moon as we work by the fireside in the firelight"), it interchanges with the present progressive ("The kitchen is growing dark"). When the durative span begins in the past and comes up to the present or beyond, any tense is possible: "Just today the fireplace commenced its seasonal roar," "The hat is found, a straw cartwheel corsaged with velvet roses out-of-doors has faded," "I am building her a kite," and so on. Duratives beginning in the past and ending there are conveyed by present per-

fects (". . . how hard [pecans] were to find (the main crop having been shaken off the trees and sold by the orchard's owners))" or simple preterites with explanatory adverbs ("[the hat] once belonged to a more fashionable relative"). The indication of future time in this kind of story is a problem, since the present tense can also have future reference. Adverbs become crucial: "We eat our supper (cold biscuits, bacon, blackberry jam) and discuss tomorrow. Tomorrow the kind of work I like best begins: buying." Capote also includes a genuine future tense to keep things clear: ". . . why, we'll need a pony to pull the buggy home."

It is commonplace to say that the cinema can only occur in the present time. Unlike the verbal medium, film in its pure, unedited state is absolutely tied to real time. To read "John got up, dressed, and took a taxi to the airport" takes only a fraction of a second; to watch it could theoretically take as long as to do it. But, of course, almost all films are elliptically edited (Andy Warhol's and Michael Snow's experiments are rare exceptions). Like the author the filmmaker routinely counts on the viewer's capacity to reconstruct or supply deleted material that he feels is too obvious to show. How much or how little is a matter of style. Filmmakers are cutting more radically as audience sophistication grows.

Narrative Macrostructure and the Typology of Plot

So far we have focused on the formal nature of the molecular units of plot, the principles of their organization, including negative possibilities (antistories), and their manifestation in actual media. These subjects comprise the microstructure of narratives, how their individual pieces fit together. Obviously, a general theory of narrative needs also to account for macrostructures, that is, the general designs of plots. Macrostructure in turn implies a theory of plot typology, how plots group together according to structural similarities.

Our present state of knowledge permits only speculations. An inspection of a few of the more celebrated schemes will demonstrate the difficulty of the problem.

Traditionally, theorists have gone to content more than to

expression for macrostructural criteria: for example, the classical *peripeteia* of tragedy, the change at some part of the action from one state of affairs to its precise opposite, or the *anagnorisis* or transition from ignorance to knowledge experienced by the protagonist. These are content-generalizations precisely because they presume to judge whether events entail large categories of behavior called "ignorance" and "knowledge."

Literary studies since Aristotle have based the analysis of plot macrostructures on the vicissitudes of the protagonist. Aristotle distinguished between fortunate and fatal plots, according to whether the protagonist's situation improved or declined. For him the most interesting forms were complex, that is, changed direction: the tragic or fatal plot line versus the comic or fortunate. These possibilities were extended according to the differing character of the protagonist. Aristotle allowed three types— the unqualifiedly good, the unqualifiedly evil, and the noble, somewhere in-between, good enough so that his miscalculation or *hamartia* will not prevent our feeling pity and fear at his downfall. There resulted six types of plots. In the realm of the fatal:

1. an unqualifiedly good hero fails: this is shockingly incomprehensible to us, since it violates probability;

2. a villainous protagonist fails; about his downfall we feel smug satisfaction, since justice has been served;

3. a noble hero fails through miscalculation, which arouses our pity and fear.

In the realm of the fortunate:

4. a villainous protagonist succeeds; but this causes us to feel disgust, because it violates our sense of probability;

5. an unqualifiedly good hero succeeds, causing us to feel moral satisfaction;

6. a noble hero (like Orestes) miscalculates, but only temporarily, and his ultimate vindication is satisfying.[41]

Clearly this categorization will accommodate only a small number of narratives, those in which notions like "good" or "succeeds" are absolutely clear.

41. Adapted from Hardison and Golden, pp. 179–185. The latter two types are not actually discussed by Aristotle but are clearly implicit in his system.

Modern attempts to analyze macrostructure and typology, like those of Northrop Frye, Ronald Crane, and Norman Friedman, increase the number of parameters and thereby extend the network of possibilities to newer kinds of narratives. Frye offers not one but two different approaches to macrostructural analysis. The first is character-centered, based on what he calls "mode," that is, "a conventional power of action assumed about the chief characters in fictional literature [which] tend to succeed one another in a historical sequence."[42] The emphasis on character resembles Aristotle's, except that the evaluative criterion is not goodness or badness but the powers of the protagonist in relation to those of the audience. If he is all-powerful, that is, divine, the macrostructure is "mythic"; if more powerful, human but marvellous, it is "romantic"; if more powerful but still only a human being, i.e., noble, it is "high mimetic"; if equal to us, it is "low mimetic"; if inferior to us, it is "ironic." These categories are crosscut by other parameters—tragic ("ostracized from society") versus comic ("integrated into society"), naive versus sophisticated, piteous versus fearsome—to provide an elaborate network of character-types and hence of plot types.

Frye's second formulation is a direct theory of mythos, attacking plot typology frontally.[43] He posits four *mythoi*: comedy, romance, tragedy, and irony-satire. Each in turn is divided into six phases, varying according to its distance from the two neighboring mythoi: hence a total of twenty-four categories. These are "narrative categories . . . broader than, or logically prior to, the ordinary literary genres." In other words, they are a set of features that combine with the genres. Novels as well as plays

42. *Anatomy of Criticism* (Princeton, 1957), First Essay, "Historical Criticism: Theory of Modes."
43. Ibid., pp. 158–239. Actually, a third basis for plot-typology is suggested in Frye's Fourth Essay, "Rhetorical Criticism: Theory of Genres" (pp. 303–314). The genres are distinguished according to the type of transmission to an audience, for instance the "radical of presentation" of "epos" is "the author or minstrel as oral reciter," while in fiction it is the "printed or written word." Subtypes of the latter include the novel, the romance (in a different sense than that used in the First Essay): these are distinguished by their treatment of characters—real versus stylized people. Other types include confession and Menippean satire or anatomy. In all there are eleven possible combinations.

can be comic or tragic, romantic or ironic-satirical. For example when the main characters in *Humphery Clinker*, drying off after their carriage accident, come to recognize each other, the "humorous society triumphs or remains undefeated," illustrating the phase of comedy nearest the pole of irony.

Frye's categories are conceptually broad and his remarkable erudition fills them with scores of examples, from *The Iliad* and Lucian's *Sale of Lives* to *Huckleberry Finn* and *Finnegans Wake*. Further, the basis of the categorization is admirably deductive. But Frye tells us little or nothing about the conceptual basis of that deduction, not even that it is arbitrary. Why four types and six phases rather than six types and four phases, or ten types and ten phases? In the titles the mythoi are equated with the four seasons, comedy with spring, romance with summer, tragedy with autumn, irony-satire with winter. But there are other numbers equally fraught with significance—the three of the holy trinity, the seven vices and virtues, the twelve signs of the zodiac. It is disturbing to be offered a typology whose basis is metaphorical if the metaphor is not explained. It is disturbing to be asked to accept a system that is hermetically sealed, whose distinctions cannot be challenged with counter-examples and thereby refined.

Ronald Crane's taxonomy also rests on tradition: three of Aristotle's six properties of poetry. Crane proposes plots of action, plots of character, and plots of thought. The first entails a change in the protagonist's situation (*The Brothers Karamazov*), the second a change in his moral character (*Portrait of a Lady*) and the third a change in his thought and feeling (Pater's *Marius the Epicurean*).[44]

To these Norman Friedman adds Aristotle's distinctions

44. "The Concept of Plot and the Plot of 'Tom Jones,'" in his *Critics and Criticism* (Chicago, 1957), pp. 66–67. Crane's formulation leaves some interesting questions. Whose "thought," the implied author's, character's, narrator's? And what are these thoughts *about*: the world of the work—events, characters, situations? Or things in general? Why, except to satisfy the benevolent ghost of the Stagirite, should "thought" be separated from other actions? If speech acts are kinds of acts, why not also thought acts? And why stop with the first three? Why are there not plots of diction too, for instance the narratives of Gertrude Stein, or *Finnegans Wake*? Or plots of spectacle and melody?

among three kinds of protagonist and two kinds of fate and comes up with fourteen types (mathematically one would expect a richer haul). Thus, for example, the "admiration" plot is a plot of action containing a "change for the better . . . caused by a sympathetic protagonist's nobility of character" (for example, *Mister Roberts*). The "maturing" plot is a plot of character in which a "sympathetic protagonist whose goals are mistakenly conceived" changes for the better (*Lord Jim*). The "education" plot is a plot in which the protagonist's thought is improved but "does not continue on to demonstrate the effects of this beneficial change on his behavior," for if it did, it would then be a maturing plot; examples are *All the King's Men* and *The Confidential Agent*.[45]

There are other schemes that we could discuss,[46] but these are sufficient to illustrate both the rewards and the risks of content-based plot-typologizing. Perhaps the first observation to make about such taxonomies is that they rest on unacknowledged cultural presuppositions. Theories based on "goodness" or distinctions between "action" and "thought" presume that these

45. "Forms of the Plot," *Journal of General Education*, 8 (1955), 241–253. The other eleven are action plots (novels of R. L. Stevenson), pathetic plots (*Tess of the D'Urbervilles*), tragic plots (*Oedipus Rex*), punitive plots (*Richard III*), sentimental plots (*Cymbeline*), reform plots (*The Scarlet Letter*), testing plots (*For Whom the Bell Tolls*), degeneration plots (*Tender Is the Night*), revelation plots (Roald Dahl, *Beware of the Dog*), affective plots (*Pride and Prejudice*), and disillusionment plots (*The Hairy Ape*).

46. For example, E. M. Forster offers spatial metaphors (*Aspects of the Novel*, p. 151): "a book the shape of an hour-glass and a book the shape of a grand chain in that old-time dance, the Lancers." Anatole France's *Thaïs* and Henry James's *The Ambassadors* are "hour-glass" novels, while Percy Lubbock's *Roman Pictures* exemplify the "grand chain" design. Other patterns are the Catherine wheel and the bed of Procrustes. Other theorists have noted the resemblance of plot structures to rhetorical tropes and figures. See citations from Shklovsky in T. Todorov, "L'Héritage methodologique du formalisme," *L'Homme*, 5 (1965), 76, and reprinted in *The Poetics of Prose* (Ithaca, N.Y., 1977; trans. Richard Howard). The essay in question is a chapter in *O teorii prozy* (*Theory of Prose*) (Moscow, 1929), translated as "La Construction de la nouvelle et du roman," in *Théorie de la littérature*, pp. 170–196. But the resemblances can hardly be causal or genetic. It seems more likely that our minds contain open patterns of a highly general sort that can be manifested at both local and global levels of narratives, and indeed of texts in general. Kenneth Burke argued this point as early as 1931 in his "Lexicon Rhetoricae," "Psychology and Form," and "The Poetic Process" (*Counterstatement*).

are in fact generally understood and agreed upon primitive terms. That may be generally true or it may only be true for a certain set of classic texts. And only if we also ignore how the audience knows and imaginatively accepts the postulated background. But in a full theory, the fact of cultural presupposition should somehow be accounted for, since it entails an interesting complex of audience behavior. The set of traits constituting a man's goodness changes from century to century, from society to society. To understand that a given trait or action is in fact good requires familiarity and imaginative sympathy with traditions other than one's own. Greek and Christian virtues tend to resemble each other and to differ from those honored by African or Amerindian civilizations. But even within the Western tradition it is easy to forget that we must learn many presuppositions. To grasp that Oedipus is basically good and noble despite his penchant for killing older gentlemen at crossroads may require some realignment of our early upbringing.

Thus, the relativism inherent in comprehending narratives, not to speak of analyzing and taxonomizing them, makes itself deeply felt. If we are serious about theory, we must question how in fact we do make such decisions. Are we forever condemned to Aristotle's moral presuppositions, no matter how poorly they fit modern characters or situations? If not, how shall we go about finding new and more adequate taxonomic features? And at the other pole, how do we guard against runaway proliferation? What is our instrument of control? How do we find our way amid so many potential variables with so few persuasive diagnostic tests? I cannot pretend an answer, but I think it is instructive to look at the successes of the Formalists and Structuralists in the macrostructural analysis of certain homogeneous texts. We can ask whether the principles informing their research are applicable to other kinds of narratives.

Structuralist taxonomies rest on the *forms* rather than substances of narrative content. Vladimir Propp was first to argue the point:

The most common [previous] division is . . . into tales with fantastic content, tales of everyday life, and animal tales. At first glance everything appears to be correct. But involuntarily the question arises,

"Don't tales about animals sometimes contain elements of the fantastic to a very high degree?" And conversely, "Don't animals actually play a large role in fantastic tales?" Is it possible to consider such an indicator as sufficiently precise?[47]

He recognized that below irrelevant biological and physical considerations, diverse characters—say an old woman, a bear, a forest spirit, or a mare's head—could perform the "same" action in different but related tales, say to test and reward a hero, could in short be similar "functors" of a single function. How did he do this? By discovering and demonstrating that there was a code implicit in each story in the corpus, a code that devotees of the Russian fairy tale know and expect. Just as speakers of a language can recognize that different pronunciations of a phoneme and different variants of a morpheme "amount to the same thing," the audience of Russian tales have learned that different actors and classes of action "amount to the same thing." The name assigned to them is not important, but the interchangeability of the functors within a function is. In fact it is precisely that interchangeability that keeps the genre alive for its audience, who recognize both the comforts of the old (the function itself) and the imaginative delights of the new (a Martian can be a villain, too). Propp as analyst looked to the behavior of the "native speaker" of the narrative "language" of the Russian fairy tale. His success was clearly facilitated by the relative simplicity of the tales and their large number, large enough to formulate and test hypotheses about the nature and sequencing of the kernels.[48] Todorov, who persuasively applies a similar technique to the *Decameron*, asserts the principle clearly:

47. *Morphology of the Folktale*, p. 5.
48. It is unfortunate that Propp should claim more for his analysis than it will bear. One can only regret the acceptance of Veselovskij's prediction with which he ended his *Morphology*: "'Is it permissible in this field also to consider the problem of typical schemes . . . giving rise to new formations? . . . Contemporary narrative literature, with its complicated thematic structure and photographic reproduction of reality apparently eliminates the very possibility of such a question. But when this literature will appear to future generations as distant as antiquity, from prehistoric to medieval times, seems to us at present —when the synthesis of time, that great simplifier, in passing over the complexity of phenomena, reduces them to the magnitude of points receding into the distance, then their lines will merge with those which we are now uncover-

The recurrence of relations is necessary if one is to identify a narrative structure. . . . We cannot speak of the structure of a short story if we limit ourselves uniquely to that story . . . a large number is also a guarantee: it permits us to proceed to verifications which will prove or disprove our hypotheses. Only an extended corpus will allow one to pose questions about the organization of the system; one of the criteria for choosing between two equally faithful descriptions is that of simplicity.[49]

Like Propp (and other recent narratologists), Todorov presents the plot recurrences of Decameron stories in algebraic formulae. First he reduces a story to its paraphrase. From the paraphrased sentence, he extracts three basic symbols—the narrative noun-subjects (for characters), narrative adjectives (their traits or situations), and narrative predicates (the actions performed). Obviously symbols in themselves are of little importance: one does not perform significant analysis by simply converting names and words into capital and lower case letters, minus and plus marks, arrows and the like. These reductions are useless unless they lead to new insights. Now reduction is a mixed blessing. On the positive side it provides, nay insists upon a decision: characters, qualities, situations, actions must be replaced by symbols. From their array an otherwise invisible pattern may emerge, and the pattern can be checked against other stories in the corpus. Classification of this sort provides a fund of hypotheses to be tested. "New" Decameronesque stories can be invented. But there is no guarantee that the reduc-

---

ing when we look back at the poetic traditions of the distant past—and the phenomena of schematism and repetition will then be established across the total expanse'" (p. 116). Fortunately Propp rectified this absurd view later, in the Italian translation of the *Morphology*: "The methods proposed in this volume before the appearance of structuralism . . . are . . . limited in their application. They are possible and profitable, wherever one has repeatability on a large scale, as in language or in folklore. But when art becomes the sphere of action of an unrepeatable genius, the use of exact methods will give positive results only if the study of the repeatable elements is accompanied by the study of that which is unique, which we observe as a manifestation of an unknowable miracle" (translated into English by D'Arco Silvio Avalli, to appear in *Proceedings of the First International Congress of Semiotics*).

49. Tzvetan Todorov, *Grammaire du Décameron* (The Hague, 1969), p. 11. Cf. Todorov, "Narrative Transformations," in *The Poetics of Prose*, pp. 218–233, and Part III of A.-J. Greimas, *Du Sens* (Paris, 1970).

tion has not been too powerful. Paraphrase is not an innocent procedure, nor are its principles well understood. A potentially criterial element may be eliminated. Propp's and Todorov's safeguard is their strong intuition, as "native speakers," of how the pattern *should* work, and the symbols are introduced to test that intuition. Thus their "grammars" are not discovery procedures: algebra did not unearth the structures of the Russian fairy tale and the Decameronesque story. It only *accounted* for the analyst's previous sense of pattern.

(In a way, though prescriptively, this is what Aristotle was also doing. He supposed that the ancient dramatic plots made up a coherent universe of texts. Thus, he could incorporate constancies of subject like "men," traits like "noble" and "fortunate," and predicates like "rise" and "fall." But he must have intuited the structure before formulating its rules. The rules work to the extent that they account for all and only Greek dramas.)

But to transfer Propp's and Todorov's method to any narrative macrostructure whatsoever is questionable. Most do not have the necessary overarching recurrences. The worlds of modern fiction and cinema are not two-valued, black and white, as are the Russian fairy tales and the *Decameron*. Who are the heroes and who the villains, say, in Mauriac's *Noeud de vipères* or Unamuno's *Abel Sanchez*? Or to revert to Aristotle's basic dichotomy, how can we know whether a character's situation has improved or worsened in a narrative whose very point is to question the values of the society depicted (for example, Sartre's *Les Chemins de la liberté*)?

Nor are we likely to have the contextual support of externally circumscribed corpora. Most narratives do not occur within enclosing and explicating frameworks like *The Decameron*'s. Nor does modern culture at large provide stereotypes of character and action for most narratives, or at least narratives of literary quality. Though stories are being churned out daily in Hollywood (and Moscow) that follow the same kind of relentless format as the Russian fairy tale, the art-narrative is valued precisely because it cannot be reduced to a formula.

I do not mean that Formalist-Structuralist theories of macro-

structural analysis are not valuable and should not be pursued wherever applicable. I only mean that they must not form Procrustean beds that individual narratives cannot sleep in. Here are two cautionary examples: (1) Whatever success Robert Scholes achieves in his recent application of Todorov's algebra to "Eveline"[50] depends on his knowledge of the overriding thematic framework of the *Dubliners*. The very decisions about what the symbols should stand for were obviously inspired by a theory of what *all* the stories are about. For example, the choice of traits to attribute to Eveline—"A = Dubliner" and "B = celibate"—was clearly made with an eye to the rest of the collection. Why "a Dubliner" instead of "an Irishwoman" or "a European" or "a female"? Why "celibate" instead of "poor" or "humble"? Scholes acknowledges as much: "This attribute [being a Dubliner], built up over the whole sequence of stories, is in fact what the stories are about. . . . Dubliners tend to be either celibate or unhappily married. . . . " But clearly narratives need not be part of larger thematic wholes, and so the selection of attributes is more problematic. The controls on interpretation are vaguer, and an algebraic model may be exactly the wrong one to use. (2) Some French structuralists, like Claude Bremond, have gone far beyond Propp and Todorov to argue the applicability of taxonomic method to all narratives; they maintain that there exist sets of general categories into which every action whatsoever may be placed. In this view, any narrative can ultimately be analyzed as an assemblage of a dozen or so constant micronarrative elements, corresponding to certain "essential" life situations: "trickery," "contract," "protection," or whatever. The narrative analyst's task is to work out the set of those basic situations. Like all hypotheses, this deserves consideration: it might lead to interesting insights and provocative counterexamples, that is, narratives not foreseen by Bremond's dozen, thereby suggesting potentially new and more inclusive categories. However, one cannot help feeling uneasy. General categories can be used not merely to explain plots, but to explain them away, to reduce their complexities to the simplicity of a

50. "Semiotic Approaches to a Fictional Text: Joyce's 'Eveline,'" *University of Idaho Pound Lectures in the Humanities*, April 8, 1976.

preexistent formula. Or the categories may become so broad as to be inane, virtually identical with those of narrative structure itself, that is, existent plus event.

Nor should the set of *mots-clefs* or descriptive terms naming the kernels of a large group of narratives be accounted categories to which any story whatsoever may be reduced. Kernels are real properties of plots; they exist, may be isolated, and should be named. For many narratives what is crucial is the tenuous complexity of actual analysis rather than the powerful simplicity of reduction. Culler and others have pointed out that a given event cannot be classified separately from its context, especially the final event. A killing may not be a murder but an act of mercy, or a sacrifice, or a patriotic deed, or an accident, or one or more of a dozen other things. No battery of preestablished categories can characterize it independently of and prior to a reading of the whole. The literary theoriest will not find much of interest in preexistent semantic categorizations of possible narrative events. As opposed to the anthropologist (and without denying the legitimate interest of such questions), he will not relish forced decisions about whether a given event is best called "revenge," "denial," "separation," or some other ready-made term. The "making" is precisely a part of an interpretation of the whole. He wants rather to understand how kernels get named by analysts in terms of the total story, on the basis of how each connects with all the others. He is willing to entrust the general categorization of behavior to the capable hands of the anthropologist as another kind of research. It is not taxonomizing the codes per se that is interesting but learning how the codes indicate the resemblance of narratives to each other, why *Tonio Kröger* seems more like *Huckleberry Finn* than like *War and Peace*, that is, how a literary historian recognizes a plot-type like *Bildungsroman*. Perhaps the best way to understand taxonomies is to treat the historian or critic as "native speaker," a user proficient in a code. It is his behavior, as much as the work itself, that we need to examine. That does not at all mean that narrative theory dissolves into literary history; on the contrary, the theorist should study literary history as a reservoir of distinctions whose viability depends not on their "real" nature but on

convention. It is not important that Othello's jealousy score at an appropriate level on the *hamartia* scale in some absolute sense; it is only important that the audience think it does. Or more exactly: that the audience understand and accept the terms of a code in which jealousy is an emotion capable of driving husbands to murder.

In short, the characterization of plot into macrostructures and typologies depends upon an understanding of cultural codes and their interplay with literary and artistic codes and codes of ordinary life. It relies heavily on verisimilitude. Until we can begin to formulate *all* the cultural codes, our deliberations must remain impressionistic compared to studies like Propp's and Todorov's. Plot-typologists must recognize the conventional nature of their basic units. The units only materialize when an audience enters into a contract with the author on the basis of known or learnable conventions. This is a mechanism whose details we know all too little about. It is clear that the categorization of plot-types is the most problematic area of narrative studies and may well have to wait until we have a number of in-depth analyses like *S/Z* and access to a general semiotics of culture. But even then our goal must never be reductionist.

For the present, the notion that all narratives can be successfully grouped according to a few forms of plot-content seems to me highly questionable. Work should proceed genre by genre, for much is to be learned in comparing narratives from a content-formal point of view. We are not ready yet for a massive assault on the question of plot macrostructure and typology.

3 STORY:

Existents

Our deeds determine us, as much as
we determine our deeds.

> George Eliot,
> *Adam Bede*

Story-Space and Discourse-Space

As the dimension of story-events is time, that of story-existence is space. And as we distinguish story-time from discourse-time, we must distinguish story-space from discourse-space. The distinction emerges most clearly in visual narratives. In films explicit story-space is the segment of the world actually shown on the screen; implied story-space is everything off-screen to us but visible to the characters, or within earshot, or alluded to by the action.

A major difference between seeing a set of objects in real life and on film is the arbitrary cutting-off performed by the frame. In real life there is no black rectangular edge sharply delimiting a visual sector but a gradual defocusing that we sense as much as see; we know we can bring peripheral objects into focus by a slight turn of the head. Nor, obviously, do we always see things while seated in a darkened room.

Story-space contains existents, as story-time contains events. Events are not spatial, though they occur in space; it is the entities that perform or are affected by them that are spatial.[1]

Story-space in cinema is "literal," that is, objects, dimensions and relations are analogous, at least two-dimensionally, to those

1. Physicists (who fortunately will not read this book) would be right to smile at the naïveté of the distinction. Everything in the universe, of course, is an event in some sense; not only the sun but each stone consists ultimately of a series of electric charges. The event-existent distinction is a purely folk ("commonsense") attitude taught us by the codes of our culture. The culture can "naturalize" events into existents: "fist" in English is a noun, hence we think of it as an object; in other languages it is a verb, hence an event. Narrative analysis is based on folk, not scientific, physics.

in the real world. In verbal narrative it is abstract, requiring a reconstruction in the mind. Thus, a discussion of story-space begins most conveniently with the cinema.

Story-Space in Cinematic Narrative

Let us consider the several spatial parameters that communicate story in film. As has been noted, these must be specified when shown—they are *bestimmt* in the cinema. Most film handbooks provide ample discussion of such distinctions;[2] I only wish to emphasize the difference between story- and discourse-space.

1. *Scale or size*. Each existent has its own size, which is a function of its "normal" size in the real world (as compared to other recognizable objects), and its distance from the camera's lens. Proximity can be manipulated for both natural and supernatural effects. Small-scale models of Spanish galleons in a bathtub photographed at relatively close range will seem like the real things when enlarged in projection. A two-inch lizard shot close up will glower like a dinosaur on the screen when superimposed, by back-projection, against Tokyo skyscrapers.

2. *Contour, texture, and density*. The linear outlines on the screen are strictly analogous to the objects photographed. But the cinema, a two-dimensional medium, must project its third dimension. The texture of surfaces can only be conveyed by shadow-modeling on the flat screen.

3. *Position*. Each existent is situated (a) in the vertical and horizontal dimension of the frame, and (b) in relation to other existents within the frame, at a certain angle from the camera: head on or from the rear, relatively high or low, to the left or to the right.

4. *Degree, kind, and area of reflected illumination (and color in color films)*. The existent is lit strongly or weakly, the source-light is focused or diffused, and so on.

2. See, for example, Alan Casty, *The Dramatic Art of the Film* (New York, 1971), chs. 4, 5, 6, 7, 11, 12; Raymond Spottiswoode, *A Grammar of the Film* (Berkeley and Los Angeles, 1965); Noël Burch, *Theory of Film Practice* (New York, 1973).

5. *Clarity or degree of optical resolution*. The existent is in sharp or "soft" focus (corresponding to the effect of *sfumato* in painting), in or out of focus, or shown through a distorting lens.

The borders between story-space and discourse-space are not so easy to establish as those between story-time and discourse-time. Unlike temporal sequence, placement or physical disposition has no natural logic in the real world. Time passes for all of us in the same clock direction (if not psychological rate), but the spatial disposition of an object is relative to other objects and to the viewer's own position in space.[3] Angle, distance, and so on are controlled by the director's placement of the camera. Life offers no predetermined rationale for these placements. They are all choices, that is, products of the art of the director. Take the scene in *Citizen Kane* when Jed Leland asks to be transferred to the Chicago branch of the *Inquirer*. A narrative choice of the normal narrative "chrono-logic" is posed—Kane can accede to the request, or he can refuse. He refuses. Leland then can elect to remain on the New York *Inquirer* or quit. He threatens to quit. Kane then can either accept his resignation or approve his transfer. He agrees to the latter. Here is the typical branching of the temporal structure of narrative events. But there is no comparable logic that will tell us whether Leland should stand on the left or on the right of Kane when he makes his request, or that he should even be in the frame: the whole thing could be done by focusing on Kane's face and watching his expression as he hears Leland's request from off-screen.

Presented here is a frame from that scene, shot from a low angle, the two men looming over us. Clearly the effect is a greater dramatization of the moment, intensifying the conflict between the two estranged friends. Leland feels that Kane has sold out, so the conflict is as much ideological as personal. The low angle makes the figures towering, larger-than-life emblems of principle rather than private individuals.

Let us consider the frame further in terms of the parameters listed above. (I do not mean to suggest that information about

3. E. H. Gombrich has explained this phenomenon beautifully in *Art and Illusion* (Princeton, 1972) and other works.

Frame reproduced from Orson Welles's *Citizen Kane* courtesy of RKO
General Pictures.

the existents is uniquely provided by these features—only that they confirm what we are also piecing together from the dialogue, story context, and so on.) Scale: Hollywood jargon calls this a "two-shot." The screen is filled by as much of two bodies as it can accommodate, roughly from the top of heads to thighs, thus, medium-close camera distance. There is a sense of tension created by the crowding of the bodies at the edges, exaggerating the conflicted empty space between the two characters. Contour: Leland's defiance is confirmed by his erect if drunken bearing. Kane, on the other hand, stands with head slightly bent, which in context reads as an attitude of defeat. Texturally, both are disheveled, Leland drunkenly so (dinged hat, collarless shirt), Kane exhaustedly so (his clothes preserve some elegance). Position: Leland is to the left, and both (with the exception of Kane's head) are parallel to the vertical lines of the frame. Leland's coat, though hanging open, also parallels the frame edges, while the pin stripes on Kane's vest, coat, and trousers are "deviant," perhaps to support the "uprightness" of Leland's moral vision. The physical gap between the two characters, which accentuates the rupture of their friendship, is not mollified by the whisky bottle. Its angle is tentative; it does not bridge the gap. The two men are connected only by the hostile diagonals of the two rafters in the ceiling, their intersection blocked by Leland's body. Though the torsos stand at an angle half-opened to the camera, Leland's face is turned accusatorily. Kane's eyes, on the other hand, are downcast, confirming his unwillingness to fight. Lighting: the sense of estrangement is enhanced. Deep shadows obscure Leland's eyes, sharpen his nose (a kind of converse projectile to that formed by the rafters), accentuate his scowl and bitterly set chin. Kane's face is also spot-lit. The lines of his face are hardened, especially at the temples and left cheekbone, showing his fatigue and reluctance to fight back. Focus: the focus is sharp and clean. Details can be made out clearly—Leland's Adam's apple and collar button, the buttonholes on Kane's vest. The starkness reflects the stark reality of the moment, the definitive rupture of an old friendship.

Movies of course are more than the set of individual frames:

the existents move, in any direction, including off-screen, and the camera can move with or against them in an infinity of combinations. Further, movement can be suggested by editing. Constant mobility makes cinematic story-space highly elastic without destroying the crucial illusion that it is in fact *there*. One can even embed a second fictive screen within the screen forming our presumed discursive limit, as one verbal narrative can be embedded within another. *Citizen Kane* utilizes such intradiegesis in the opening newsreel account of Kane's life. Unbeknownst to the viewer, the two screens exactly coincide until the newsreel concludes; then the trick is revealed as the "real" camera moves left to show the final titles of the newsreel, now distorted in oblique angle. The conical "throw" of the projector is marked by the cigarette smoke that has accumulated in the screening room.

Story-Space in Verbal Narrative

In verbal narrative, story-space is doubly removed from the reader, since there is not the icon or analogy provided by photographed images on a screen. Existents and their space, if "seen" at all, are seen in the imagination, transformed from words into mental projections. There is no "standard vision" of existents as there is in the movies. While reading the book, each person creates his own mental image of Wuthering Heights. But in William Wyler's screen adaptation, its appearance is determined for all of us. It is in this sense that verbal story-space is said to be abstract. Not nonexistent, but a mental construct rather than an analogon.

Verbal narratives can also depict movement through story-space, even in cinematic ways. In William Golding's *Lord of the Flies*, story-space is circumscribed by the shores of the desert island upon which the boys are stranded. Given that space, the novel is frequently "framed," very much like a film.

Piggy looked up miserably from the dawn-pale beach to the dark mountain.
"Are you sure? Really sure, I mean?"
"I told you a dozen times now," said Ralph, "we saw it."
"D'you think we're safe down here?"

"How the hell should I know?"

Ralph jerked away from him and walked a few paces along the beach. Jack was kneeling and drawing a circular pattern in the sand with his forefinger. Piggy's voice came to them, hushed.

"Are you sure? Really?"

The effect is like a "pan" in a film. The action follows Ralph from the encounter with Piggy to that with Jack. Our focus of attention is continuously moved, leaving Piggy behind. "Piggy's voice came to them, hushed"—that is, from "off-frame."

Thus, discourse-space as a general property can be defined as *focus of spatial attention*. It is the framed area to which the implied audience's attention is directed by the discourse, that portion of the total story-space that is "remarked" or closed in upon, according to the requirements of the medium, through a narrator or through the camera eye—literally, as in film, or figuratively, as in verbal narrative.

How do verbal narratives induce mental images in story-space? One can think of at least three ways: the direct use of verbal qualifiers ("huge," "torpedo-shaped," "shaggy"); reference to existents whose parameters are "standardized," by definition, that is, carry their own qualifiers ("skyscraper," "1940 Chevrolet coupe," "silver-mink coat"); and the use of comparison with such standards ("a dog as big as a horse"). These are explicit, but images can also be implied by other images ("John could lift a 200-pound barbell with one hand" implies the size of John's biceps).

Another important consideration is whose sense of space is being depicted. We depend on the "eyes" we are seeing with—narrator, character, implied author. Are we inside or outside the character? And "outside" in what sense? Completely separate from, alongside, or what? Here we plunge into the murky realm of *point of view*. In Chapter 4 I try to disentangle its senses and relation to narrative *voice*, with which it is often confused.

A character can perceive only that which is in the world of the story, through a perceptual narrative predicate. The object of this predicate appears within his *perceived* story-space, and his point of view is from his *occupied* story-space: "Richard Dalloway and Hugh Whitbread . . . looked in at a shop window. . . .

Richard was aware that he was looking at a silver two-handled Jacobean mug, and . . . Hugh Whitbread admired . . . a Spanish necklace. . . ." We infer Dalloway's and Whitbread's purview—its distance (say three or four feet), angle (obliquely downwards), size (a shop window, say one hundred square feet), and so on.

Once a verbal narrative has established a locus in a character's mind, it may communicate his perceptual space without explicit perceptual verbs (just as it can render inner views without explicit cognitive verbs). Rezia and Septimus, sitting forlornly on chairs in Regent's Park, are asked directions to the tube station by Maisie Johnson, fresh from Edinburgh:

> . . . how queer it was, this couple she had asked the way of, and the girl started and jerked her hand, and the man—he seemed awfully odd; quarreling, perhaps; parting for ever, perhaps; something was up, she knew; and now all these people (for she returned to the Broad Walk), the stone basins, the prim flowers, the old men and women, invalids most of them in Bath chairs—all seemed, after Edinburgh, so queer.

Not a single "she saw" but such is the set of discursive expectancies that the mere mention of the couple, the stone basins, the flowers, old people in Bath chairs presupposes Maisie's vision of them and their environs.

On the other hand a narrator may delimit story-space, whether in direct description, or obliquely, *en passant*. Observations may be presented by a narrator who assumes that people and places need to be introduced and identified. The narrator may be omnipresent (a power separate from omniscience). Omnipresence is the narrator's capacity to report from vantage-points not accessible to characters, or to jump from one to another, or to be in two places at once. In the opening sentences of *Jude the Obscure*, our attention is first directed to the village of Marygreen where a small cart and horse stand in front of the schoolhouse. The narrator's visual relation to the objects is vague; the passage does not emphasize how things looked but rather their significance and history (it is the miller's cart and horse, the schoolmaster never studied the piano, etc.). We do not know exactly where the narrator stands, or indeed if he "stands" anywhere. The second paragraph is also vague spa-

tially: "The rector had gone away for the day. . . ." The space of the rector is "allotopic"; still it exists somewhere in the world of the story. The space of the third paragraph is concrete, firmly within the schoolhouse: our imagined visual frame is now precisely that which would accommodate three men and a piano (and no more).[4]

Verbal story-space then is what the reader is prompted to create in imagination (to the extent that he does so), on the basis of the characters' perceptions and/or the narrator's reports. The two spaces may coincide, or the focus may shift back and forth freely, as in this example from *Madame Bovary*:

> One day he arrived about three o'clock. Everyone was in the fields. He went into the kitchen, and at first didn't see Emma. The shutters were closed; the sun, streaming in between the slats, patterned the floor with long thin stripes that broke off at the corners of the furniture and quivered on the ceiling. On the table, flies were climbing up the sides of glasses that had recently been used, and buzzing as they struggled to keep from drowning in the cider at the bottom. The light coming down the chimney turned the soot on the fireback to velvet and gave a bluish cast to the cold ashes. Between the window and the hearth Emma sat sewing; her shoulders were bare, beaded with little drops of sweat.

The first two sentences are ambiguous from the strict perceptual point of view. Charles's entrance is either seen from the outside, the narrator's vantage, or from the character's (we share *his* sense of arrival, we see the door and move into the room with him). But in the third sentence story-space is clearly the narrator's: ". . . at first [Charles] didn't see Emma," though Emma was in the room. The next sentences, however, suggest Charles's perception. The order of presentation—the closed shutters, beam of sunlight streaming through the slats, and so on—records the temporal order in which they came into his

4. "Butor explains: just as every organization of time-spans within a narrative or a musical composition . . . can only exist by virtue of the suspension of the habitual time of reading or listening, so all the spatial relations of characters or adventures narrated to me can only reach me through the intermediary of a distance which I hold in relation to the place which surrounds me." As quoted by F. Van Rossum-Guyon, *Critique du roman* (Paris, 1970), p. 25n. (original in "L'Espace du roman," *Répertoire* II, 43).

vision. Completing its circuit back to the window, Charles's glance falls at last on Emma.

The reader does not go through such speculative gyrations as he reads, but the logic of his acquisition of story-space must be something like that. Certainly one of the values of scrutinizing cinematic narratives—where discourse-space is analogous— is to make us conscious of how scenes change, characters get from one spot to another, and so on. Verbal and cinematic narratives share an agile fluidity in depicting space not available to the traditional stage. In the classic stage-play a single set may suffice for a scene, an act or even a whole play. Dialogue alone will imply "other parts." Further, the relation of the characters' distance, angle of vision, and so on are relatively fixed. Even when a character moves through the greatest distance that the stage permits, say from extreme background right to extreme foreground left, the audience cannot see much more of his person than if he had remained where he was. But in film we can literally (and in novel, figuratively) see the very pores of a character's face if the camera wishes to exhibit them.

The affinity between cinematic and verbal narrative has been frequently noted. Indeed, "camera eye" is a comfortable metaphor in traditionalist literary criticism: "The omniscient eye which surveys the scene in the first chapter of *Bleak House* is like the lens of a film camera in its mobility. It may encompass a large panoramic view or, within a sentence, it may swoop down to a close scrutiny of some character or local detail."[5] How precisely is this done in verbal narratives, where all the artist can command are words? The answer must lie in the words themselves. The "survey" of Southern England on the first page of *Bleak House* is achieved by nouns whose very sense implies pervasiveness, expanse: "Fog everywhere . . . up the river . . . down the river . . . on the Essex marshes . . . on the Kentish heights," "Gas looming through the fog in diverse places in the streets," "Mud in the streets, as if the waters had but newly retired from the face of the earth." These are "mass" nouns (denoting that which exists in an extensive continuum). The

5. W. J. Harvey, *Character and the Novel* (Ithaca, N.Y., 1966), p. 95.

"count" nouns that occur are indefinite plural, again suggesting pervasiveness, a vast collection of disparate things: "streets," "dogs, undistinguishable in mire," "horses," "foot passengers, jostling one another's umbrellas," "aits and meadows," "tiers of shipping," "marshes and heights," "cabooses of collier-brigs and gunwales of barges and small boats." The narrator's eye is omnipresent, both by its bird's-eye-view perspective and its flying movement—from streets to meadows, from shipping tiers to the firesides of Greenwich pensioners. It is this capacity for "cinematographic" surveillance (not merely "photographic" reproduction), for a picture whose canvas is dynamic, not static, that prompted Eisenstein to discover in Dickens' novels the inspiration for D. W. Griffith's films.

But there remain important differences between verbal and cinematic story-space. Recall the frame. Images evoked in my mind by verbal descriptive passages are not contained by frames, but no matter how engrossed in a movie I become, I never lose the sense that what I see is bounded by the screen's edges. Further, I "see" in my reading mind's eye only what is named. At the movies, however, I note both focal objects, a cowboy walking down a deserted street in a Western frontier town, and also peripheral objects—the sky, buildings, tethered horses. If the movie has lost its grip on me, my attention may well wander from the focal to the fringe area. Even if the fringe area is obliterated in neutral gray or black, the frame remains, sectioning off the world of the work in a spatially arbitrary way. Further, verbal narratives can be completely nonscenic, "nowhere in particular," transpiring in a realm of ideas rather than place. The movies have difficulty evoking this kind of nonplace. Even a pure black or gray or white backdrop will suggest night, or a fogged-in area, or heaven, or an overilluminated room, but rarely "nowhere."

Finally, the cinema cannot *describe* in the strict sense of the word, that is, arrest the action. It can only "let be seen." There are tricks for doing that, close-ups, certain camera movements, and so on. But these are hardly descriptions in the normal sense of the word. Filmmakers may use a narrator's "voice-over"; but

they find this effect inartistic, and generally limit it to introductions. Too much overt verbal description suggests a lack of faith in the medium, the kind that Doris Lessing would deplore. So the cinema must seek out obvious visual symbolic props. Say a young woman has motherly impulses, as in the British film *Georgy Girl*. The director shoots her in bifocal glasses, a Mother Hubbard "snood," seated in front of the television set, watching a program on childbirth, knitting something small. An important consequence of the difference between the filmic presentation and verbal description of objects: the filmed image of an object, no matter how large it is or how complex its parts, may appear whole on the screen. We form an immediate visual synthesis. Verbal description, on the other hand, cannot avoid a linear detailing through time: "Thus each part stays . . . individualized, underlined, independent. . . . The film object enjoys an *intense autonomy* . . . the described object . . . [only] a relative autonomy."[6]

Let us now turn to the objects contained in story-space, the existents, namely character and setting.

Story-Existents: Character

It is remarkable how little has been said about the theory of character in literary history and criticism. If we consult a standard handbook, we are likely to find a definition of the *genre* of "character" (Thomas Overbury, La Bruyère). If we turn to "characterization," we read: "The depicting, in writing, of clear images of a person, his actions and manners of thought and life. A man's nature, environment, habits, emotions, desires, instincts: all these go to make people what they are, and the skillful writer makes his important people clear to us through a portrayal of these elements."[7] We are left with little more than

6. Jean Ricardou, *Problèmes du nouveau roman* (Paris, 1967), p. 70.
7. William F. Thrall and Addison Hibbard, *A Handbook to Literature* (New York, 1936), pp. 74–75. W. J. Harvey, *Character and the Novel*, p. 192, comments: "Modern criticism, by and large, has relegated the treatment of character to the periphery of its attention, has at best given it a polite and perfunctory nod and has regarded it more often as a misguided and misleading abstraction. Plenty of 'character sketches' still appear which serve only as easy targets for such

the identification of characters as "persons" or "people" "depicted in writing."[8]

That characters are indeed simply "people" captured somehow between the covers of books or by actors on stage and screen seems an unspoken axiom, the mute entity following the symbol ∃ in symbolic logic. Perhaps the axiom is inevitable, but no one has argued the need to *decide* if it is, if "character" and "people" are, as Kenneth Burke would say, "consubstantial." Obviously narrative theory should at least contemplate the relationship. And whether we apply to characters the laws of the psychology of personality should be something we do consciously, not merely because we have not thought of alternatives. At the present moment, the concept of "trait" is about all we have for the discussion of character. But the conventionality (rather than inevitability) of its transfer to fictional beings must be stressed. Theory requires an open mind to other possibilities that might better suit the requirements of the narrative construct.

Aristotle's Theory of Character

Chapter II of *Poetics* begins with the statement, "Artists imitate men involved in action." According to O. B. Hardison, "In the Greek, the emphasis is on action, not on the men performing the action. . . . Action comes first; it is the object of imitation. The agents who perform the action come second." He then

---

hostility. But if I wish to refer my students to a wise and substantial general treatment of character in fiction there is relatively little to which I can direct them since E. M. Forster's deceptively light treatment of the subject more than thirty years ago."

8. M. H. Abrams, in *A Glossary of Literary Terms* (New York, 1958), p. 69, also dwells on "people": "The plot is the system of actions represented in a dramatic or narrative work; the characters are the people, endowed with specific moral and dispositional qualities, who carry on the action . . . the sphere of 'character' can be progressively widened to include even the thought and speeches in which it manifests itself, as well as the physical actions which are motivated by a person's character." It is eyebrow-raising to learn that physical actions, thought, and speeches are part of character, rather than activities performed by characters. But more deplorable is the ease with which character is explained away by "people" and "person" at the very moment that the artificial and constructive character of plot (a "system of actions") is so clearly asserted.

underlines a crucial distinction in Aristotle's theory: "Agent (*pratton*) should be carefully distinguished from character (*ethos*), for agents—people who perform actions—are necessary to a drama; but character in the technical Aristotelian sense is something that is added later and, in fact, is not even essential to successful tragedy, as we learn in Chapter VI (l. 59)."[9] "Added later . . . if at all": to Aristotle some traits are not only secondary but inessential. But clearly every agent or *pratton* must have at least one trait, namely that deriving from the action he performs, a fact implicit in the *nomina agentis*: one who commits murder or usury is (at least) murderous or usurious. No explicit statement need be made; the trait holds by the mere performance of the action. According to Hardison, "the *key* traits of the agents are determined [by function even] before 'character' [*ethos*] is added."

Nevertheless Aristotle attributes (in Chapter II) one additional trait to *pratton*: the agent "must either be noble or base, since human character regularly conforms to these distinctions, all of us being different in character because of some quality of goodness or evil." The qualities noble (*spoudaios*) and base (*phaulos*)— and these alone—are primary, belong to the agent (*pratton*) in some direct way, rather than indirectly or "additionally" to his character (*ethos*), because "they are qualities inherent in agents by virtue of the actions in which they are involved."[10] It seems reasonable to ask why the base/noble traits are the only reflexes of "action." If one trait is assigned to an action, why isn't the floodgate thereby opened? Odysseus is shown by his actions to be "subtle"—which is neither "noble" nor "base." Why is "subtle" not attributed to his *pratton*?

In addition to being "noble" or "base," an agent may or may

9. Golden and Hardison, *Aristotle's Poetics*, pp. 4, 82. The primacy of action is underlined repeatedly throughout the *Poetics*. In ch. 6, for example, plot is compared to the "over-all plan of a painting" and character to the "colors" which fill in the spaces. (But line drawings are also satisfying.) A painting with such colors alone "would not please us as much as if [the painter] had outlined the figure in black and white."

10. Ibid., pp. 5, 83. And in opposition to other commentators, Hardison notes that "nobility and baseness cannot, strictly speaking, be part of character at all." They occupy "a kind of 'no-man's land' between plot and character."

not have a character, an *ethos*, for instance, being "good" (*chrestos*). "By character," says Aristotle, "I mean that element in accordance with which we say that agents are of a certain type." The "element" is a composite of personality features, or traits, culled "from such sources as the *Nicomachean Ethics* and, especially, the type-formulas found in classical rhetoric," [11] for instance, the young, the old, the wealthy, the man of power. Aristotle speaks of four dimensions of characterization. The first is *chreston*, already discussed. The second, *harmotton*, means, according to Hardison, "'appropriate' traits [which] allow [the character's] features to be delineated in greater detail and in ways that are necessarily and/or probably related to the action." Admitting the difficulty of interpreting the third principle of characterization, *homoios*, generally translated as "like," Hardison suggests "like an individual," in other words, possessed of "idiosyncrasies that soften—without obscuring—the general outline." In a highly traditionalist art-form like Greek tragedy, this "likening" does not mean copying closely from nature, from living models. For example, "when depicting Agamemnon, the poet should use traits that are 'like' those traditionally associated with Agamemnon in legend." [12] The final principle is *homalon* or "consistency": "the traits revealed by the speeches at the end of the play should be the same sort as those revealed by the speeches at the beginning." [13]

Clearly, Aristotle's general formulation of character and characterization is not totally appropriate to a general theory of narrative, although, as usual, he provokes questions that cannot be ignored.

There seems no self-evident reason to argue the primacy of action as a source of traits, nor for that matter the other way around. Is the distinction between agent and character really necessary? Let us argue that plot and character are equally important and escape the awkwardness of explaining how and when character (*ethos*) traits are "added" to agents.

11. Ibid., p. 199.
12. Ibid., p. 203.
13. Ibid., p. 204.

Formalist and Structuralist Conceptions of Character

The views of the Formalists and (some) structuralists resemble Aristotle's in a striking way. They too argue that characters are products of plots, that their status is "functional," that they are, in short, participants or *actants* rather than *personnages*, that it is erroneous to consider them as real beings. Narrative theory, they say, must avoid psychological essences; aspects of character can only be "functions." They wish to analyze only what characters do in a story, not what they are—that is, "are" by some outside psychological or moral measure. Further, they maintain that the "spheres of action" in which a character moves are "comparatively small in number, typical and classable."

For Vladimir Propp, characters are simply the products of what it is that a given Russian fairy-tale requires them to do.[14] It is as if the differences in appearance, age, sex, life concerns, status, and so on were *mere* differences, and the similarity of function were the only important thing.

Tomashevsky's requirements were not those of the comparative folklorist, but for him too character was secondary to plot: "The presentation of the characters, a sort of living support for the different *motives*, is a running process for grouping and connecting them. . . . The character plays the role of connecting thread helping us to orient ourselves amid the piling-up of details, an auxiliary means for classing and ordering particular motives."[15] Tomashevsky concedes that since narrative appeals through the emotions and moral sense, it requires the audience to share interests and antagonisms with the characters. Thereby arises the story situation, with its tensions and conflicts and resolutions. Still the character is secondary, a derivative product of plot. Though a composite of "characteristics," that is, "the system of motifs which are indissolubly tied to him" constituting his "psyche" (a word that the structuralists reject), "the hero is scarcely necessary to the story (*fabula*). The story as a system

14. Vladimir Propp, *Morphology of the Folktale*, p. 20.
15. B. Tomashevsky, "Thématique," in Todorov, ed., *Théorie de la littérature*, p. 293.

of motifs can entirely dispense with the hero and his characteristic traits." [16]

The French *narratologistes* have largely followed the Formalist
position that "characters are means rather than ends of the
story." Though Claude Bremond shows that Propp's fairy tales
can go counter to this rule, and in fact were occasionally reorga-
nized "to demonstrate the psychological or moral evolution of
a character," [17] his own system concerns only the analysis of
possible event-sequences, disregarding characters completely.
But the role that a character plays is only part of what interests
the audience. We appreciate character traits for their own sake,
including some that have little or nothing to do with "what happens." It is difficult to see how the particularities of certain roles
can be explained as instances or even complexes of elementary
categories like "helper," "avenger," "judge." How, for example, can we account for the full irony of the role of "ambas-
sador" played by Lambert Strether—dispatched to retrieve a
prodigal New England son and becoming "prodigal" himself in
the bargain? What is the "role" of Mrs. Ramsay in *To the Lighthouse* or of Edward in *Les Faux-Monnayeurs*, or of any of the
characters of Samuel Beckett? The inappropriateness of the term
reflects the impossibility of finding sufficiently general categories to meet every case. Or to agree that a character is a case.

The differences between modern characters like Leopold
Bloom or Marcel and Prince Charming or Ivan are so great as
to be qualitative rather than quantitative. Not only are the traits
more numerous, but they tend not to "add up," or more ger-
manely, "break down," that is, reduce to any single aspect or
pattern. They cannot be discovered by ramifying dichotomies;
forcing the issue only destroys the uniqueness of characters'
identities. What gives the modern fictional character the particular kind of illusion acceptable to modern taste is precisely the
heterogeneity or even scatter in his personality.

Some critics redress the balance. Henry James asks, "What is

16. Ibid., p. 296. Barthes, *Communications*, 8: 16, notes that Tomashevsky
later modified this extreme position.
17. "Le Message narratif," in *Communications*, 4: 15 (reprinted in *Logique
du récit*, Paris, 1973).

character but the determination of incident? What is incident but the illustration of character?" Both character and event are logically necessary to narrative; where chief interest falls is a matter of the changing taste of authors and their publics. The contemplation of character is the predominate pleasure in modern art narrative. It depends on the convention of the uniqueness of the individual, but that is a convention no less than the older insistence on the predominance of action.

Aristotle and the Formalists and some structuralists subordinate character to plot, make it a function of plot, a necessary but derivative consequence of the chrono-logic of story. One could equally argue that character is supreme and plot derivative, to justify the modernist narrative in which "nothing happens," that is, the events themselves do not form an independent source of interest, for example, a puzzle or the like. But to me the question of "priority" or "dominance" is not meaningful. Stories only exist where both events and existents occur. There cannot be events without existents. And though it is true that a text can have existents without events (a portrait, a descriptive essay), no one would think of calling it a narrative.

Todorov and Barthes on Character

Others of the structuralists, interested in sophisticated narratives, have come to recognize the need for a more open, afunctional notion of character.

In his studies of *The Decameron, The Thousand and One Nights, Sinbad the Sailor*, and other "anecdotal" narratives, Todorov defends the Proppian attitude toward character, but at the same time he distinguishes two broad categories—plot-centered or apsychological, and character-centered, or psychological narratives: "Though James's theoretical ideal may have been a narrative in which everything is subservient to the psychology of the characters, it is difficult to ignore a whole tendency in literature, in which the actions are not there to 'illustrate' character but in which, on the contrary, the characters are subservient to the action." [18] Texts like *The Thousand and One Nights* and *The Sara-*

18. "Narrative Men," in *The Poetics of Prose*, p. 66.

gossa Manuscripts are *cas limites* of literary apsychologism. Take the narrative statement "X sees Y." Where psychological narratives like James's would stress the experience of X, the focus for apsychological narratives is the action of seeing. For psychological narratives, actions are "expressions" or even "symptoms" of personality, hence "transitive"; for apsychological narratives they exist in their own right, as independent sources of pleasure, hence "intransitive." In narrative-grammatical terms, the focus of the former falls on the subject, of the latter on the predicate. Sinbad is the most impersonal of heroes: the model sentence for his tales is not "Sinbad sees X" but rather "X is seen."

Todorov further discovers that when a trait is cited in an apsychological narrative, its consequence must immediately follow (if Hasim is greedy, he embarks at once in search of money). But then the trait has virtually amalgamated with its consequent action: the relation is now not *potential/fulfillment* but *durative/punctual* or even *iterative/instance*. The anecdotal trait is always provocative of action; there can be no unacted-upon motives or yearnings. Second, only the psychological narrative manifests a trait in different ways. If the narrative statement "X is jealous of Y" occurs in a psychological narrative, X may (a) become a hermit, (b) kill himself, (c) court Y, (d) try to harm Y. In an apsychological narrative like *The Thousand and One Nights*, however, he can only try to harm Y. What was only implied before (as a potential, hence a property of the subject) is reduced to a subordinate part of the act. The "characters" are deprived of choice, and become in a real sense mere automatic functions of the plot. In apsychological narratives, the character is himself the "virtual story that is the story of his life."[19]

Roland Barthes has also shifted from a narrow functional to something like a psychological view of character. His introduction to the famous 1966 issue of *Communications* argued that "the notion of character is secondary, entirely subordinated to the notion of plot," and hinted that historically a belief in "psychological essence" was only the product of aberrant bourgeois influences. But even then he admitted that the problem of character doesn't go away easily:

19. Ibid., pp. 68–70.

On the one hand the characters (whatever the names given to them: *dramatis personae* or *actants*) constitute a necessary plane of the description, outside of which the commonplace "actions" that are reported cease to be intelligible, so that it may safely be assumed that there is not a single narrative in the world without "characters," or at least without "agents." Yet . . . these numerous "agents" cannot be either described or classified in terms of "persons," whether one considers a "person" as a purely historic form restricted to certain genres . . . or . . . one takes the view that the "person" is but a convenient rationalization superimposed by our epoch on otherwise pure narrative agents.

Yet he concludes that Bremond, Todorov, and Greimas correctly "define a character . . . by his participation in a sphere of actions, such spheres being limited in number, typical, and subject to classification," and that the problems of such a formulation (inability to cope with "a great number of narratives," "difficulty [in] accounting for the multiplicity of participatory acts as soon as one starts analyzing them in terms of perspectives," "and [fragmentation of]the system of characters") "can be smoothed over fairly rapidly."[20] That prediction, by any fair estimate, has not materialized. And Barthes himself has changed his tune.

His analysis of Balzac's "Sarrasine," *S/Z*, is monumental, brilliant, and a bit maddening in its elliptical, throwaway style. It deserves itself a booklength study, but I limit myself to remarks on its implications for character analysis. Barthes no longer argues that character and setting are subservient to action. They are narrative properties revealed by their own "code"—the so-called "semic" code (abbreviated SEM).[21] His 1966 attack on "psychological essence" is contradicted by the actual use of words like "trait" and "personality" in *S/Z*: "character is a product of combinations: the combination is relatively stable (denoted by the recurrence of the seme) and more or less complex (involving more or less congruent, more or less contradictory figures [traits]); this complexity determines the charac-

20. "Introduction . . . ," pp. 256–259.
21. *S/Z*, trans. Richard Miller, p. 17 and *passim*. The use of the term "seme" is questionable on several counts. A seme in the Hjelmslevian-Greimasian theory is what is usually called in American linguistics an "elementary semantic feature," a single component of the total sense of a word. For example, a word (or "semanteme" in Greimas' terminology) like English "colt" consists of at least

ter's 'personality,' which is just as much a combination as the odor of a dish or the bouquet of a wine." [22]

Barthes by 1970 is not only stressing the legitimacy of terms like "trait" and "personality": he is arguing that reading narratives is nothing less than a "process of nomination," and that one element to be named is the trait. "To read is to struggle to name, to subject the sentences of the text to a semantic transformation. This transformation is erratic; it consists in hesitating among several names: if we are told that Sarrasine had *'one of those strong wills that know no obstacle,'* what are we to read? *will, energy, obstinacy, stubbornness,* etc.?" [23]

Are Characters Open or Closed Constructs?

Another restriction on character derives from a confusion between story and the verbal manifestation of discourse. A com-

---

two semes—/young/ and /equine/. (Not the phonetic component /yəŋ/ as it appears in "youngster," but the semantic component /young/, which also appears in "boy," "calf," "chick," etc.) Barthes applies the term metaphorically to character without explaining exactly why. To refer to traits as "semes" rather than simply "traits" or "characteristics" implies that they are parts of a "meaningful whole." But is a character, in fact, a "semanteme" in any sense? The "seme" is a content (rather than expression) element, and to a certain extent, I suppose, that which is "meant" by a trait in narrative is a component of the unique referent of the proper name (which Barthes discusses fruitfully—see below). Finally, why should "seme" refer to existents alone and not equally to events (the elements of Barthes's "action" code)? One can decompose a narrative action in precisely the same "semic" way; "to present somebody with a book" could be analyzed into /to hand over/ + /to yield ownership of/ + /to honor/, etc. So it is not clear that the term "seme" is illuminating for narrative analysis.

22. *S/Z*, p. 67. Richard Miller confuses what is already a difficult text by translating French *traits* as "figures." But "figure," in the latter part of this same section, is something more like "temporary personality feature," "role," or "stance." Indeed, it may be precisely an *actantiel* element—that which is required by the plot at the moment, but not necessarily intrinsic to the character. Barthes writes, "The figure is altogether different: it is not a combination of semes concentrated in a legal Name, nor can biography, psychology or time encompass it. . . . As figure, the character can oscillate between two roles, without this oscillation having any meaning. . . . Thus, the child-woman and the narrator-father . . . can overtake the queen-woman and the narrator-slave" (*S/Z*, p. 68). Figure is "a symbolic ideality" (marked in the SYM code), as opposed, presumably, to the "semantic reality" of the character. This clearly distances the later *trait*-Barthes from the earlier *actantiel*-Barthes and enables his theory to deal with richer narratives.

23. Ibid., p. 92.

mon sentiment: "it is characteristic of a fiction that certain questions cannot appropriately be asked about it. We cannot ask how many children Lady Macbeth had; or what courses Hamlet pursued at the University of Wittenberg."[24] But because one question is idle, does it mean that all questions concerning characters are idle? How about "Is Lady Macbeth a good mother, and if so, in what sense of 'good'?" Or, "What is there in her character to explain her bloodthirsty ambition, yet relative lack of staying power once the battle is joined?" Or about Hamlet: "What sort of a student was he? What is the relation between his scholarly interests and his general temperament?" In short, should we restrain what seems a God-given right to infer and even to speculate about characters if we like? Any such restraint strikes me as an impoverishment of aesthetic experience. Implication and inference belong to the interpretation of character as they do to that of plot, theme, and other narrative elements. O. B. Hardison's observations relating to this subject trouble me:

When we consider human actions, we think of them as the outcome of the character and intelligence—the 'personalities'—of the individuals who perform them. Character and thought are the 'natural causes' of actions. When we read a tragedy, we carry this preconception with us. That is, we think of the actions of Hamlet or Macbeth as the results of the personalities of these two dramatic figures. A little consideration, however, will show that this is a false reasoning. Hamlet and Macbeth exist only as words on a printed page. They have no consciousness, and they do whatever the dramatist requires them to do. The feeling that they are living people whose personalities determine the actions they perform is an illusion.[25]

I have done more than a little consideration of this point and cannot agree. Of course Hamlet and Macbeth are not "living people"; but that does not mean that as constructed imitations they are in any way limited to the words on the printed page. Of course their existence at the purely verbal level is relatively superficial. Why should we be any less inclined to search

24. Quoted by David Lodge, *The Language of Fiction* (London, 1967), p. 39, from J. M. Cameron's lecture, "Poetry and Dialectic," in *The Night Battle* (London, 1962).

25. Hardison, *Aristotle's Poetics*, p. 122.

through and beyond the words of Shakespeare for insights into the construct "Hamlet" than through and beyond the words of Boswell for insights into the construct "Samuel Johnson"? Samuel Johnson did indeed live, but any current attempt to "know" him requires reconstruction, inference, and speculation. No matter that the facts and views provided by Boswell are more numerous than those provided by Shakespeare—there is always more to reconstruct, to speculate about. The horizons of personality always recede before us. Unlike geographers, biographers need never worry about going out of business. No one would ever accuse *their* objects of being mere words. The same principle operates with new acquaintances: we read between their lines, so to speak; we form hypotheses on the basis of what we know and see; we try to figure them out, predict their actions, and so on.

The equation of characters with "mere words" is wrong on other grounds. Too many mimes, too many captionless silent films, too many ballets have shown the folly of such a restriction. Too often do we recall fictional characters vividly, yet not a single word of the text in which they came alive; indeed, I venture to say that readers generally remember characters that way. It is precisely the medium that "falls away into dimness and uncertainty," as Lubbock puts it,[26] though our memory of Clarissa Harlowe or Anna Karenina remains undimmed.

As a stylistician, I would be the last to suggest that the interesting configurations of the medium, the words that manifest the character in the verbal narrative, are therefore less worthy of study than other parts of the narrative composite. I only argue that they are separable, and that plot and character are independently memorable.

Some characters in sophisticated narratives remain open constructs, just as some people in the real world stay mysteries no matter how well we know them. Therein perhaps lies the annoyance of enforced visualization of well-known characters in films. The all too visible player—Jennifer Jones as Emma Bovary, Greer Garson as Elizabeth Bennet, even a superb actor like

26. Lubbock, *Craft of Fiction*, p. 4.

Laurence Olivier as Heathcliff—seems unduly to circumscribe the character despite the brilliance of the performance.[27] Where the character is simpler, "flatter," the problem is less acute: Basil Rathbone is easier to accept as Sherlock Holmes because Conan Doyle's character is more limited to begin with. The predictability of Holmes's behavior (his power to collect clues, his teasing of Watson) is agreeably matched by the predictable appearance of the actor.

Toward an Open Theory of Character

A viable theory of character should preserve openness and treat characters as autonomous beings, not as mere plot functions. It should argue that character is reconstructed by the audience from evidence announced or implicit in an original construction and communicated by the discourse, through whatever medium.

What is it that we reconstruct? An unsophisticated answer must do for a start: "What the characters are like," where "like" implies that their personalities are open-ended, subject to further speculations and enrichments, visions and revisions. Of course, there are limits. Critics correctly resist speculations that overflow the bounds of the story or seek superfluous or over-

27. Cf. Wolfgang Iser, *The Implied Reader* (Baltimore, 1974), p. 283: "The truth of this observation is borne out by the experience many people have on seeing . . . the film of a novel. While reading *Tom Jones*, they may never have had a clear conception of what the hero actually looks like, but on seeing the film, some may say 'That's not how I imagined him.' The point here is that the reader of *Tom Jones* is able to visualize the hero virtually for himself, and so his imagination senses the vast number of possibilities; the moment these possibilities are narrowed down to one complete and immutable picture, the imagination is put out of action, and we feel we have somehow been cheated. This may perhaps be an oversimplification of the process, but it does illustrate plainly the vital richness of potential that arises out of the fact that the hero in the novel must be pictured and cannot be seen. With the novel the reader must use his imagination to synthesize the information given him, and so his perception is simultaneously richer and more private; with the film he is confined merely to physical perception, and so whatever he remembers of the world he had pictured is brutally cancelled out" (p. 283). Flaubert refused to allow his books to be illustrated for the same reason: "A woman drawn resembles one woman, that's all. The idea, from then on, is closed, complete and all the sentences are useless" (letter to Ernest Duplan, quoted by Ricardou, *Problèmes*, p. 79).

concrete detail. The kinds of insight desired are "deep" rather than inconsequently broad or unnecessarily specific; they are enriched by experience in life and art, not by self-indulgent flights of fancy. A trip to Dublin cannot but help us understand the special quality of paralysis attributed to its denizens by Joyce, and meeting a Dublin working-class girl, even in 1978, will give us deeper insight into Eveline's predicament and personality. We will more precisely infer traits that we missed or were vague about. We will learn about the distinctively Irish way of being trapped—the religious overtones, the close family ties, the sense of guilt, the sentimental admixtures that make the prison comfortable (like the sense of "fun"—"her father putting on her mother's bonnet to make the children laugh"), and so on. I have never been to Ireland, but I know that the peculiar sort of "strutting" that Eveline's father does would be clearer if I had. Narrative evokes a world, and since it is no more than an evocation, we are left free to enrich it with whatever real or fictive experience we acquire. Yet somehow we know when to stop speculating. Did Ernest smoke? What was the color of Eveline's hair? There is obviously a line that separates the worthwhile from the trivial. (But if we must choose, let us risk irrelevancy rather than exclude potentially rich inferences and speculations about characters.)

We reconstruct "what the characters are like." But what is that? What is the relation between real and fictional personality? We are offered this short definition of "character" by the *Dictionary of Philosophy*:[28] "The totality of mental traits characterizing an individual personality or self. See *Self*." Forgiving the author the repetition of the word-to-be-defined in the definition, and looking up "self," we find a definition most useful for our purposes: "The quality of uniqueness and persistence through changes . . . by virtue of which any person calls himself I and leading to the distinction among selves, as implied in

28. Edited by Dagobert Runes (Totowa, N.J., 1975), p. 230. Perhaps "personality" is a mistake for "person": the *Dictionary* tells us that "person" means "The concrete unity of acts." That commits us to a radically behaviorist view which might satisfy Aristotle and Formalists and structuralists, but for reasons advanced above is not appropriate to a general and open theory of narrative.

such words as myself, yourself, himself, etc." [29] The terms that need particular examination are *totality*, *mental traits*, and *uniqueness . . . leading to the distinction among selves*.

Totality: Two questions arise: (1) What is the nature of this totality? Is it ever achievable in narrative? Obviously not. "Totality" is a theoretical construct, a limit never to be reached, a horizon toward which we travel, hopefully with increasing intellectual and emotional maturity. (2) Is the totality organized in some sense? Is it a teleological set, or merely an agglomerate? This question needs full consideration; at the moment, an open theory should probably argue for both eventualities. Instances of both in fact occur in literary history.

Traits: Is personality limited to *mental* traits? Turning from philosophy, we see that psychologists generally do not limit the term, and there seems no particular reason for our doing so in respect to fictional characters. What is a trait? Is it the best name for a minimal quality of fictional character? The most useful definition I have found is J. P. Guilford's: "any distinguishable, relatively enduring way in which one individual differs from another." [30] The classic psychological characterization of "trait" was made by Gordon W. Allport. Four of the eight properties he cites seem significant for narrative theory:

1. A trait is more generalized than a habit . . . [it is a] great system . . . of interdependent habits. If the habit of brushing one's teeth can be shown . . . to be unrelated to the habit of dominating a tradesman, there can be no question of a common trait involving both these habits; but if the habit of dominating a tradesman can be shown . . . to be related to the habit of bluffing one's way past guards, there is the presumption that a common trait of personality exists which includes these two habits. . . .

29. Ibid., p. 288.
30. J. P. Guilford, *Personality* (New York, 1959), as quoted in E. L. Kelly, *Assessment of Human Characteristics* (Belmont, Ca., 1967), p. 15. Some other definitions: "consistent and stable modes of an individual's adjustment to his environment" (Gordon W. Allport and Henry S. Odbert, *Trait-Names: A Psycholexical Study, Psychological Monographs*, vol. 47 [Princeton, 1936], p. 26); "the unit or element which is the carrier of the distinctive behavior of a man" (Allport, "What Is a Trait of Personality?" *Journal of Abnormal and Social Psychology*, 25 [1931], 368); "personal disposition . . . integrated systems of action tendencies that comprise the molar units of the total structure of personality,"

2. The existence of a trait may be established empirically or statistically . . . in order to know that an individual has a trait it is necessary to have evidence of repeated reactions which, though not necessarily constant in type, seem none the less to be consistently a function of the same underlying determinant. . . .

3. Traits are only relatively independent of each other . . . [e.g.] in one study expansion correlated with extroversion to the extent of +.39, ascendance with conservatism, +.22, and humor with insight, +.83. . . .

4. Acts, and even habits, that are inconsistent with a trait are not proof of the non-existence of the trait . . . there may be opposed integrations, i.e., contradictory traits, in a single personality . . . there are in every personality instances of acts that are unrelated to existent traits, the product of the stimulus and of the attitude of the moment.[31]

The distinction between "trait" and "habit" is most helpful to narrative theory, as is the characterization of trait as a great system of interdependent habits. Narratives may not examine habits microscopically, but they do demand of the audience the capacity to recognize certain habits as symptomatic of a trait: if a character is constantly washing his hands, mopping already clean floors, picking motes of dust off his furniture, the audience is obliged to read out a trait like "compulsive."

The relative persistence of a trait is critical. Narrative audiences do not perform statistical analyses, but their evidence is empirical. And the observation that traits generally overlap is equally significant, at least for classical narratives. It contributes to that sense of the verisimilar consistency of characters that is the cornerstone of fiction, at least of the classical variety. The

---

"'permanent possibilities for action' of a generalized order . . . cortical, sub-cortical, or postural dispositions having the capacity to gate or guide specific phase reactions. . . . Traits . . . include long-range sets and attitudes, as well as such variables as 'perceptual response dispositions,' 'personal constructs,' and 'cognitive styles'" (Allport, "Traits Revisited," in *The Person in Psychology* [Boston, 1968], pp. 43, 48); "a conceptual attribute or definition of the reactive nature of an individual . . . observable [through] . . . those characteristics (1) which society regards as of sufficient importance to identify and name, and (2) which are regarded as expressions or manifestations of the constitutional nature of the individual," that is, "that characterize a given individual and differentiate him from his fellows . . . [whether] innate or acquired in respect to origin" (H. A. Carr and F. A. Kingsbury, "The Concept of Traits," *Psychological Review*, 45 [1938], 497).

31. "What Is a Trait of Personality?" *passim*.

observation that "acts, and even habits" may be inconsistent with a trait and that within a given personality there may inhere conflicting traits is absolutely vital to modern character theory. The first point explains how an essentially evil character, like Valmont in *Les Liaisons dangereuses*, may perform a virtuous act; the second accounts for complex, "rounded" characters, like Hamlet or Leopold Bloom.

Uniqueness . . . leading to distinction among selves: It goes without saying that a general theory of character would require such a criterion. We need merely recall the names of certain characters—Othello, Tom Jones, Heathcliff, Dorothea Brooke, Mr. Micawber, Julien Sorel, the March Hare, Augie March—to recognize that the names themselves are more familiar to us than those of acquaintances, or (alas) ex-students. Even where the traits of a character may be forgotten, our sense of their uniqueness rarely flags.

It is interesting to consider how traits acquire names. It turns out that they too are culturally coded. Psychologists observe that it is the

tendency of each social epoch to characterize human qualities in the light of standards and interests peculiar to the times. Historically, the introduction of trait-names can be seen to follow this principle of cultural (not psychological) determination to a striking degree. Presumably human beings through countless ages had displayed such qualities as *devotion, pity,* and *patience,* but these terms were not established with their present meanings until the Church made of them recognized and articulated Christian virtues.[32]

Other sources for our trait-names are astrology (*jovial, saturnine*), Galenian medicine (*good-humored, cold-blooded*), the Reformation (*sincere, bigoted, fanatic, self-assured*), Neoclassicism (*fatuous, callous, countrified*), Romanticism (*depressed, apathetic, diffident*), psychology and psychoanalysis (*introverted, neurotic, schizoid*), etc. These clearly form a code of interest to the semiotician. Like all important philosophical questions, they may be viewed from the polar perspectives of realism and nominalism. The former holds that the terms, from whatever source, "designate 'universals' having an existence apart from individual

32. *Trait-Names*, p. 2.

events."[33] The latter maintains that traits are "names and nothing more," and that there is no necessary "correspondence of linguistic symbols to universals," indeed, that there are no such universals.[34] Realists argue that the very fact that the Nominalist can regard "names as mere designations of a range of perceived similarities . . . is a demonstration of the objective validity of universals. . . . They are similar *in some respect*, and it is in this *respect* that the universal itself subsists."[35] Nominalists are right, however, in recognizing that the *names* for traits are "socially invented signs, by no means perfect designations of what is going on materially in the depths of nature. Trait-names are not themselves traits."[36]

This modest survey of psychological opinion suggests that the narrative theorist may justifiably rely on the rich coding of trait-names stored by history in ordinary language. The repertoire of names exactly suits a genre addressed to an audience that analyzes persons in cultural (hence language-bound) terms, that is, verisimilarly. The psychologist admits that he cannot offer better names than the traditional ones, agreeing with Francis Bacon: "The problem of human dispositions . . . is one of those things wherein the common discourse of men is wiser than books—a thing which seldom happens." And Ludwig Klages: "Language excels in unconscious insight the acumen of the most talented thinker, and we contend that whoever, having the right talent, should do nothing but examine the words and phrases which deal with the human soul, would know more about it than all the sages who omitted to do so, and would know perhaps a thousand times more than has ever been discovered by observation, apparatus, and experiment upon man."[37]

33. Ibid., p. 5.
34. Ibid., p. 6. For example, A. P. Weiss denies that there is any such trait as, say, *benevolence*: "from the sensimotor standpoint these actions [putative instances of "benevolence"] are all different." Or, as Allport and Odbert put the Nominalist position: "A trait-name . . . covers some perceived similarities in conduct, but to perceive similarity . . . is often simply a failure to perceive analytically."
35. *Trait-Names*, p. 8.
36. Ibid., p. 17.
37. Ibid., p. 4 (from *The Advancement of Learning*, Book VIII, ch. 3), and p. 1 (from *The Science of Character*), quoted by Allport and Odbert.

For narrative purposes, then, a trait may be said to be a narrative adjective out of the vernacular labeling a personal quality of a character, as it persists over part or whole of the story (its "domain"). Just as we define "event" at the story level as a narrative predicate (DO or HAPPEN), so we can define "trait" as the narrative adjective tied to the narrative copula when that replaces the normal transitive predicate. The actual verbal adjective, of course, need not (and in modernist narratives will not) appear. But whether inferred or not, it is immanent to the deep structure of the text. In "Eveline," for example, no such word as "timid" or "paralyzed" appears. But clearly we must infer these traits to understand the narrative, and comprehending readers do so. Thus the traits exist at the story level: indeed, the whole discourse is expressly designed to prompt their emergence in the reader's consciousness.

The definition of narrative trait as an adjective, which in turn is defined as a personal quality, may seem question-begging or a mere trading in names. But it usefully emphasizes the transaction between narrative and audience. The audience relies upon its knowledge of the trait-code in the real world. This code is enormous.[38] In naming, we identify the trait recognized by the culture. At the same time, narrative theory does not need the psychologists' distinctions among moral virtues and vices, behavior predispositions, attitudes, motives and so on. All relatively persistent personality features can be lumped together as traits in a rough-and-ready fashion if all we care about is what the characters are like. I do not think that this recourse to audience and trait-code evades the issue. On the contrary, it assigns the decision-making function of character interpretation exactly to that party in the narrative transaction who makes it, and is

38. A list of 17,953 trait-names was gleaned from *Webster's Unabridged Dictionary* by Allport and Odbert. A four-part distinction was made (p. 38): I. "Neutral Terms Designating Possible Pertinent Traits" (e.g., abrupt, absent-minded, abstinent); II. "Terms Primarily Descriptive of Temporary Moods or Activities" (abashed, absent, absorbed); III. "Weighted Terms Conveying Social or Characterial Judgements of Personal Conduct, or Designating Influence on Others" [see Allport's exclusion of "moral qualities," in item six in his list of trait-properties above] (abnormal, absorbing, absurd, acceptable); and IV. "Miscellaneous: Designations of Physique, Capacities, and Developmental Conditions; Metaphorical and Doubtful Terms" (able, abortive, abrasive, absolute).

content to leave the study of mechanisms of judgment to others (reader-response theorists, hermeneutists, or whomever).

I have used traditional terms like "trait" with the full consciousness that they may sound old-fashioned and hence suspicious in a theory that pretends to be new and rigorous. My reasons are relatively simple. For one thing, new terms should not be introduced unless new conceptual distinctions warrant them. Insofar as the narrative audience is asked to read out characters in the same way as it does real people, words like "trait" and "habit" are perfectly acceptable, and I see no reason for introducing more or less arcane synonyms. It is enough to distinguish the narrative from the real-life case by adding "narrative" or "fictive" to remind us that we are not dealing with psychological realities but artistic constructs, yet that we understand these constructs through highly coded psychological information that we have picked up in ordinary living, including our experiences with art.

Character: A Paradigm of Traits

I argue—unoriginally but firmly—for a conception of character as a paradigm of traits; "trait" in the sense of "relatively stable or abiding personal quality," recognizing that it may either unfold, that is, emerge earlier or later in the course of the story, or that it may disappear and be replaced by another. In other words, its domain may end. Pip's trait of shyness is replaced by one of snobbishness after his inheritance, and that in turn ultimately changes into one of humility and gratitude after his discovery of the source of his good fortune. At the same time, traits must be distinguished from more ephemeral psychological phenomena, like feelings, moods, thoughts, temporary motives, attitudes, and the like. These may or may not coincide with traits. Elizabeth Bennet, though basically a kind and generous person, has her moments of prejudice. On the other hand, the hectic agitation exhibited by the hero of Knut Hamsun's *Hunger* strikes us as merely an exaggeration, caused by malnutrition, of a general and abiding disposition toward intense feeling and romantic euphoria—the temporary spells of

hunger-induced madness differ from the hero's trait of passionate commitment more in degree than in kind.

As for transient moods and feelings, perhaps they are what Aristotle meant by *dianoia*, "thought," that is, what is passing through a character's mind at a specific moment, not his general moral disposition—that which "is pertinent and fitting to the occasion," rather than a permanent quality. As such, it is related to the *topoi*, the lines of argument and general truths that exist quite independent of character.

The paradigmatic view of character sees the set of traits, metaphorically, as a vertical assemblage intersecting the syntagmatic chain of events that comprise the plot. There is an important difference between this notion and that of paradigm in linguistic analysis, however. In structural linguistics, an individual item— word, morpheme, or whatever—was thought to occur in a given position in the absence of, indeed, in opposition to the totality of others that could potentially fill the position it occupies. Thus:

The	cat	runs	bad	ly
	dog		smooth	ly
	man		slow	ly
	horse		quick	ly
	car		angri	ly
	[etc.]		[etc.]	

In ordinary discourse, one given item, say *man* or *bad*, does not evoke the rest. In poetry, however, there may well be an evocation or reverberation among other possibilities, because of the general heightening of sensibility, effected by phonetic correspondences and so on, as I. A. Richards and others have shown.[39] In narratives, too, the whole set of a character's traits established up to that moment is available to the audience. We sort through the paradigm to find out which trait would account for a certain action, and, if we cannot find it, we add another trait to the list (or at least put ourselves on guard for further evidence of the one we impute). In short, the trait paradigm,

39. "Poetic Process and Literary Analysis," *Style in Language* (New York, 1960).

like the poetic paradigm, but unlike the linguistic paradigm, tends to operate *in praesentia*, not *in absentia*.[40]

This practice does not seem to differ in kind from our ordinary evaluations of human beings that we meet in the real world. As Percy Lubbock puts it:

Nothing is simpler than to create for oneself the idea of a human being, a figure and a character, from a series of glimpses and anecdotes. Creation of this kind we practise every day; we are continually piecing together our fragmentary evidence about the people around us and moulding their images in thought. It is the way in which we make our world; partially, imperfectly, very much at haphazard, but still perpetually, everybody deals with this experience like an artist.[41]

We can now perceive a fundamental difference between events and traits. The former have strictly determined positions in story (at least in classical narratives): X happens, then Y happens because of X, then Z as a final consequence. The order in story is fixed; even if the discourse presents a different order, the natural order can always be reconstructed. Further, events are discrete; they may overlap, but each has a clear-cut beginning and end; their domain is circumscribed. Traits are not subject to these limitations. They may prevail throughout the work and beyond, indeed, as long in our memory as does the work itself. Eveline's fear of the world outside Dublin is "permanent" in this sense. Passing or temporary moods, on the other hand, have limited time domains in the text: Eveline is "tired" only in the beginning, not on the quay. How far her tiredness extends into the story is not clear; perhaps she has forgotten it when she begins to think about Frank and her imminent departure, or perhaps even earlier, as she remembers the good times

40. Barthes finds this *presence* of elements of the narrative mysterious, a kind of mirage: "we use Code here not in the sense of a list, a paradigm that must be reconstituted [that is, it is already constituted]. The code is a perspective of quotations, a mirage of structures; we know only its departures and returns, the units which have resulted from it (those we inventory) are themselves, always, ventures out of the text, the mark, the sign of a virtual digression toward the remainder of a catalogue (*The Kidnapping* refers to every kidnapping ever written); they are so many fragments of something that has always been *already* read, seen, done, experienced; the code is the wake of that *already*" (*S/Z*, p. 20).

41. *The Craft of Fiction*, p. 7. Kenneth Burke writes about the genesis of trait patterns in "Lexicon Rhetoricae," *Counterstatement*, p. 152.

the children used to have in the field. "Tiredness" is temporary rather than permanent; it is not a trait; its domain is fleeting. Unlike events, traits are not in the temporal chain, but coexist with the whole or a large portion of it. Events travel as vectors, "horizontally" from earlier to later. Traits, on the other hand, extend over the time spans staked out by the events. They are *parametric* to the event chain.[42] The communication of existents is not tied rigorously to the chrono-logic, as are the events. Consider again our elementary story about Peter (Chapter 1), and the observation that

was superior to the straight-line diagram because it indicated the fact that the third statement—"Peter had no friends or relatives"—does not refer to an event and hence should not be displayed along the event axis. Now we see the error of even connecting nodes two to three and three to four by arrows, since no narrative *movement* passes through the third node. The following is more accurate:

But if the trait "lonely" (node three) is unconnected sequentially with the events (nodes one, two, and four), it may be misleading to give it any specific position on the diagram at all, since the exact moment when the quality "lonely" enters this narrative may not be particularly significant.

Saying that a trait or other existent is not local in domain does not mean that its moment of expression in the discourse is of no significance. For example, the sequence "Peter fell ill; he had no friends or relatives; he died" might very well imply that it

42. Barthes, "Introduction . . . ," p. 249, who cites Nicole Ruwet's musical reference as analogical: "an element which remains constant throughout the duration of a musical piece."

was *because* he had no friends or relatives that his illness was not attended to and then he died. Whereas the sequence "Peter had no friends or relatives. He fell ill. He died" may, by similar logic, be taken to imply that he fell ill because he had no one to care for him. And "Peter fell ill. He died. He had no friends or relatives" might suggest that nobody mourned his passing. The relative position of a stasis statement of a trait may turn out to be significant at the event-level as well. This fact does not invalidate our previous characterization. Discourse statements often communicate in both event and existent dimensions at once. Thus Peter's friendless, family-less state is an abiding attribute; it is only the *because*-element that belongs in the event chain.

So perhaps the best way to diagram traits is as follows:

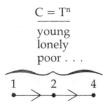

where C = the character, T^n = a given trait, and the brace detaches existents from the temporal sequence of story but does not interfere with their parametric reference to it. This diagram makes it clear that traits are both paradigmatic *and* parametric. The trait-paradigm is marked T^n to show its open-endedness, to allow for unrecognized traits that may suggest themselves in later readings. One is able to call up increasingly accurate descriptive adjectives the deeper one gets into the narrative.

Barthes interestingly suggests that not-yet-named traits abide in the proper name of the character, as a mysterious residue:

Character is an adjective, an attribute, a predicate. . . . Sarrasine is the sum, the point of convergence, of: *turbulence, artistic gift, independence, excess, femininity, ugliness, composite nature, impiety, love of whittling, will,* etc. What gives the illusion that the sum is supplemented by a precious remainder (something like *individuality,* in that, qualitative and ineffable, it may escape the vulgar bookkeeping of compositional

characters) is the Proper Name, the difference completed by what is *proper* to it. The proper name enables the person to exist outside the semes, whose sum nonetheless constitutes it entirely. As soon as a Name exists (even a pronoun) to flow toward and fasten onto, the semes become predicates, inductors of truth [the truth of fiction, of course], and the Name becomes a subject: we can say that what is proper to narrative is not action but the character as Proper Name: the semic raw material . . . *completes* what is proper to being, *fills* the name with adjectives.[43]

The proper name in this sense is precisely the identity or quintessence of selfhood property discussed in Chapter 1. It may well be what Aristotle meant by *homoios*. It is a kind of ultimate residence of personality, not a quality but a locus of qualities, the narrative-noun that is endowed with but never exhausted by the qualities, the narrative-adjectives. Even where the name is highly suggestive of or conformable to a quality, that is, where it is onomatopoetic or symbolic—Pecksniff, Volpone, Allworthy—it does not thereby lose its "precious remainder." The man identified as "Pecksniff," though thoroughly "nosey," is still a man and must have other qualities, however rigorously Dickens refuses to mention them. (I do not mean that the implied reader will insist upon these other traits; he, of course, will go along with the implied author's wishes.)

Names are deictic, that is, pointing, marked out as definite, "(de-)finited" or cut out of infinity, hypostatized, and catalogued (be it ever so minimally). Thus, narratives do not need proper names in the strict sense. Any deictic mark will do; a personal pronoun, an epithet ("the man with a beard," "the lady in blue") or even a demonstrative pronoun or definite article. (The character is referred to as "a man" only once—in the first sentence. Thereafter, he will be called "the man.")

Kinds of Character

If the functional or *actantiel* theory is inadequate, does that mean that all attempts to distinguish kinds of characters are doomed? One that has weathered the hurricanes of literary debate is E. M. Forster's distinction between "round" and "flat"

43. *S/Z*, pp. 190–191.

characters. Does it find convenient expression in an open structuralist theory?

Yes, as I understand it, since the distinction is precisely for-
mulatable in terms of traits (Forster uses the words "idea" or
"quality" but they are clearly equivalent). And that in two respects: for one thing, a flat character is endowed with a single
trait—or very few: "There is Mrs. Micawber—she says she
won't desert Mr. Micawber; she doesn't, and there she is." [44]
This does not mean that the flat character is not capable of great
vivacity or power, nor even that he need be "typed," though
frequently he is (I presume by "typed" Forster means "easily
recognizable with reference to familiar types in the real or fictive
world"). Secondly, since there is only a single trait (or one
clearly dominating the others), the behavior of the flat character
is highly predictable. Round characters, on the contrary, pos-
sess a variety of traits, some of them conflicting or even contradictory; their behavior is not predictable—they are capable of
changing, of surprising us, and so on. In structuralist vocabulary we could say that the paradigm of the flat character is directed or teleological, whereas that of the round is agglomerate.
The effect of the flat character is that it has a clear direction,
and so, as Forster remarks, is more distinctly (if not more easily)
remembered—there is simply *less* to remember, and that less is
very clearly structured. Round characters, on the other hand,
may inspire a stronger sense of intimacy, despite the fact that
they do not "add up." We remember them as real people. They
seem strangely familiar. Like real-life friends and enemies it is
hard to describe what they are exactly like.

Saying that characters are capable of surprising us is another
way of saying that they are "open-ended." We come to anticipate, indeed to demand, the possibilities of discovering new
and unsuspected traits. Thus, round characters function as open
constructs, susceptible of further insight. Our "readings out"
are not limited to the actual period of immediate contact with
the text. The character may haunt us for days or years as we try
to account for discrepancies or lacunae in terms of our changing

44. *Aspects of the Novel* (Harmondsworth, 1962), p. 75.

and growing insight into ourselves and our fellow beings. The great round characters seem virtually inexhaustible objects for contemplation. We may even remember them as presences with (or in) whom we have lived, rather than as separate objects.

The ineffability of round characters results in part from the large range and diversity or even discrepancy among traits. But other factors may contribute, too. The evidence for their traits may be indeterminate in some way. For instance, the medium may only hint at crucial data. Films are particularly versatile in exhibiting the unspoken inner lives of characters laconically. The jaded, apathetic, mysteriously troubled heroes and heroines of Michelangelo Antonioni's *L'Avventura, La Notte, L'Eclisse, Il Deserto Rosso, Blow-Up,* are intriguing precisely because we have no direct access to their minds. Their dialogue only hints, tantalizingly, at the complexities below the skin.

Even where the medium does permit deep psychological plunges, they may be expressly avoided by an opacifying discourse. Conrad's *Lord Jim* is an obvious example: by making the source for all information about Jim a narrator who continually admits his inability to plumb Jim's depths, to reconcile his inconsistencies, any ultimate tally is blocked. "Enigmatic," in effect, becomes the last but most potent of Jim's traits. Or, among more modern narratives, the reticences of Hemingway and Robbe-Grillet are obvious examples of "enrichments by silence."

Where a character is open-ended, our speculation, of course, is not limited to traits but also to possible future actions. It is all very well to think that we leave Eveline in a kind of time-bubble on the quay, or that it is Giuliana's permanent fate in *Il Deserto Rosso* to walk with her child under the polluted sky. Indeed, Truffaut seems to have intended just such an effect in freezing the last frame of *The Four Hundred Blows*, fixing the young hero, Antoine, in permanent flight from authority. But our minds do not necessarily accept the confines of the bubble. We may understand that "fleeing authority" will characterize much of Antoine's future behavior, but we refuse to give up the right to think about the specifics of that flight: more misunderstandings with relatives, friends, well-wishers, more trouble

with the law, despite the intrinsic sweetness and decency of his character. Like Guido, the director-hero of Federico Fellini's *8-1/2*, we cannot help wondering what will become of them, these dear creatures who have joined our fantasy world. The public demand for sequels and serials is not to be written off as naive Philistinism. It represents a legitimate desire, of theoretical interest, to extend the illusion, to find out how fate disposes of characters in whom we have come to invest emotion and interest. Whether the author elects to respond or not is, of course, his own aesthetic affair.

A. C. Bradley and the Analysis of Character

Barthes describes the uncertain pursuit of traits, provocatively, as a "metonymic skid." In searching out traits (semes), we often find ourselves discovering not names but

synonymic complex[es] whose common nucleus we sense even while the discourse is leading us toward other possibilities, toward other related signifieds: thus, reading is absorbed in a kind of metonymic skid, each synonym adding to its neighbor some new trait, some new departure. . . . This expansion is the very movement of meaning: the meaning skids, recovers itself, and advances simultaneously; far from analyzing it, we should rather describe it through its expansions, lexical transcendence, the generic word it continually attempts to [form].[45]

The motive for "skidding" is the search for the key to the character, the exact combination of trait-names to sum him up. This kind of critical activity has fallen on bad times. After reaching a high point in A. C. Bradley's famous work on Shakespearean tragedy, it came under attack for neglecting the verbal "surface." But Bradley's work remains something of a model of open trait-analysis and deserves reconsideration.

His method is simple and effective. Basically, it consists of a careful re-scanning of the text, especially in places where tradition may have blinded us by simplistic attitudes: "Iago is evil and that's that." Bradley wanted to specify Iago's exact sort of evil, hoping to find thereby the genuine mainsprings of his character. So he carefully perused what Iago does and does not do, does and does not say, what is said to and about him, to

45. *S/Z*, p. 92.

"read out" and to speculate about these data. If he could establish an independently coherent view of Iago's traits Bradley felt he could discover the motive for his plot against Othello. Bradley's efforts resulted in a formulation of character which is at once immanent and highly sophisticated, and going through his set of descriptive adjectives is a valuable exercise.

He starts by naming the traits of Iago's public image, what others thought of him. To them he is "courageous," "vulgar," "blunt," yet "jovial," "a plain-dealer . . . and . . . liked . . . for it," "humorously satiric," but "serious" when necessary, and above all "honest." It is here that the others are most taken in by his hypocrisy.

Iago, of course, is quite another person, and his real character shows "prodigious powers of dissimulation and of self-control." Thus caustic speech is not a product of blunt honesty, but a relief from the elaborate "hypocrisy" of his stance, a kind of "safety-valve." Indeed, Bradley surmises, he is not "a man of strong feelings and passions," but "cold," one who might have avoided crime were it not for an ultimate "temptability." To effect what he does, Iago must also be remarkably intelligent, "insightful into human nature," "zealous in working upon it," "quick and versatile in response to sudden difficulties and opportunities," "untemptable by indolence or sensuality," "without conscience, honor, or regard for others." These traits argue a "deadness of feeling" rather than "positive ill-will." Bradley denies that Iago is an unusually "envious" or "ambitious" man; rather he is "keenly sensitive to anything that touches his pride or self-esteem." He feels "superior" to others and is "irritated" by "whatever disturbs or wounds his sense of superiority." Goodness "annoys his intellect as a stupidity."

Having established a profile of Iago's traits, Bradley goes on to his main business—the search for motives to explain Iago's heinous plot against Othello. Given what he is, Bradley asks, why does he elect to do what he does? Most critics feel he is provoked by hatred of Othello and a desire for military advancement, but Bradley argues that Iago is not driven by passions but lured on by the prospect of delight: "The most delightful thing to such a man would be something that gave an extreme

satisfaction to his sense of power and superiority; and if it involved, secondly, the triumphant exertion of his abilities, and thirdly, the excitement of danger, his delight would be consummated."[46] Indeed, Bradley sees him as a twisted artist: his evil manipulations bring him "the tension and the joy of artistic creation."[47]

Bradley's assessment of Iago's personality is an act of interpretation, just as are the "close readings" of a lyric poem and of the plot of an enigmatic novel like *The Turn of the Screw*. He undertook such an interpretation because he thought previous interpretations had been mistaken. My concern with his interpretation is not to defend its substance (which is a literary-critical question), but rather its legitimacy *as an operation* (which is a metacritical or theoretical question).

Bradley was attacked by critics of the *Scrutiny* group, in particular L. C. Knights, for stressing character at the expense of the verbal texture of Shakespeare's poetry. Bradley's devotion of "so many of his pages to detailed psychological and moral analyses of the characters of the plays, to the exclusion of any serious concern with their language" and especially his continuation of the "bad tradition of writing about Shakespeare's *dramatis personae* as if they were real persons whose lives could be properly thought of as extending beyond the plays in which they are involved" did "grave disservice to Shakespeare." For Knights, "the 'characters' of a drama or novel, as well as its 'plot,' have no existence except as 'precipitates' from the reader's memory of the successive words he has read and . . . as such they are mere critical 'abstractions' to which we can attend only at the cost of impoverishing our 'total response' to the work."

Obviously no one wants to denude Shakespeare's play of its exquisite stylistic surface. But the poetry, if our argument is correct, exists in the manifestation, the substance of the expression. Attention to the medium, though completely justified as one sort of critical act, in no way discounts the real existence of other structures in plays and narratives—character, setting,

46. A. C. Bradley, *Shakespearean Tragedy* (New York, 1955), p. 185.
47. Ibid., p. 187.

and plot—or the right of critics to be concerned with them. I find nowhere in Bradley a denial of the poetry—the worst that can be said about his studies is that their focus is elsewhere. As R. S. Crane points out, the two sides are really talking about two different things. There is nothing wrong with "concentrating on the characters as the main source of 'the tragic fact' . . . not as 'abstractions' from the words of the plays as finally written but as the concrete semblances of real men and women, each with a being more or less independent of the particular actions he performs in the completed drama."[48] Here is another unnecessary argument between critics about whether certain aspects of works of art are intrinsically more valuable than others. It is absurd to describe characters as "abstractions" or "precipitates" from words; it is like saying that a statue is a "precipitate" from marble. The story structure (of which characters are a part), the discourse structure, and the manifestation structure achieve interdependence only because they are independently systematic. No hierarchy of value exists among them—they all serve the common end of the whole work. Words actualize characters; but so do the visual images of actors in silent movies or mimes on the stage, and no one would claim that *they* are abstractions or verbal precipitates. Crane correctly labels them "concrete semblances," stressing at once their real and their fictional nature; they are sets of traits attached to a name, but to the name of someone who happened never to exist (that is, about whom no truth-claim is made or makeable).[49]

An argument for the "code of traits" of personality as a useful and natural way to analyze characters in no way implies that

48. Ronald Crane's *The Languages of Criticism and the Structure of Poetry* (Toronto, 1953), p. 16.

49. A character is "something more than a creation of language or a function in the total context of the play. 'He is the sort of man who in such-and-such situation would do so-and-so'—this is the kind of remark we constantly use in real life, when discussing somebody's character. If this is permissible with a Shakespearian character it is even more legitimate when applied to the larger scope of the novel. The novelist, because he has more time and space, can frame the situation to justify the *would do such-and-such* in our reaction. Indeed he may do more than this; as we have seen he may also leave room enough for us to speculate and to frame other situations than those actually existing in the novel. In other words, we may sometimes legitimately assume a character's

their "lives" extend "beyond the [fictions] in which they are involved." Characters do not have "lives"; we endow them with "personality" only to the extent that personality is a structure familiar to us in life and art. To deny that seems to deny an absolutely fundamental aesthetic experience. Even fantastic narratives require inferences, guesses, and expectations according to one's sense of what *normal* persons are like. Our behavior may or may not have implications for the formal study of psychology: that is beside the point. I am arguing simply that the character-interpretive behavior of audiences is structured. But that in no way says that characters are "alive"—they are only more or less lifelike. When fictional characters are psychoanalyzed as if they were real people, hard-nosed critics may be right to challenge the effort. But characters as narrative constructs do require terms for description, and there is no point in rejecting those out of the general vocabulary of psychology, morality, and any other relevant area of human experience. The terms themselves do not claim psychological validity. Validity is not at issue: a fictional-character trait, as opposed to a real-person trait, can only be a part of the narrative construct. All we need is some orthographic device like quotation marks to remind ourselves of that fact: Iago is "cold," not cold.

Setting

Characters exist and move in a space which exists abstractly at the deep narrative level, that is, prior to any kind of materialization, like the two-dimensional movie screen, the three-dimensional proscenium stage, the projected space of the mind's eye. Abstract narrative space contains, in clear polarity, a figure and a ground. Just as we can distinguish, in a painted portrait, the person from the background against which he or she is posed, so we can distinguish the character from the setting in a story. The setting "sets the character off" in the usual figurative sense of the expression; it is the place and collection

autonomy, and there may be a proper place for a kind of speculation and inference not vulnerable to the anti-Bradleyan critic's attack. Such speculative activity may, in fact, compose a large part of the character's reality for us" (W. J. Harvey, *Character and the Novel*, Ithaca, N.Y., 1966), pp. 204–205.

of objects "against which" his actions and passions appropriately emerge.

But in working out the details of this division, some questions
arise. Are there clear criteria for distinguishing between minor
characters and human beings—"walk-ons"—who are mere elements of the setting? This forms a critical boundary, and the
fate of any strict categorization would seem to rest on its articulation. One can think of at least three possible criteria, no one
of which is adequate in itself: (1) biology, (2) identity (that is,
nomination), (3) importance.

1. Clearly the biological criterion is not independently satis-
factory. It makes no sense to treat crowds of walk-ons or extras
as characters. In *Slaughterhouse-Five* the narrator recalls "Russian soldiers guarding . . . Englishmen, Americans, Dutchmen,
Belgians, Frenchmen, Canadians, South Africans, New Zea-
landers, Australians, thousands of us." These hordes, though
human, are obviously not characters; they are parts of the dismal setting, along with the rain, the beetfield, the Elbe, against
which the narrator and his buddy O'Hare stand out. The opposite is equally true. it is easy to think of narratives whose protagonists are animals—Aesop's fables, for example—or even
inanimate. Not only friendly or hostile robots in science-fiction
stories can be characters, but even primal forces, like fires,
winds and storms, the sun and the moon. One can imagine
a narrative that told the history of the solar system, with the
Earth as protagonist. Thus, it is not clear that characters need
be anthropomorphic (although in most cases they are).

2. By identity or nomination, I mean Barthes's residue, discussed above, the mysterious property of having a name. If the
name is a locus or nucleus around which circulate traits, perhaps we could propose that feature as criterial of characterhood.
A moment's reflection will scotch this theory as well. There are
too many examples in fiction of named human beings whom it
would be counterintuitive to call characters, who are simply part
of the ambience in which a character finds himself. André
Gide's *Lafcadio's Adventures* begins: "In 1890, during the pontifi-
cate of Leo XIII, Anthime Armand-Dubois, unbeliever and Free-
mason, visited Rome in order to consult Dr. X, the celebrated

specialist for rheumatic complaints." Leo XIII is clearly not a character in this novel (in any meaningful sense of "character") nor is Dr. X, even though both are named. Unlike Anthime, neither "enters the action," although they are present, in some sense, in the world of the work. Their noncharacterhood is a function of their nonreappearance. Similarly, the general failure to appear independently in a scene, in the world of the work, which we may call "absence," seems to exclude from character-hood those named human beings who exist only in the reminiscence or fantasy of a character, as in "Eveline." Eveline's memory is populated by mother, father, brothers and sisters, family priest, old playmates, and so on, many of them named; but clearly we would not want to call these characters. They are part of the furniture, the bric-à-brac, of Eveline's mind, but only she is a character.

3. Importance to the plot might seem to be the most fruitful criterion. We can define it as the degree to which the existent takes or is affected by plot-significant action (that is, performs or is affected by a kernel event). But here again counterexamples immediately suggest themselves. Objects can be absolutely crucial to a plot and yet clearly remain props, even gimmicks. Hitchcock is the great master of such devices: he calls them "MacGuffins." A MacGuffin is "something that the characters in the film care a lot about," a poisoned coffee-cup, a wine-bottle filled with uranium ore, the plans for the forts, "an airplane engine or a bomb-bay door or something."[50] "Or something": the author treats the MacGuffin's substance with appropriate formalist disdain. It is only a device for putting the characters in jeopardy. Only the jeopardy counts, a life-and-death matter. But its importance hardly qualifies the MacGuffin for characterhood.

Someone might interject: "What about a human being important to the action?" But we can think about human MacGuffins too—Godot, for example. He's as human as a Beckett character can be, and he satisfies the requirement "something that the characters . . . care about." But does that make him a character?

50. *Focus on Hitchcock*, ed. Albert J. La Valley (New York, 1972), p. 43.

At best perhaps, a potential character, a character *manqué*. What is missing is his presence.

What we see in these musings, I think, are problems attendant upon categorizing narrative elements, instead of investigating the features that mark them. The above fail as criterial marks of character, but they seem relevant as features. Again, evidentially narrative elements are composites of features: the more characterial the features, the more fully emergent the character. Characterhood, in this view, would be a question of degree: a human being who is named, present and important is *more likely* to be a character (be he ever so minor) than an object that is named, present, and important, or a human being who is named, present, but unimportant, or whatever. Though there may be no single feature, a battery of cumulative features may do the trick. The class of narrative existents could be said to contain two subclasses whose demarcation is not a simple line but, again, a continuum.

A final difference between characters and setting-elements seems to be that characters are difficult to presuppose. Characters are only there, on the scene, when their presence is announced or strongly implied. But we can always "fill in," so to speak, whatever is needful to authenticate a setting. If we are told in a novel that the scene is a New York street, we can mentally provide it with stock details: cars, pedestrians, shops, policemen. But we cannot provide a hero: he is too special to "fill in."

A normal and perhaps principal function of setting is to contribute to the mood of the narrative. The brevity of "Eveline" again makes it a good example. It starts in a quiet, reflective, reminiscent mood. The setting is evening, few people are in the avenue, and the houses call attention to themselves, provoke fond reminiscence. The few people in the street make it lonely, and Eveline's decision is a lonely one. The cretonne is dusty, not because Eveline is a poor housekeeper, but because it is an old house in a decrepit neighborhood, the kind of environment she wishes to escape. It is cretonne, a cheap fabric, rather than some other material. There is decrepitude elsewhere too: the photograph is yellow and the harmonium broken.

The scenic props in "Eveline" are of three sorts. In her home everything is grimy and poverty-ridden. Cretonne curtains and broken harmonium, "her entire wages—seven shillings," her black leather purse (she would not permit herself a more cheerful color), the crowds at the market, the load of provisions (no delivery boy for her), the two children "in her charge," the "close dark room on the other side of the hall" in which her mother died, and so on. But in her internal, mental setting we find some pleasant, homey elements: before the fire, the picnic on the Hill of Howth, her mother's bonnet that her father playfully dons.

Outside her home, everything is exotic, frightening, and finally unacceptable. Chief is the night-boat itself (not a *day*-boat), whose dark mass and illuminated portholes lurk beyond the wide doors of the sheds. The boat is suitably shrouded in mist. The soldiers with their brown baggage invoke far-away and hence meaningless violence and threat.

Elements of setting can serve multiple functions. The street organ's rich evocation derives from all three complexes of setting—poverty, homey comforts, and the exotic. The street-organ is commoner in poor sections of the city than in rich, where policemen keep the streets free of beggars. More especially, Eveline associates it with the painful memory of her mother's death. But there is also a bit of comfort in a street-organ tune to one who has heard it all her life above the noise and tumult of a working-class street. And, finally, the organ is exotic: it is operated by an Italian and plays Italian airs. Equally remarkable is the way setting gets promoted to a symbolic dimension in the finale. The normally effaced narrator cannot resist several climactic metaphors precisely at the moment of the heroine's greatest anguish. The extremity of her situation validates the suddenly transcendent diction: "A bell clanged upon her heart. . . . All the seas of the world tumbled about her heart. He was drawing her into them: he would drown her. . . . Amid the seas she sent a cry of anguish." A real bell sounds the boat's departure and a real sea lies beyond the harbor. The metaphors inhere in the juxtapositions: "the seas tumbled about her heart," "he would drown her." What makes the metaphors

powerful is the way they fuse character and setting, subject character to the onslaught of setting, make setting almost a character—Frank and the seas collude, the strange and sinister outer world threatens to overwhelm her. The narrator permits himself the luxury of clustered metaphors only once in this story, and it is at the most telling point.

A few critics have proposed categorizations of the way in which setting may be related to plot and character. Robert Liddell, concentrating on natural setting, distinguishes five types.[51] The first, or utilitarian, is simple, low keyed, minimally necessary for the action, and generally untouched by emotion. The novels of Jane Austen provide examples. The second, or symbolic, stresses a tight relation with action; here setting is not neutral but *like* the action. Tempestuous happenings take place in tempestuous places, like the marshes in *Great Expectations*; the rainy weather in *Bleak House* corresponds to the rain in Lady Dedlock's heart. Liddell's third type is "irrelevant"; the landscape is not supposed to matter. The characters are not particularly conscious of it. An example is that portion of *Madame Bovary* which follows Charles Bovary around the countryside. A subclass or adjacent type is the ironic, where the setting jars with the character's emotional state or the prevailing atmosphere. In *The Ambassadors*, Strether, exhilarating in the discovery of "that French ruralism . . . with its cool special green" reminiscent of a landscape by Lambinet seen years before in a Boston art gallery, stumbles upon the boat-tryst of Mme. Vionnet and Chad. For Strether "it was a sharp, fantastic crisis that had popped up as if in a dream." "Countries of the mind" is Liddell's fourth type: the kind of inner landscape of Eveline's reminiscences. The fifth is "kaleidoscopic," a rapid shifting back and forth from the outside physical world to the world of the imagination. The novels of Virginia Woolf provide examples. Doubtless other types of setting can be distinguished: here again we need some heuristic principles for categorization.

Roland Barthes argues that it is only meaningful to discuss setting as a function of classical (*lisible*) narratives. His reasoning

---

51. Robert Liddell, *A Treatise on the Novel* (London, 1947), ch. 6.

takes us back to verisimilitude and ties setting together with plot and character. In Flaubert's "Un Coeur Simple," for example, Mme. Aubain's room contains a piano under a barometer supporting a pyramid of boxes. Barthes calls the exact detail of the barometer "useless," a kind of luxury of narration. Though the piano indexes Mme. Aubain as a bourgeois, and the boxes illustrate the disorder of her household, the barometer has no contributory justification except the "real," the verisimilar. It thereby raises the "cost" of narrative information, makes it somehow more precious (and not only in the simple sense of delaying it). From the strictly narrative point of view these descriptions seem simply enigmatic. For Barthes narrative per se is "predictive." Its implication is: The hero does X, and Y is the consequence. "Everything else is description . . . or 'analogical.'" The source of apparently insignificant details is the ancient rhetorical genre of the epideictic, the discourse for pomp or show, the set-piece to inspire admiration for the orator, and within that genre, specifically the figure of ecphrasis, "a brilliant detachable morsel, sufficient unto itself." In *Madame Bovary*, Barthes feels, the description of Rouen is introduced solely for the pleasures of verbal portraiture. Quite independently of its relation to plot or character, it finds its justification in "cultural rules of [what constitutes] representation." But the depiction of the irrelevant but realistic detail serves to harness the fantasy, to keep the narrative from running out of control. It is the resistance of the senses to the unbridled intellect, of the actually lived to the intellectually potential. Here we have an important influence of history on fictional narratives. The ancients made a clear distinction between the genuinely real, the province of History, and the probable, the verisimilar, the seeming-real, the province of Fiction: the latter was always based on public notions of likelihood. It was general, and it always allowed of the contrary—"The great word which is presupposed at the beginning of every classical discourse submitted to the probable was *Esto* ('Let us admit that . . .')."[52] Barthes contends that modern discourse

52. Roland Barthes, "L'Effet du réel," *Communications*, 11 (1968), p. 88. Kenneth Burke says similar things, but calls preoccupation with description for its own sake a "disease" of narrative form (*Counterstatement*, p. 144).

abolishes this preamble and admits only the "objectively" real. But it thereby creates a new kind of probability, the real "itself." The new style, he argues, eliminates the signified, goes directly from the signifier to the referent. This new verisimilitude is a "referential illusion." Things depicted no longer need meaning: they simply *are*: that is their meaning. "It is the category of the real itself (and not its mere accidental contents) that is finally what is signified."

However one formulates the questions of the functions of setting and its relation to character, of the nature of character and its constitution by features of identity and trait, it seems clear that the notion of existent is no less critical than that of event, and that narrative theory cannot neglect it.

4 DISCOURSE:

Nonnarrated Stories

Silence is become his mother tongue.
Oliver Goldsmith,
The Good-Natured Man

Every narrative—so this theory goes—is a structure with a content plane (called "story") and an expression plane (called "discourse"). Having examined story in Chapters 2 and 3, we turn to the other half of the narrative dichotomy. The expression plane is the set of narrative statements, where "statement" is the basic component of the form of the expression, independent of and more abstract than any particular manifestation—that is, the expression's substance, which varies from art to art. A certain posture in the ballet, a series of film shots, a whole paragraph in a novel, or only a single word—any of these might manifest a single narrative statement. I have proposed that narrative statements are of two kinds—process and stasis—corresponding to whether the deep narrative (not the surface linguistic) predicate is in the mode of existence (IS) or action (DOES).

Crosscutting this dichotomy is another: Is the statement directly presented to the audience or is it mediated by someone—the someone we call the narrator? Direct presentation presumes a kind of overhearing by the audience. Mediated narration, on the other hand, presumes a more or less express communication from narrator to audience. This is essentially Plato's distinction between *mimesis* and *diegesis*,[1] in modern terms between showing and telling. Insofar as there is telling, there must be a teller, a narrating voice.

The teller, the transmitting source, is best accounted for, I think, as a spectrum of possibilities, going from narrators who are least audible to those who are most so. The label affixed to

1. These terms are revived by Gérard Genette in "Frontières du récit," *Communications*, 8 (1966).

the negative pole of narratorhood is less important than its reality in the spectrum. I say "nonnarrated": the reader may prefer "minimally narrated," but the existence of this kind of transmission is well attested.

The narrator's presence derives from the audience's sense of some demonstrable communication. If it feels it is being told something, it presumes a teller. The alternative is a "direct witnessing" of the action. Of course, even in the scenic arts like drama and the ballet, pure mimesis is an illusion. But the degree of possible analogy varies. The main question is how the illusion is achieved. By what convention does a spectator or reader accept the idea that it is "as if" he were personally on the scene, though he comes to it by sitting in a chair in a theater or by turning pages and reading words. Authors may make special efforts to preserve the illusion that events "literally unfold before the reader's eyes," mostly by restricting the kinds of statements that can occur.

To understand the concept of narrator's voice (including its "absence") we need to consider three preliminary issues: the interrelation of the several parties to the narrative transaction, the meaning of "point of view" and its relation to voice, and the nature of acts of speech and thought as a subclass of the class of acts in general. These topics form a necessary prolegomena to the analysis of narrator's voice, upon which any discussion of narrative discourse rests.

Real Author, Implied Author, Narrator, Real Reader, Implied Reader, Narratee

That it is essential not to confuse author and narrator has become a commonplace of literary theory. As Monroe Beardsley argues, "the speaker of a literary work cannot be identified with the author—and therefore the character and condition of the speaker can be known by internal evidence alone—unless the author has provided a pragmatic context, or a claim of one, that connects the speaker with himself." [2] But even in such a context,

---

2. In *Aesthetics* (New York, 1958), p. 240. Cf. Walker Gibson, "Authors, Speakers, Readers, Mock Readers," *College English*, 11 (1950), 265–269; and Kathleen Tillotson, *The Tale and the Teller* (London, 1959).

the speaker is not the author, but the "author" (quotation marks of "as if"), or better the "author"-narrator, one of several possible kinds.

In addition, there is a demonstrable third party, conveniently dubbed, by Wayne Booth, the "implied author":

As he writes, [the real author] creates not simply an ideal, impersonal 'man in general' but an implied version of 'himself' that is different from the implied authors we meet in other men's works. . . . Whether we call this implied author an 'official scribe', or adopt the term recently revived by Kathleen Tillotson—the author's 'second self'—it is clear that the picture the reader gets of this presence is one of the author's most important effects. However impersonal he may try to be, his reader will inevitably construct a picture of the official scribe.[3]

He is "implied," that is, reconstructed by the reader from the narrative. He is not the narrator, but rather the principle that invented the narrator, along with everything else in the narrative, that stacked the cards in this particular way, had these things happen to these characters, in these words or images. Unlike the narrator, the implied author can *tell* us nothing. He, or better, *it* has no voice, no direct means of communicating. It instructs us silently, through the design of the whole, with all the voices, by all the means it has chosen to let us learn. We can grasp the notion of implied author most clearly by comparing different narratives written by the same real author but presupposing different implied authors. Booth's example: the implied author of *Jonathan Wild* "is by implication very much concerned with public affairs and with the effects of unchecked ambition on the 'great men' who attain to power in the world," whereas the implied author "who greets us on page one of *Amelia*" conveys rather an "air of sententious solemnity."[4] The implied author of *Joseph Andrews*, on the contrary, sounds "facetious" and "generally insouciant." Not merely the narrator but the whole design of *Joseph Andrews* functions in a tone quite different from that of *Jonathan Wild* or *Amelia*. Henry Fielding created three clearly different implied authors.

The distinction is particularly evident in the case of the "unre-

3. *Rhetoric of Fiction*, pp. 70–71.
4. Ibid., p. 72.

liable narrator" (another of Booth's happy coinages). What makes a narrator unreliable is that his values diverge strikingly from that of the implied author's; that is, the rest of the narrative—"the norm of the work"—conflicts with the narrator's presentation, and we become suspicious of his sincerity or competence to tell the "true version." The unreliable narrator is at virtual odds with the implied author; otherwise his unreliability could not emerge.

The implied author establishes the norms of the narrative, but Booth's insistence that these are moral seems unnecessary. The norms are general cultural codes, whose relevance to story we have already considered. The real author can postulate whatever norms he likes through his implied author. It makes no more sense to accuse the real Céline or Montherlant of what the implied author causes to happen in *Journey to the End of the Night* or *Les Jeunes Filles* than to hold the real Conrad responsible for the reactionary attitudes of the implied author of *The Secret Agent* or *Under Western Eyes* (or, for that matter, Dante for the Catholic ideas of the implied author of the *Divine Comedy*). One's moral fibre cannot really be "seduced" by wily implied authors. Our acceptance of their universe is aesthetic, not ethical. To confound the "implied author," a structural principle, with a certain historical figure whom we may or may not admire morally, politically, or personally would seriously undermine our theoretical enterprise.[5]

There is always an implied author, though there might not be a single real author in the ordinary sense: the narrative may have been composed by committee (Hollywood films), by a disparate group of people over a long period of time (many folk ballads), by random-number generation by a computer, or whatever.[6]

The counterpart of the implied author is the *implied reader*—not the flesh-and-bones you or I sitting in our living rooms read-

5. There is an interesting discussion of the question in Susan Suleiman, "Ideological Dissent from Works of Fiction: Toward a Rhetoric of the *Roman à thèse*," *Neophilologus* (April 1976), 162–177. Suleiman thinks that the implied author, as well as the narrator, can be unreliable, and thus we can accept imaginatively a narrative that we reject ideologically.

6. Christian Metz, *Film Language*, p. 20.

ing the book, but the audience presupposed by the narrative itself. Like the implied author, the implied reader is always present. And just as there may or may not be a narrator, there may or may not be a *narratee*.[7] He may materialize as a character in the world of the work: for example, the someone listening to Marlow as he unfolds the story of Jim or Kurtz. Or there may be no overt reference to him at all, though his presence is felt. In such cases the author makes explicit the desired audience stance, and we must give him the benefit of the doubt if we are to proceed at all. The narratee-character is only one device by which the implied author informs the real reader how to perform as implied reader, which *Weltanschauung* to adopt. The narratee-character tends to appear in narratives like Conrad's whose moral texture is particularly complex, where good is not easily distinguished from evil. In narratives without explicit narratees, the stance of the implied reader can only be inferred, on ordinary cultural and moral terms. Thus, Hemingway's "The Killers" does not permit us to assume that we too are members of the Mob; the story just will not work if we do. Of course, the real reader may refuse his projected role at some ultimate level—nonbelievers do not become Christians just to read *The Inferno* or *Paradise Lost*. But such refusal does not contradict the imaginative or "as if" acceptance of implied readership necessary to the elementary comprehension of the narrative.

It is as necessary to distinguish among narratees, implied readers (parties immanent to the narrative), and real readers (parties extrinsic and accidental to the narrative) as it is among narrator, implied author, and real author. The "you" or "dear reader" who is addressed by the narrator of *Tom Jones* is no more Seymour Chatman than is the narrator Henry Fielding. When I enter the fictional contract I add another self: I become an implied reader. And just as the narrator may or may not ally himself with the implied author, the implied reader furnished by the real reader may or may not ally himself with a narratee. In *Tom*

7. The term was first coined, so far as I know, by Gerald Prince, "Notes Toward a Categorization of Fictional 'Narratees,'" *Genre*, 4 (1971), 100–105. Booth's "postulated reader" (157) is what I call the implied reader.

Jones or *Tristram Shandy* the alliance is reasonably close; in *Les Liaisons dangereuses* or *Heart of Darkness* the distance is great.

The situation of the narratee is parallel to that of the narrator: he ranges from a fully characterized individual to "no one." Again, "absence" or "unmarkedness" is put in quotation marks: in some sense every tale implies a listener or reader, just as it implies a teller. But the author may, for a variety of reasons, leave these components unmentioned, indeed, go out of his way to suggest that they do not exist.

We can now diagram the whole narrative-communication situation as follows:

Narrative text

Real author ---→ Implied author →(Narrator)→(Narratee)→ Implied reader ---→ Real reader

The box indicates that only the implied author and implied reader are immanent to a narrative, the narrator and narratee are optional (parentheses). The real author and real reader are outside the narrative transaction as such, though, of course, indispensable to it in an ultimate practical sense.

I shall take up the "nonnarrated" forms in this chapter and reserve the discussion of covert and overt narrators and narratees for the final chapter.

Point of View and Its Relation to Narrative Voice

It is the task of narrative theory, like any theory, to deal with the ambiguities and unclarities of terms passed down to it. To understand the concept of narrator's voice—including the case where one is "not" (or minimally) present—we must first distinguish it from "point of view," one of the most troublesome of critical terms. Its plurisignification must give pause to anyone who wishes to use it in precise discussion. At least three senses can be distinguished in ordinary use:

(a) literal: through someone's eyes (perception);
(b) figurative: through someone's world view (ideology, conceptual system, *Weltanschauung*, etc.);

(c) transferred: from someone's interest-vantage (characterizing his general interest, profit, welfare, well-being, etc.).
The following sentences will illustrate these distinctions:

(a) From John's point of view, at the top of Coit Tower, the
panorama of the San Francisco Bay was breath-taking.

(b) John said that from his point of view, Nixon's position,
though praised by his supporters, was somewhat less than
noble.

(c) Though he didn't realize it at the time, the divorce was
a disaster from John's point of view.

In the first sentence, "The panorama of the Bay" is reported as
actually seen by John; he stands at the center of a half-circle
of vision. Let us call that his *perceptual* point of view. In the
second, there is no reference to his actual physical situation in
the real world but to his attitudes or conceptual apparatus, his
way of thinking, and how facts and impressions are strained
through it. We can call that his *conceptual* point of view. In the
third, there is no reference to John's mind at all, either to perceptual or conceptual powers. Since John is unaware of the
mentioned consequences, he is not "seeing," in either the actual
or the figurative sense; the term then is a simple synonym for
"as far as John is concerned." Let us call this his *interest* point
of view. What is confusing is that "point of view" may thus
refer to an *action* of some kind—perceiving or conceiving—or to
a *passive state*—as in the third sense.

Now texts, any kind of text, even ordinary conversation, may
entail one or any combination of these senses. A simple description of an experiment or an explorer's account of a new island
may convey only the literal perceptions of the author, but it
may also entail his *Weltanschauung*, or his practical interests.
A philosophical treatise on abstract issues does not usually entail perceptual point of view, but may express quite eloquently
the author's personal interests in the matter, along with his
ideology.

When we turn to narrative texts, we find an even more complicated situation, since as we have seen there is no longer a
single presence, as in expository essays, sermons, political
speeches, and so on, but two—character and narrator—not to

speak of the implied author. Each of these may manifest one or more kinds of point of view. A character may literally perceive a certain object or event; and/or it may be presented in terms of his conceptualization; and/or his interest in it may be invoked (even if he is unconscious of that interest).[8]

Thus the crucial difference between "point of view" and narrative voice: point of view is the physical place or ideological situation or practical life-orientation to which narrative events stand in relation. Voice, on the contrary, refers to the speech or other overt means through which events and existents are communicated to the audience. Point of view does *not* mean expression; it only means the perspective in terms of which the expression is made. *The perspective and the expression need not be lodged in the same person.*[9] Many combinations are possible. Consider just literal, that is perceptual, point of view. Events and existents may be perceived by the narrator and recounted by him in his own first person: "I felt myself fall down the hill" or "I saw

8. Another ambiguity of "point of view" was recognized by Sister Kristin Morrison in "James's and Lubbock's Differing Points of View," *Nineteenth-Century Fiction*, 16 (1961), 245–256. Lubbock and his followers used the term in the sense of the narrative perspective of the speaker (the narrator), while James usually used it in the sense of the perspective of the knower or reader. Boris Uspensky in *Poetics of Composition*, trans. Valentina Zavarin and Susan Wittig (Berkeley, 1974), ch. 1, distinguishes various kinds of point of view along lines similar to mine. Some alternatives to "point of view" have been proposed: for instance, James's "central consciousness," Allen Tate's "post of observation," and Todorov's "*vision*" (derived from Jean Pouillon). The latter two continue the confusion between cognition and interest.

9. For example a recent article misreads "Eveline" by confusing character's point of view and narrator's voice (Clive Hart, "Eveline," in *James Joyce's Dubliners: Critical Essays*, London, 1969, p. 51). The author argues that Eveline is shallow and incapable of love—which may be true—but supports his argument with questionable evidence: "She over-dramatizes her association with Frank, calls it an 'affair' and him her 'lover'; she thinks of herself in pulp-literature terms as 'unspeakably' weary. But most obvious of all is the strong note of falsity in the language of the passage in which she reasserts her choice to leave: 'As she mused the pitiful vision of her mother's life laid its spell on the very quick of her being . . .' Dublin has so paralysed Eveline's emotions that she is unable to love, can think of herself and her situation only by means of a series of tawdry clichés." Surely the objectionable words are not Eveline's but the narrator's. It is he who is parodying pulp-literature sentimentality in tawdry clichés (as does the narrator of the "Nausicaa" section of *Ulysses*). Eveline may indeed feel maudlin sentiments, but "mused," "pitiful vision," "very quick of her being" are not in her vocabulary.

Jack fall down the hill" (in the first case, the narrator is protagonist, in the second, witness). Or the point of view may be
assigned to a character who is not the narrator: then the separate
narrating voice may or may not make itself heard—"Mary, *poor
dear*, saw Jack fall down the hill" versus "Mary saw Jack fall
down the hill." Or the event may be presented so that it is not
clear who, if anyone, perceived it (or perception is not an issue):
"Jack fell down the hill."

The "camera eye" names a convention (an "illusion of mimesis") which pretends that the events just "happened" in the
presence of a neutral recorder. To call such narrative transmission "limited third person" is wrong because it specifies only
the point of view, not the narrative voice. It is necessary to
distinguish between "limited third person point of view voiced
by a covert narrator," "limited third person point of view voiced
by an overt narrator," and so on.

Perception, conception, and interest points of view are quite
independent of the manner in which they are expressed. When
we speak of "expression," we pass from point of view, which
is only a perspective or stance, to the province of narrative
voice, the medium through which perception, conception, and
everything else are communicated. Thus point of view is *in* the
story (when it is the character's), but voice is always outside,
in the discourse. From *A Portrait of the Artist as a Young Man*: "A
few moments [later] he found himself on the stage amid the
garish gas and the dim scenery." The perceptual point of view
is Stephen's, but the voice is the narrator's. Characters' perceptions need not be articulated—Stephen is not saying to himself the *words* "garish gas and dim scenery"; the words are the
narrator's. This is a narrator's report. But in " 'He shivered a
little, and I beheld him rise slowly as if a steady hand from
above had been pulling him out of the chair by the hair' " (*Lord
Jim*), not only the voice, but the perceptual point of view is the
narrator's, Marlow's, not Jim's. And in "Coffin now. Got here
before us, dead as he is. Horse looking round at it with his
plume skewways. Dull eye: collar tight on his neck, pressing on
a bloodvessel or something. Do they know what they cart out
here every day?" ("Hades," *Ulysses*), the perceptual point of

view is Leopold Bloom's, and so are the words, but he is no narrator. He is not telling a narratee anything. Indeed, he is not speaking even to himself: the convention argues that he is directly perceiving the coffin and the nag's dull eye, and nothing more. There *is* no narrator.

In all these cases the character perceives: his senses are directed outward upon the story-world. But when that perception is reported, as in the first two examples, there is necessarily presupposed another act of "seeing" with an independent point of view, namely that of the narrator, who has "peered into" the character's mind (metaphors are inevitable) and reports its contents from his *own* point of view. Can this kind of point of view be called "perceptual"? The word sounds strange, and for good reason. It makes sense to say that the character is literally perceiving something within the world of the work ("homo-diegetically," as Genette would say). But what the narrator reports from his perspective is almost always outside the story (heterodiegetic), even if only retrospective, that is, temporally distant. Typically, he is looking back at his own earlier perception-as-a-character. But that looking-back is a conception, no longer a perception. The completely external narrator presents an even more purely conceptual view. He never *was* in the world of the work: discourse-time is not a later extension of story-time. He did not "perceive" in the same direct or diegetic sense that any character did. Literally speaking, he cannot have "seen" anything in that other world.

Thus the use of terms like "view" and "see" may be dangerously metaphorical. We "see" issues in terms of some cultural or psychological predisposition; the mechanism is entirely different from that which enables us to see cats or automobiles. Though it is true that preconceptions of various sorts affect our strictly physiological vision too (people may not see what is literally before their noses because they have compelling personal reasons not to), there remains an essential difference between perceptions and conceptions. Further, the narrator's is second-order or heterodiegetic conceptualizing *about* the story— as opposed to the first-order conceptualizing of a character within the story. These distinctions most clearly emerge where

the two conflict, where the narrator is operating under a clearly different set of attitudes than those of the character. Then the narrator's conceptual point of view (except when he is unreliable) tends to override the character's, despite the fact that the latter maintains the center of interest and consciousness. An example is Conrad's *The Secret Agent*: the narrator is clearly unsympathetic to Verloc. Or, more precisely, the character has a conceptual point of view undermined by the narrator's manner of depicting it. Verloc's ideology (such as it is) reeks of indolence; the narrator carefully picks words to so characterize it. For example, Verloc does not simply stay in bed, he "wallows" in it. But the narrator (like all Conrad's narrators) is on the side of vigorous achievement. Similarly, he tells us that Verloc "remained undisturbed by any sort of aesthetic doubt about his appearance." From the narrator's conceptual point of view, implicitly communicated, Verloc's physical messiness is reprehensible and a clear analogue to moral sloth and political dishonesty. Or consider the difference between Verloc's and the narrator's attitudes toward female psychology. Verloc's unpleasant encounter with Mr. Vladimir brings him home in a towering rage. Forgetting that his wife is mourning the death of her brother, for which he is responsible, he is disappointed that she does not soothe him. Yet, immediately, he realizes that she is "a woman of few words." But his notion of his relationship with her, his conceptual point of view, is paraphrased in the narrator's superior diction: "[Winnie's] reserve, expressing in a way their profound confidence in each other, introduced at the same time a certain element of vagueness into their intimacy." Though the "profound confidence in each other" is the narrator's expression, not Verloc's, whose verbal style we know to be less elegant, it can only be Verloc's sentiment. His complacency, of course, turns out suicidal.

Disparity between the character's point of view and the narrator's expression of it need not entail ironic opposition. The narrator may verbalize neutrally or even sympathetically what (for reasons of youth, lack of education or intelligence, and so on), the character cannot articulate. This is the whole structural principle of James's *What Maisie Knew*. Maisie's uncertainty

about when next she will visit her mother is expressed thusly: "Mama's roof, however, had its turn, this time, for the child, of appearing but remotely contingent. . . ." Clearly these are not phrases in Maisie's vocabulary. We accept them only because a sensitive little girl might have feelings that somehow matched the narrator's elegant terms. That is, we can "translate" into more childlike verbiage—for instance, "I don't expect to be at Mama's again very soon." The diction is sanctioned only by the convention of the "well-spoken narrator."

"Point of view" expressing someone's interests is even more radically distanced, since there is not even a figurative "seeing." The subject may be completely unconscious that events work for or against his interests (welfare, success, happiness). The identification of interest point of view may follow the clear specification of the character's perceptual and conceptual points of view. Once they are established, we continue identifying with his interests, by a process of inertia, even if he is unaware of something. In *The Ambassadors*, the narrator speaks of Maria Gostrey's powers of "pigeon-holing her fellow mortals": "She was as equipped in this particular as Strether was the reverse, and it made an opposition between them which he might well have shrunk from submitting to if he had fully suspected it." The narrator informs us of aspects of Maria's character that Strether does not know, yet it makes perfect sense to say that the sentence is "from his point of view." The focus of attention remains on him. Maria's traits are significant only in their implications for him—even though he is not aware of them.

Access to a character's consciousness is the standard entree to his point of view, the usual and quickest means by which we come to identify with him. Learning his thoughts insures an intimate connection. The thoughts are truthful, except in cases of willful self-deception. Unlike the narrator, the character can only be "unreliable" to himself.

At the same time, interest point of view can be established quite independently. The point of view may reside in a character who is "followed" in some sense, even if there is no reference at all to his thinking. If Jack and Peter are in the first scene, and Jack and Mary in the second, and Jack and Joseph in the

third, we identify with Jack simply because he is the one continually on the scene. This has nothing to do with whether or not we care for him on human or other grounds.

The notion of interest point of view is not very meaningfully applied to an external narrator. His only interest is to get the narrative told. Other sorts of interest arise only if he is or was also a character. Then he may use the narrative itself as vindication, expiation, explanation, rationalization, condemnation, or whatever. There are hundreds of reasons for telling a story, but those reasons are the narrator's, not the implied author's, who is without personality or even presence, hence without motivation other than the purely theoretical one of constructing the narrative itself. The narrator's vested interests may be so marked that we come to think of him as unreliable.

The different points of view usually combine, but in important and interesting cases, they do not. Consider "autobiographical" or first-person narration, as in *Great Expectations*. The protagonist-as-narrator reports things from the perceptual point of view of his younger self. His ideology on the other hand tends to be that of his older self. The narrator is older and wiser for his experiences. In other narratives the ideology may not change; the narrator may exhibit substantially the same traits as characterized his earlier self. Where the narrator is a different person than the hero, he may present his own ideology, against which he judges his hero's actions, either overtly, as in *Tom Jones*, or covertly and inferentially, as in *The Ambassadors*. The narrator may utilize a perceptual point of view possible to no character, for example when he describes a bird's-eye view, or a scene with no one present, or what the character did *not* notice.

Point of View in Film

Films endow narrative with interesting new possibilities of point of view manipulation, since they have not one but two, cotemporal information channels, visual and auditory (and in the auditory, not only voices but music and noises). These can occur independently (sound track with black screen or full picture with complete silence), or they can be combined in various ways. The sound may be fully synchronized, as when lip move-

ments coincide with the speaker's words, or unsynchronized, as when no one's lips move yet we hear a voice: the convention is that we are hearing unuttered thoughts (or the like). The situation may be rendered even more complex by having voice-over and voice-on running concurrently. It may even be the same voice, as in Robert Bresson's *Le Journal d'un curé de campagne* where the voice-over represents the priest's diary commenting on the very action in which we are watching him play his part.

The simplest film situation presents a bare visual record of what happened "out there," as in "The Killers." Though it may move, the camera must shoot from some single position. This position need not coincide with the perceptual point of view of any character. The whole movie may pass before us in pure visual objectivity, the camera identified in no way with any character. Whatever identification we feel for the hero issues from thematic empathy, or perhaps merely from the fact that he is on camera more than anyone else.

If he wishes to underline a character's point of view, however, the director has two options. The actor can be so placed in the frame as to heighten our association with him. For example, his back or side profile may appear on an extreme margin of the screen. As he looks into the background we look with him. The other (or "montage") convention uses a simple match-cut: if in the first shot the character looks off-screen, to right or left or front or back, and there follows a cut to another setup within his eyeshot, we assume that he has in fact seen that thing, from that perceptual point of view. And we have seen it with him. (Or vice versa: we may see the thing first and secondly cut to the character looking at it.)

Even so, it is not always clear whether we have seen the object separately from the character, conjointly with him, or through him. We are sure only of a perceptual sympathy with him. In *Citizen Kane*, Thompson, the reporter, is trying to discover the secret of "Rosebud" in the banker Thatcher's memoirs. The camera focuses on the lowering statue, then moves down to the inscription WALTER PARKS THATCHER. The curator, Bertha, says off camera, "The directors of the Thatcher Memorial Library

have asked me . . ."—at which point the camera, tracking back, reveals Thompson in the foreground, Bertha at her desk. In context, the viewer feels awe, amusement, and slight depression at this spectacle of plutocratic self-adulation. The backward movement of the camera to reveal Thompson, looking up at the statue, suggests that he feels this way too. Of course that is an inference; we see Thompson, just as we see the statue. But we see the statue with him: his perceptual point of view is dominant. This odd phenomenon—a character who is both object and mediator of our vision—occurs regularly in the visual narrative arts. It is much rarer in verbal narrative since we do not normally observe a scene through a narrator's eyes at the very moment that he is part of the scene. As a perceptual object in the picture that the narrator is drawing, he cannot also be perceptual subject. Even if they are the same person (the character-narrator), as in "The Pit and the Pendulum" or "The Tell-Tale Heart," the narrating half describes the situation of the other-half-self-as-character after the fact, and hence as object, not subject. The gap between the time of the discourse-telling and the time of the story-events is crucial. Most first-person accounts are retrospective.

But if he wishes, the director of the film can completely identify our vision with the character's, positioning his camera's lens not only alongside the character, but inside, literally behind his eyes. This is the so-called subjective camera technique, employed intermittently in many films, but continuously in only one (as far as I know), *The Lady in the Lake*. The actor playing the hero carried the camera strapped to his chest. The film restricts the point of view in obvious ways: for example by eliminating any glimpse of the character's body unless he is looking in a mirror, by showing extremities of his body at the edges and corners of the screen (much distorted, of course), by having characters who speak to him look directly into the camera, and by letting approaching objects, like fists, block out the lens.

The camera can make very fluid changes in point of view because of its ability to move abruptly or smoothly in any direction. The shift in point of view can be effected by a simple cut or by a track or pan of the camera in a visual *glissando*. A classic

example occurs in Fellini's *La Dolce Vita*: Marcello, the hero, arrives at his friend Steiner's apartment. We see only the door, which opens. Then Steiner's wife looks directly into the camera, so we know that the shot is subjective, that the perceptual point of view is Marcello's, that we are seeing through his eyes. We are carried along into the room: Marcello is greeted by Steiner who is also looking straight into the camera. But then Steiner turns his eyes to the right, and the camera in a graceful and perfectly smooth movement pans left to reveal Marcello emerging on the left side of the frame. A transition has been made from a subjective to an objective shot, and from now on Marcello is fully visible at the party. An analogous sliding change of viewpoint sometimes occurs in modernist verbal narratives; in *Mrs. Dalloway*, a perception may shift from one character to another or to the narrator's report even within the bounds of a single sentence.

Narrators' and Characters' Speech Acts

A final bit of ground-clearing before I take up the central topic of these next two chapters, namely, the transmission of the story, with or without an intervening narrator. We must first consider the nature of accounts of speech, thought, and physical action in general, since in verbal narrative, these are all the audience can utilize to decide whether it is a narrator or a character speaking, thinking, or acting.

A convenient basis for such distinctions is provided by a recent development in philosophy called "speech act" theory. This is not linguistics in the strict sense. It is not concerned with the grammatical composition of sentences in a language, but rather with their role in the communication situation, as actual acts by speakers. We owe the theory to the English philosopher John Austin.[10] Roughly, what sentences intend to do —what Austin calls their "illocutionary" aspect—is to be sharply distinguished from their mere grammatical, or "locutionary" aspect, and from what they do in fact do, their effect on the hearer, or "perlocutionary" aspect. Thus, when a speaker utters

10. John Austin, *How to Do Things with Words* (New York, 1962).

a sentence in English (or any natural language), he is doing at least two, and possibly three things: (1) he is making that sentence, that is, forming it according to the rules of English grammar ("locuting" it), (2) he is performing a quite separate act *in* saying it, an act which might equally be performed by non-linguistic means ("illocuting" it). For example, if he says "Jump into the water!" he is forming (1) the locution "Jump into the water" according to the standard English rules for imperative constructions, etc. At the same time, he is performing (2) the illocution of *commanding*, an act that could also be communicated by making jumping motions near the edge of the pool. If he accomplishes the intention of the illocution, if he succeeds in getting his interlocutor to jump into the pool, he has achieved (3) the perlocution of *persuading*.

One illocution may entail a wide variety of locutions and perlocutions. An illustrative table for the illocutionary act of *predicting* follows.[11]

Locution	Illocution	Possible Perlocutions
"John will doubtless go mad" "It is probable that John will ultimately be crazy" "John's insanity probably will manifest itself" "John's getting nutty" etc.	predict	teach persuade deceive irritate frighten amuse etc.

That is, any given illocution, like *predicting*, can be couched in any one of a number of locutions, using different syntactic and lexical elements. And it can give rise to a wide variety of perlocutions in an addressee (including no effect at all), depending upon the context.

The theory of speech acts provides a useful tool for distin-

11. William Alston, in *Philosophy of Language* (Englewood Cliffs, N.J., 1964), p. 25, proposes this as one of a number of illocutionary acts. Others include reporting, announcing, admitting, opining, asking, reprimanding, requesting,

guishing the language of the narrator vis-à-vis his narrative audience from that of characters vis-à-vis each other. Consider the first three sentences of *The Brothers Karamazov*:

Alexey Fyodorovitch Karamazov was the third son of Fyodor Pavlovitch Karamazov, a landowner well known in our district in his own day, and still remembered among us owing to his gloomy and tragic death, which happened thirteen years ago, and which I shall describe in its proper place. For the present I will only say that this "landowner" —for so we used to call him, although he hardly spent a day of his life on his own estate—was a strange type, yet one pretty frequently to be met with, a type abject and vicious and at the same time senseless. But he was one of those senseless persons who are very well capable of looking after their worldly affairs, and, apparently, after nothing else.

Despite the varied syntax, the following illocutions of *identification* occur:

> There was a man named Alexey Fyodorovitch Karamazov.
> There was a man named Fyodor Pavlovitch Karamazov.
> Alexey was the third son of Fyodor.
> Fyodor was a landowner.

These identify, in a logical sense of the word: that is, "a" is said to be "b," where both "a" and "b" are entities. Other existence statements are, illocutionarily, *descriptions* (or *attributions*), that is, a quality in the predicate is attributed to an entity that is subject:

> He was a strange type.
> He was abject and vicious, yet senseless.

Certain other statements, though their syntax might suggest process statements, are also descriptions:

> Fyodor was well known in our district in his day.
> Fyodor is still remembered among us.

Speech act theory helps us understand that fundamental narrative units—the story statements—cannot be equated with sentences, either their surface or underlying deep structures. Here, it is the items "known" and "remembered" that function as the

---

suggesting, ordering, proposing, expressing, congratulating, promising, thanking, and exhorting.

significant qualities or traits attributed to Fyodor. For the narrative, it is not important that "we" knew or remembered him, but simply that he was so known and remembered. The surface features, the verbs "known" and "remembered," translate into traits in the narrative statement. "We used to call him 'landowner'" and "He hardly spent a day of his life on his own estate" are similarly "disguised" for the narrative. The important point for story is not that "we" called him "landowner," but rather that he was usually so called, that that was one of his attributes. The sentence as sentence is cast as an event; that is its locutionary aspect. But illocutionarily, its function is descriptive.

"Owing to his gloomy and tragic death," on the other hand, does not function descriptively. It is rather a speech act informing us of the event of his death. The purely narrative statement would be something like *He died, gloomily and tragically*. (I am not, of course, presuming to rewrite Dostoevsky, but simply to highlight the narrative thrust of these sentences.)

Other speech acts in this passage *generalize* or *opine*, for instance, "yet one pretty frequently to be met with" and "he was one of those senseless persons who. . . ." The second may seem to take the form of identification, say "There exists a class of senseless persons who. . . ." But it differs in an important way from a clear-cut identification such as "There was a man named Fyodor Pavlovitch Karamazov." A true identification is always integral to the story and cannot be questioned by a reader, since to do so is to prevent the narrative from proceeding, to deny its very fabric. The author must be granted, by convention, the right to posit all those entities and actions necessary to his narrative. But statements that are the narrator's opinions do not have this warranty. They refer to his view of the real world, not to the inner world of the story, and the reader can immediately recognize this departure from the necessities of the story world.[12] When the narrator says that there *are* persons who are

12. "Opining" is an instance of Barthes's "referential" or "cultural" or "gnomic" code (*S/Z*, trans. Richard Miller, p. 20)—"referential" because it permits the discourse to refer outward to the real world, to some kind of scientific or moral authority.

both senseless and yet capable of looking after their affairs (note present tense), and that such fellows are frequently met with, he is presumably referring to the real world of nineteenth-century Russia. Since it bears on the outside world, *opining*, in the strict speech-act sense, makes an apparent truth-claim; one can reasonably ask whether the narrator is right or wrong on independent grounds. But it would not be meaningful to ask whether there was or was not a person named Fyodor Pavlovitch Karamazov. A statistical survey of Russian personality types of the nineteenth century is a logical possibility, but since no one claims that Fyodor ever existed, it is impossible to judge whether or not he was vicious. (We shall return to this question in Chapter 5 when we take up "commentary.")

The speech acts of characters differ logically from those of narrators. Even when a character is telling a story within the main story, his speech acts always inhabit the story, rather than the primary discourse. Like his other acts, they directly interact with other characters, not with the narratee and/or implied reader. So there is a wider range of illocutions open to him than to the narrator. When Clarissa Harlowe writes "I beg your excuse for not writing sooner," the purported illocution is *apologizing*. When her mother writes "I cannot but renew my cautions on your master's kindness," there is a *warning*. And so on. Now of course a narrator can—and Fielding's and other authors' narrators often do—apologize and warn, but only and necessarily about their narrative encounter with the narratee. They can only apologize or warn about the narrative itself. In Book II of *Tom Jones*, the narrator performs the speech act of *intending*, but the intention clearly refers to the narrative: "Though we have properly enough entitled this our work, a history, and not a life; nor an apology for a life, as is more in fashion; yet we intend in it rather to pursue the method of those writers, who profess to disclose the revolutions of countries, than to imitate the painful and voluminous historian." Clearly *intending* and other such speech acts are ancillary to a narrator's central speech act, namely *narrating*. Contrarily, *narrating* can never be a character's central function without his thereby becoming a narrator, hence leaving the story and entering a secondary discourse.

Characters use language to argue, to make love, to carry on business, to rhapsodize, to cogitate, to promise, to make commitments, to lie, and so on, always within the boundaries of the world of the story.[13]

Having examined the preliminary areas—the parties of narrative discourse, the meaning of point of view, and the nature of speech and thought as illocutionary acts—we can proceed to the vocal manifestations of the narrator, in order, so to speak, of advancing degrees of narratorhood. We must recall that our basic concern is discourse *features* that combine in various ways, rather than fixed genres (although a rough generic classification as a composite of features may be possible after isolating the features). By discourse feature I mean a single property of the narrative discourse, for example, the self-reference of the narrator by first person pronoun, or the use or avoidance of time summary. Variety among discourse styles can then be accounted for in terms of mixtures of independent features. Narrative theory has suffered from too great a reliance on categories, so that the full discursive complexities of individual narratives are sometimes missed because they do not "fit."

"Nonnarrated" Representation in General

The negative pole of narrator-presence—the pole of "pure" mimesis—is represented by narratives purporting to be untouched transcripts of characters' behavior. At the positive pole of pure diegesis, on the other hand, the narrator speaks in his proper voice, uses the pronoun "I" or the like, makes interpretations, general or moral observations, and so on.

The non- or minimally-mediated narrative records nothing beyond the speech or verbalized thoughts of characters. Such minimal marks of narrative presence or tags as "he thought" or "he said" may be deleted: this effect is usually called free style. But even if the tags are employed, they are purely conventional; separate paragraphing could as easily indicate a change of speaker.

13. An analysis of the speech acts of characters can be found in Richard Ohmann, "Literature as Act," in Seymour Chatman, ed., *Approaches to Poetics, English Institute Essays* (New York, 1973).

To say that only the speech or thoughts of characters is imitated is not to imply that the mimesis is simply in its underlying semantics. Mikhail Bakhtin, in an important theoretical work, shows that quotations are really duplex. On the one hand, like other conventional signs, they are oriented toward their signification, just as if they appeared in ordinary texts like newspapers, textbooks, and so on. On the other, they are "objectivized," understood "not only . . . from the point of view of [their] object, [but] become [themselves] object[s] as . . . characteristic, typical, or picturesque" that is, reflective of the characters. Thus each speech or thought of a character always presupposes *two* "speech centers and two speech unities"—even if the implied author does not admit a narrator. An "ultimate semantic authority, which requires a purely object-oriented understanding"—the implied author—"exists in every literary work, but it is not always represented by the direct authorial word." The implied author's

foreign intention does not penetrate inside the objectivized [speech]; it takes it rather as a whole and without altering the sense or tone, subordinates it to its own tasks. It does not invest [the speech] with another object-oriented meaning. It is as if the [speech] is not aware of the fact that it has become an object; it is like a person who goes about his business and is not aware of the fact that he is being watched.[14]

Theoretically, a copied text is the minimal case. The discourse pretends merely to transmit already written materials, like letters or a character's diary. At one remove is quoted dialogue, whose only necessary assumption is that someone has transcribed the speech of the characters. All we are given is the written version of a sound recording. The presupposed device is a stenographer. We cannot avoid the implication that somebody has done the transcription, but the convention ignores the act and assumes that the expression is a pure mimesis. Still, logically, there is a transformation, from the modality of oral to that of written speech.

14. Mikhail Bakhtin, *Problems of Dostoevsky's Poetics*, trans. R. W. Rotsel (Ann Arbor, 1973), pp. 154, 155, 156. I have substituted "speech" for the translator's "word"—which I find unnecessarily metaphorical for Bakhtin's concerns.

Somewhat more distant from the pure objective pole are non-speech actions—bodily and other movements and internal processes, thoughts, feelings, sense impressions. Among the latter, the convention is that what is going on in the mind of a character can be copied out in words. This presupposes a device more complex than a stenographer—one that reads thoughts—not only verbal ones, but perceptions, sensations, and unarticulated feelings, and puts them into linguistic form.

As for external physical actions, narrative, unlike drama, cannot directly imitate physical movements. When an actor sits down, he imitates with his body the character's movements. It is he, not the playwright, who embodies the character. In verbal narrative, however, "John fell into the chair" or "John lounged about" give us an interpretation, obviously a narrator's. This is logically true even if the term is as neutral as can be—"sat" rather than "lounged." "Sat" implies a neutral depiction, namely that other, more loaded terms have been avoided. That too can be called interpretation: "John [simply] sat down"; but by convention neutral words for actions tend to suggest a conscious avoidance of narrator mediation. The bare description of physical action is felt to be essentially unmediated, without overt thematic interpretation. The reader must infer themes from a bare account of purely external behavior. The verbs of Hemingway's "The Killers," a standard example of sheer reportage, convey only overtly visible actions, strenuously avoiding even a hint of inner behavior: "Nick walked up the street beside the car-tracks and turned at the next arc-light down a side-street," or "Nick walked up the dark street to the corner under the arc-light, and then along the car-tracks to Henry's eating house," or "Ole Andreson said nothing." We must always guess at what Nick or Ole is thinking.

Further, sentences separately describing the setting for its own sake tend to be avoided. Hemingway's story mentions the car-tracks and the arc-light only because they frame Nick's actions: they are spatial markers of his movements. They are mentioned leanly and purposively, tucked away in the syntax, never—as Barthes says about Flaubert's descriptions of Rouen—gloriously irrelevant to the plot, never "set" descriptions.

In another impersonal narrative style, that of certain *nouveaux romans*, description is widely prevalent, in fact becomes dominant. Jean Ricardou[15] has shown that in some of these novels the writing seems to take over from the author (or implied author), becoming autonomous, or in his word *scriptural* (compare Barthes's notion of *scriptible* narratives). Rather than starting with some previous conception and putting it into words, the convention is that the pen traces the lineaments of things on its own. Things depicted in this flat way are emptied of human significance; they become mere functions of the writing rather than vice versa. Philippe Sollers' *Drame* gets fixated on the color red. Ricardou's *L'Observatoire de Cannes* goes from triangle to triangle. And so with works of Claude Mauriac, Alain Robbe-Grillet, Claude Ollier, and others.

Nonnarrated Types: Written Records

In a progression from minimal to maximal narrator-mediation, from features that signal the least to those that signal the greatest audibility of his voice, "already written documents" should be examined first. Of all the forms of literary narrative those that pretend to be constituted by found letters and diaries least presuppose a narrator. If we insist upon an agent beyond the implied author, he can only be a mere collector or collator. His power is the trivial one of having collected (and perhaps edited) the letters or journal for the typesetter. He is not even responsible for direct reports of characters' physical actions, but presents only their literal written artifacts. The sole purported change is from handwriting to print. But he may not even allow himself a stenographer's options about punctuation and so on. His presence can only be made known by means of footnotes or a preface. The *redacteur* of Laclos' *Les Liaisons dangereuses* tells us that he has changed the names of persons referred to in the letters and asks permission to delete whatever seems superfluous. The editor of *La Nausée* writes about the problem of dating Roquentin's early pages, the physical condition of the manuscript, and the interpretation of certain words. He identifies

15. Jean Ricardou, *Problèmes du nouveau roman* (Paris, 1967), ch. 2.

characters (the "Self-Taught" man) and gives a bibliographical reference to Roquentin's reading.

But if the external narrator is reduced or nonexistent, can we not posit some kind of internal narrator? Is it not the case that most epistolary or diary narratives are constructed to frame a narration by correspondents or diarists? If so, why are they not simply a subclass of first-person or autobiographical narrative? Though letters or diary-entries may and often do narrate, they need not. A story can be cast in epistolary form in which every sentence expresses only the then-and-there relationship between the correspondents. In that instance, it is no less "dramatic" than if the interchange were through pure dialogue marked off by quotation marks. A recent novel by Mark Harris, *Wake Up, Stupid*, is of this order. The letters of the hero concern matters of current practical importance to him; they are not reports of what has happened since the last letter. The reader must piece that out for himself.

And even where letters contain a great deal of narrating, we may find many here-and-now elements. In *Pamela* there is a more or less constant movement between narrations and other kinds of speech acts proper to the story—requests, commands, laments, questions, and so on.

Pamela's first speech act is *announcing her present intentions*: "I have great trouble, and some comfort, to acquaint you with." The mode is then switched to *narrating*, as the topic of this announcement is presented in summary preterite: "The trouble is, that my good lady died of the illness I mentioned to you, and left us all much grieved for the loss of her." Then *describing* a character: "for she was a dear good lady, and kind to all us her servants." After more narrating, we are given an *assessment* of the mother's situation: ". . . who have enough to do to maintain yourselves. . . ." This assessment is not narrative (discoursive) but actual (diegetic), that is, an estimate of the present state of affairs in the story-world. Pamela is not telling her father and mother a story they do not know, but rather considering their actual situation with them, weighing its import.

Another important characteristic: unlike genuine narrators, the correspondent or diarist cannot know how things will ulti-

mately turn out. Nor can he know whether something is important or not. He can only recount the story's past, not its future. He can only have apprehensions or make predictions. Suspense derives from our curiosity about whether or not his hopes or fears materialize. Pamela expresses her apprehensions, and later we discover, from further letters, what ultimately happens.

Of course, an interval must elapse between the events recounted and the appearance of the letter or entry in the diary. But these intervals tend to be much shorter than those between the story-time and discourse-time of a genuine retrospective account, for example an autobiographical novel. Moments of composition appear as lulls amidst the storms of the story. Pamela sometimes cannot even enjoy that respite; her letter is regularly interrupted by some onslaught by Mr. B. Richardson captures the immediacy of the event by having her add a postscript to a letter: "I have been scared out of my senses; for just now, as I was folding up this letter in my late lady's dressing room, in comes my young master! Good sirs! how I was frightened!"

Thus, epistolary narrative is an enactment, an unmediated narrative text—although secondary mediation is always possible and indeed generally occurs. But it is incorrect or at least oversimplified to argue, as Jean Rousset does,[16] that characters in epistolary narratives "tell the story of their lives at the same time that they live them," that the reader "is made contemporaneous with the action," that he sees the character's life "at the very moment when it is lived and written by the character." The moment of writing, yes, but the moment of living, no. Just after it. The act of writing is always distanced from the correspondent's life, be it ever so minimally. The correspondent has intruded upon the "liver." Even if the delay between the event and its transcription is very brief—if the events are "seized while hot" (*saisie à chaud* as Rousset puts it)—it is still a delay. It is precisely this delay that separates epistolary and diary narratives from true story-contemporaneous forms like the interior monologue.

Further, epistolary and diary narratives are *accounts*: they

16. Jean Rousset, "Le roman par lettres," *Forme et signification* (Paris, 1960), p. 67.

strongly presuppose an audience. Interior monologue, on the other hand, has no conscious sense of audience. It is expressive, not communicative, of the character's thoughts.

The diary narrative differs from the epistolary in its narratee. The narratee of a letter is the addressed correspondent; the narratee of a private diary is usually the writer himself, though the diary may ultimately be intended for someone else's eyes (*Noeud de vipères, The Key, Abel Sanchez*). The diarist may narrate events for his own edification and memory. But he may also be working out his problems on paper. Still, he is talking to himself. Most of the entries in Roquentin's diary in *La Nausée* are of an expository, not a narrative cast:

I don't think the historian's trade is much given to psychological analysis. In our work we have to do only with sentiments in the whole to which we give generic titles such as Ambition and Interest.

When narrative does appear, it often serves the function of example:

The thing is that I rarely think; a crowd of small metamorphoses accumulate in me without my noticing it, and then, one fine day, a veritable revolution takes place. This is what has given my life such a jerky, incoherent aspect. For instance, when I left France, there were a lot of people who said I left for a whim. And when I suddenly came back after six years of traveling, they still could call it a whim. I see myself with Mercier again in the office of that French functionary who resigned after the Petrou business last year. Mercier was going to Bengal and he pressed me to go with him. Now I wonder why.[17]

Film offers some interesting twists on the diary convention. The best example I have seen is Robert Bresson's version of Georges Bernanos' *Le Journal d'un curé de campagne* (1950).[18] Especially at the beginning, brief shots illustrating the quality

17. Translated by Lloyd Alexander.
18. In the novel, according to Raymond Durgnat, "the diary is 'transparent,' a convention, [since] the priest would a) have had to have been born a novelist and b) spent most of the day writing up his diary" (*The Films of Robert Bresson*, New York, 1969, p. 46). Durgnat argues that the film journal is more realistic in this respect. The visual image of the curé scribbling a "few trite words" can be followed instantaneously by a cut, a purely "showing" cinematic device, which takes over the burden of exposition.

of the curé's bleak life in his tiny vicarage are interlaced with shots of his hand writing the journal (his physical and mental distress reflected in frequent blottings). At the same time his own voice-over reads what the hand is writing in the diary. But the diary can continue to "speak," by the voice-over effect, even when the camera leaves it, and returns to the action, "back then," which it recounts. At such moments the actions that we see, in the screen's usual "present tense," are the visual counterpart of what we hear, in the past tense, as the curé's offscreen voice speaks the diary. The words are kept, yet also transformed, by a routine cinematic convention, into their corresponding flashbacked images. And certain odder effects are also possible. At one point, accompanying the visual image of his hand writing the diary, his voice-over breaks off and says that he must write down immediately what is happening. But as the voice-over describes that current action, the visuals show the action itself, not his hand writing in the diary. The account of "life" is suppressed by "life" itself.

Another interesting effect is utilized several times to show that the mind of the curé is unable to grasp what is being said to him (not only illness but naiveté plagues him: he says, plaintively, that he will never understand human beings). The action proceeds in the completely dramatic mode, that is, the narrative voice-over is still, for instance, as the curé (as character) talks with the countess. The camera focuses on him as he listens to her, though it is her voice we hear. Then her voice becomes weaker, though still audible, and the curé's diary voice-over starts speaking conjointly with it, though louder, explaining why, at that moment in the story, he could not understand what she was saying.

Pure Speech Records

A step further, the transcription of speech presupposes not only a collator but a stenographer. The record of speech can be that of a single character, the classic dramatic monologue, or of two or more, that is, unmediated dialogue.

Dramatic monologues subsume that a character speaks to an-

other, silent, character.[19] The essential limitation is that the speaker's central activity not be narration, since in that case, he would be a narrator, and the scene would be merely a frame for a secondary narrative. An example of rather pure dramatic monologue is Dorothy Parker's story "Lady with a Lamp," the record of the speech of an unnamed character to her friend Mona, who is suffering a nervous breakdown, whom she ostensibly tries to comfort but only manages to make worse. The story is in the character's direct free speech (that is, in the present tense, with first-person pronoun reference and without quotation marks or dialogue tags like "she said"):

Well, Mona! Well, you poor sick thing, you! Ah, you look so little and white and *little*, you do, lying there in that great big bed. That's what you do—go and look so childlike and pitiful nobody'd have the heart to scold you. And I ought to scold you, Mona. Oh, yes, I should so too. Never letting me know you were ill.

(The expression "I should so too" implies that at this point Mona has protested that she should not be scolded. Her verbal reactions never actually appear in print but are inferrable from what her friend says.)

I was mistaken, that's all. I simply thought that after—Oh, now, you don't have to do that. You never have to say you're sorry, to *me*. I understand.

(Mona's apology must interrupt the speaker at "after.") At the end the speaker has so upset Mona that she becomes alarmed herself at the reaction:

Mona, don't! Mona, stop it! Please, Mona! You mustn't talk like that, you mustn't say such things.

(Mona has perhaps threatened to do herself in.) In desperation, the speaker calls to Mona's maid, Edie, the change of interlocutor being indicated by italics:

19. There is no point in limiting "dramatic monologue" to poetry merely because its most famous exemplars were the poems of Browning. A simple but useful definition appears in Joseph Shipley, *Dictionary of World Literature* (Paterson, N.J., 1960), p. 273: "The dramatic monologue is a character sketch, or a drama condensed into a single episode, presented in a one-sided conversation by one person to another or to a group." Bakhtin refers to the dramatic monologue as "the phenomenon of hidden dialogicality" (p. 163).

Edie, Oh, Edie! Edie, I think you'd better get Dr. Britton on the telephone, and tell him to come down and give Miss Morrison something to quiet her. I'm afraid she's got herself a bit upset.

Obviously, the dramatic monlogue is so special an effect that there must be some overwhelming reason for its employment. In "Lady with a Lamp" a character's moral and psychological obtuseness and possible malice is supported by the technique of keeping her interlocutor—her victim—unheard.

Most dramatic monologues leave the interlocutor's comments completely out of the text, but there is a short story by Katherine Mansfield called "Two Tuppenny Ones, Please," in which the interlocutor is given a simulacrum of voice through dots of ellipsis:

Lady. . . . You've heard about Teddy—haven't you?
Friend. . . . .
Lady. He's got his . . . He's got his . . . Now what is it? Whatever can it be? How ridiculous of me!
Friend. . . .?
Lady. Oh, no! He's been a Major for ages.
Friend. . . .?
Lady. Colonel? Oh, no, my dear, it's something much higher than that . . .

The friend is allowed an intonation and nothing more, as if she turned away from us and we could only catch the interrogative intonation at the end of her utterances.

Though pure dialogue between characters is more common than dramatic monologue, its apparent structural simplicity is an illusion. Much could be said about dialogue as a source of narrative information, but I shall limit myself to questions of inference and taxonomy. Stories that are uniquely dialoguic or rely heavily on it require the implied reader to do more inferring than other kinds, or if not more, at least a special kind. Speech act theory clarifies the issue. To a greater degree than normal, the reader must divine for himself the illocutionary force of the sentences spoken by characters to each other, that is, what they "mean" as a function of what they *do* in the context of the action, since there are no direct reports of that doing. It is as if we were supposed to supply, metatextually, the correct verb

tag—"complained," "argued," "pleaded,"—to characterize the speech act. Consider for example the following sentences from Hemingway's "Hills Like White Elephants":

The girl was looking off at the line of hills.
They were white in the sun and the country was brown and dry.
    "They look like white elephants," she said.
    "I've never seen one." The man drank his beer.
    "No, you wouldn't have."
    "I might have," the man said. "Just because you say I wouldn't have doesn't prove anything."

Illocutionarily, the girl first *poeticizes* or the like. The man seems to be *admitting ignorance* but the later context tells us that he is *rejecting* her flight of fancy. She then *criticizes* or *belittles* him. He in turn *defends* himself and *challenges* her authority to make judgments about him.

A crucial element in the representation of dialogue is the identification of the speaker. The least obtrusive marking is simple position: the ordinary convention is that speakers alternate from paragraph to paragraph. In the passage from "Hills Like White Elephants," we know that the girl is saying "No, you wouldn't have" because it is her "turn"—hers are the odd paragraphs. If the text had read

    "They look like white elephants," she said. "I've never seen one."
    The man drank his beer. "No, you wouldn't have,"

we would assume that it was the man who accused the girl of lacking visual imagination rather than vice versa.

We make these inferences about speech acts as we make all our inferences in reading—in terms of our ordinary coded knowledge of the world and our expectations about human behavior in society as we know it. That is why pure speech-report narratives would be particularly difficult to understand across great cultural divides.

Of all narrative theoreticians, Bakhtin has been most concerned with questions of dialogue. Though he often used the word in a very expanded sense (for example, the "dialogue" of the author with society), he also studied the ordinary intradiegetic situation closely. He recognized a wide range of effects

possible in the dialogue,[20] for example how Dostoevsky's characters are intensely preoccupied with their interlocutors' potential replies. Obviously, a great deal of the tension in the Hemingway passage above stems from our sense of the pregnancy of each speech for the interlocutor. "I've never seen one" is clearly a chip-on-the-shoulder remark: the girl promptly knocks it off. Her rejoinder in turn is phrased to solicit a counterrejoinder. The couple are caught up in one of those endless wrangles that intimates wage so viciously because they know each other's weak points and struggle for the last word.

Quite different is what Bakhtin calls the "servile" or "cringing" attitude, the "timid and bashful stifled cry of defiance" so common in Dostoevsky. From *Poor Folk*:

I live in the kitchen, or, more correctly speaking, here next to the kitchen is a little room (and I would like to point out that our kitchen is clean and bright, a very good one), a small nook, a humble little corner. . . . Well, so, this is my little corner. . . .

The "halting speech and . . . interruptions [and] reservations" characterize Devushkin's "sideward glance" at his epistolary interlocutor Varenka Dobroselova, reflecting his nervousness about her potential disdain. "The other person's words as it were wedge their way into his speech, and although they are in reality not there, their influence brings about a radical reorganization of that speech."

Such dialogues may go inward, the two "interlocutors" actualizing different facets of the same personality. Golyadkin, in *The Double*, has dialogues with an alter ego. His own tone is one of hollow independence and indifference ("he's his own man, he's all right"), designed to reassure himself. The double he himself creates, "an older, more confident person," begins by comforting him, but ends (usurping the function of ironic narrator) by turning Golyadkin's own blustering words against him. Similar effects occur in *Notes from Underground, The Idiot, Crime and Punishment, The Brothers Karamazov*.

When we know more about textual and semantic analysis, it may be possible to develop viable taxonomies of dialogue types.

20. Bakhtin, *Dostoevsky's Poetics*, pp. 110ff.

Usefully, if impressionistically, Maurice Blanchot has already proposed a three-way distinction. His exemplars are Malraux, James, and Kafka. In Malraux's work, dialogue serves the function of genuine discussion, in the traditional Socratic sense. His characters, despite their passionate intensity, become "at moments of clarity . . . suddenly and naturally, the voices of the great ideas of history." They discuss because they want to find the truth, even if the pressures of the time prevent them from reaching accord. The characters of James, on the other hand, carry on dialogues in a spirit of idle conversation, "around the tea in an old lady's cup" (as Hawthorne put it). But there may suddenly emerge in such a conversation an "extraordinary explanation in which the protagonists understand each other, wonderously, through a hidden secret which they feel they have no right to know, communicating for the moment around the incommunicable, thanks to the reserve they surround themselves with and the mutual understanding that permits them to speak without seeming to speak." Kafka's characters, for their part, are doomed forever to talk at cross purposes, past each other: "the characters are not really interlocutors; speeches cannot really be exchanged, and though resemblant in surface meaning, they never have the same import or the same reality: some are words above words, words of judgment, of commandment, of authority or temptation; others are words of ruse, flight, deceit, which keep them from ever being reciprocated."[21]

Soliloquy

Narrative theorists have used the word *soliloquy* to describe another sort of unmediated presentation of a character's speech, citing such works as Virginia Woolf's *The Waves* and Faulkner's *As I Lay Dying*.[22] Is the transfer of the term to narrative structure useful? Is it a viable narrative feature? Let us recall the

21. Maurice Blanchot, "La douleur du dialogue," *Le Livre à venir* (Paris, 1959), pp. 223–234. I am grateful to Jonathan Culler for calling this and other references to my attention.

22. For example, Robert Humphrey, *Stream of Consciousness in the Modern Novel* (Berkeley and Los Angeles, 1959), pp. 35–38. Humphrey defines soliloquy as "the technique of representing the psychic content and processes of a character directly from character to reader without the presence of an author, but

meaning of "soliloquy" in the drama. The standard examples—
Hamlet's and Macbeth's—contain (at least) the following features:

(1) the character does in fact speak (in the cinematic version,
by a technical trick, his lips remain closed but we hear his
voice);

(2) either he is alone on stage, or if there are others they
show by their demeanour and actions that they do not hear
him;

(3) he traditionally faces the audience;

(4) but he does not necessarily name the audience; the second person pronoun or the imperative is addressed either
to himself or, in formal apostrophe, to someone not present
("ye Gods," or the like);

(5) thus the audience is not addressed but rather overhears
the character's address to himself or to someone not present;

(6) the style and diction of the soliloquy tend to be very
much of a piece with the character's ordinary dialogue; thus
if he speaks in a formal and poetic manner to the other
characters, that is the style of the soliloquy, too; there is
no attempt to modify his language to show that it is an
inner phenomenon;

(7) the content often constitutes an explanation of or comment on the character's situation.

Features (1) and (2) are obligatory, the rest optional but usual.

Now in what sense can passages in narrative be called soliloquies? *The Waves* and *As I Lay Dying* do in fact exhibit some of
these features.[23] In *The Waves* characters are said to speak: the
tag "he (she) said" is usually present, and passages attributed
to each character are always in quotation marks. Thus, the style
is direct tagged ("tagged" means marked by the *verbum dicendi*).

---

with an audience tacitly assumed" (whereas interior monologue does not
acknowledge the presence of an audience). The character does not necessarily
name an audience; rather, because he is explaining or commenting upon what
is happening, we presume that he is doing it for one.

23. Thus L. E. Bowling is incorrect in referring to *The Waves* as an interior
monologue novel ("What Is the Stream of Consciousness Technique?" *PMLA*,
65 [1950], p. 339). See the discussion of interior monologue below.

"Susan has passed us," said Bernard. "She has passed the tool-house door with her handkerchief screwed into a ball. She was not crying, but her eyes, which are so beautiful, were narrow as cats' eyes before they spring. I shall follow her, Neville. I shall go gently behind her, to be at hand, with my curiosity, to comfort her when she bursts out in a rage and thinks, 'I am alone.'"

As I Lay Dying uses not tags but name-captions to identify each speaker:

DARL

Jewel and I come up from the field, following the path in single file. Although I am fifteen feet ahead of him, anyone watching us from the cotton-house can see Jewel's frayed and broken straw hat a full head above my own.

In neither novel do other characters respond directly to the statements of the speaker; thus we infer that the others have not heard them. So the form cannot be "dramatic monologue". Though Bernard seems to be addressing Neville directly, there is nothing in Neville's own speech (which occurs no less than four pages and ten speakers later) to suggest an acknowledgement of what Bernard has said. Indeed, the speech implies that Bernard is not even present:

"Where is Bernard?" said Neville. "He has my knife. We were in the tool-shed making boats, and Susan came past the door. . . ."

Nor is the reader named or addressed in either *The Waves* or *As I Lay Dying*. In the rare cases that "you" occurs, it serves as apostrophe, as in Louis' speech upon finishing school:

"I am most grateful to you men in black gowns, and you, dead, for your leading, for your guardianship. . . ."

Soliloquies, then, are in fact possible in narrative, providing they are tagged, never free, for the simple reason that they must be recognized unambiguously as speech, not thought, or as a stylized, expressionistic form beyond mere thinking or speaking. In this sense, *As I Lay Dying* is more ambiguous than *The Waves*, since it gives only name-captions and does not specify whether the named character thinks or speaks the words that follow. My own feeling is that we are to assume that the words in Faulkner's novel are neither spoken nor thought but rather

attributed to characters in some extranaturalistic way. But the expression is always external, and for that reason belongs here in the discussion of unmediated speech.

Soliloquy is perhaps best used as a term to refer to nonnaturalistic or "expressionistic" narratives in which the only informational source is that of characters formally presenting, explaining, and commenting upon things. These are formal declamations— not speech or thought in the ordinary sense but a stylized merging of the two. As with dramatic monologue and dialogue, the convention is that they have been "heard" by someone and transformed into a written text.

Records of Thought: Direct Free Style=Interior Monologue

We turn now to characters' thoughts. The representation of a character's consciousness may also be unmediated (although the very fact that it is revealed implies a shade more mediation than that in a strict speech record). But "consciousness" as a narrative concept needs circumspection and circumscription. Some plain-sense observations might help distinguish cases often confusingly lumped together.

Without plunging into psychology,[24] one can separate two kinds of mental activity: that which entails "verbalization," and that which does not—roughly, the distinction between cognition and perception. I am sometimes conscious of saying to myself as I pass a market the *words* "I must get milk and bread," but rarely of saying, as I pass a garden, "That rose is red" or "Look at that red rose" or "The redness of that rose." The latter is something "felt" rather than said.

Since a cognition is already a verbal constitute, or is easily

24. As does Erwin Steinberg in "The Stream-of-Consciousness Novelist: an Inquiry into the Relation of Consciousness and Language," *Etc.* 17 (1960), 423–439. Steinberg searches through a variety of psychological theories, old and new, but comes up with little more than the observation that some part of consciousness is nonverbal; hence the author's task is to simulate nonverbal as well as verbal elements as they traverse the character's mind. But this point was already affirmed by Bowling (p. 342) without the need for documentation from the psychologists. What is important for narrative theory is only what authors, film-makers, cartoonists, and their audiences *assume* the mind to be like. Their assumptions may be quite wrong scientifically and still function verisimilarly, as a cultural commonplace.

reduced to one, its transference to verbal narrative is simple and immediate. But the communication of perceptions requires a transformation into language. A visual medium like the cinema can imitate a red rose directly, nonverbally, and noncommittally, and it can show that it is the object of a character's perception by simple conventions, like having the character look off-screen, and then cutting to the rose itself. But the verbal medium necessarily presupposes a verbalization of that which is not in essence verbal.

Now an important question is whether this verbalization does or does not necessarily assign the words to a narrator. Can nonverbal sensations be transformed into "unassigned" words? The answer is yes: by means of the "interior monologue."

The most obvious and direct means of handling the thoughts of a character is to treat them as "unspoken speech," placing them in quotation marks, accompanied by tags like "he thought." From *Pride and Prejudice*, "'Can this be Mr. Darcy!' thought she." This is direct tagged thought: the tense of the report clause is present, not past as it would be in the case of indirect style, a tag is used, and the thought appears in quotation marks. To the function of stenographer has been added that of mind-reader. But no more than that. There is no interpretation. Only the words—the exact words, diction, and syntax, as "spoken" in the character's mind—have been taken down. The narrator is a bit more prominent by assuming this function, but only a bit. We have moved along the spectrum only a notch or two.

Further, it is very easy—and has long been commonplace in Western fiction—to drop the quotation marks. And more recently the tag has also been eliminated. The result is *direct free thought*. This is a form of enactment that in extended form is called "interior monologue."[25] The criterial features are:

   (1) The character's self-reference, if any, is first person.
   (2) The current discourse-moment is the same as the story-

25. Cf. Scholes's and Kellogg's definition: "a direct, immediate presentation of the unspoken thoughts of a character without any intervening narrator" (p. 177). But inadequate definitions are the rule, rather than the exception. Typical is Dorothy Van Ghent's: "The technique of the 'interior monologue' is

moment; hence any predicate referring to the current moment will be in the present tense. This is not an "epic present" depicting past time, but rather a real present referring to contemporary time of the action. Memories and other references to the past will occur in the simple preterite, not the past perfect.

(3) The language—idiom, diction, word- and syntactic-choice—are identifiably those of the character, whether or not a narrator elsewhere intervenes.

(4) Allusions to anything in the character's experience are made with no more explanation than would be needed in his own thinking, that is,

(5) There is no presumptive audience other than the thinker himself, no deference to the ignorance or expository needs of a narratee.

Conditions (1), (2), and (4) are not, of course, unique to direct free thought. They apply equally to any form of unmediated speech—dramatic monologue, dialogue, and soliloquy (but not to indirect free thought and speech, which are narrator-mediated, albeit minimally and sometimes ambiguously so).

It is important to note that this characterization of interior monologue includes the enactment of both perceptions and cognitions. In this respect it differs from previous opinions (like Lawrence Bowling's), which use the perception/cognition distinction to contrast interior monologue with "stream of consciousness."

For an example of direct free thought, consider this extract from the "Calypso" section of *Ulysses*. We first meet Leopold Bloom in the kitchen (I number the sentences for the reader's convenience):

[1] Kidneys were in his mind as he moved about the kitchen softly, righting her breakfast things on the humpy tray. [2] Gelid light and

a modification of the subjective point of view. It is not a departure from traditional convention, for even Fielding used this point of view when he wanted to show 'from the inside' how a character's mind worked; but it is an employment of the subjective point of view throughout the entire novel—instead of sporadically" (*The English Novel: Form and Function*, New York, 1953, p. 267). The "modification" is certainly more than merely quantitative.

air were in the kitchen but out of doors gentle summer morning everywhere.

[3] Made him feel a bit peckish.

[4] The coals were reddening.

[5] Another slice of bread and butter: three, four: right. [6] She didn't
like her plate full. [7] Right. [8] He turned from the tray, lifted the kettle
off the hob and set it sideways on the fire. [9] It sat there, dull and
squat, its spout stuck out. [10] Cup of tea soon. [11] Good. [12] Mouth
dry. [13] The cat walked stiffly round a leg of the table with tail on high.

[14] —Mkgnao!

[15] —O, there you are, Mr. Bloom said, turning from the fire.

Such passages, though often cited as standard examples of
interior monologue are by no means uniformly pure direct free
thought. The first four sentences communicate the straightforward report of an effaced narrator. The character is referred to
by the third person and his actions and thoughts represented
in the past tense. Actually, the narrator's voice is more audible
than in "The Killers." In the third sentence the deletion of "it"
hints at the direct style, but the tense remains preterite.

In sentence five, however, there is a shift to direct free
thought, not because of the truncated syntax (the third sentence
is truncated without a shift in transmissional mode), but rather
because what is deleted is clearly a tag like "He thought" and
the pronoun "I." The deleted predicate, we infer, is the present
tense: "[He thought, 'I need to add] another slice of bread and
butter'" (or the like). Why are we so certain that these are the
exact words that pass through Bloom's mind? (1) Because the
words "right" cannot be attributed to the narrator: in this context, the narrator cannot reasonably be imagined to be weighing
the "rightness" of anything. Only Bloom can do so. (2) Because
narrators conventionally do not speak in truncated syntax.
(3) Because there is no audience: Bloom is not his own narratee.
(4) Because of the semantics: three plus another slice makes four;
that's "right," the exact number to suit Molly's taste. Only
Bloom would be interested in the arithmetic.

Sentence six, on the other hand, is indirect free style, since
the predicate is "didn't" rather than "doesn't." Seven is verb-
less again, so we assume direct free thought. Eight and nine
resume the narrator's voice. "Soon," in ten, however, is a pres-

ent time adverb, and with the absent predicate, which might be present, brings us back to a quotation of words passing through Bloom's mind: "[I'll have a] cup of tea soon." Similarly eleven is short for "That's good." Sentence twelve, however, differs in an interesting way. All the direct free thought sentences so far—five, seven, ten, and eleven—have communicated cognitions. The words say what Bloom's mental voice seems unequivocally to say. But "Mouth dry" may simply mean that Bloom's mouth *feels* dry, in which case the words, by the standard convention discussed above, translate an unarticulated sensation. Or he may (also) be *saying* to himself, in response to the dry sensation, "My mouth is dry." There seems no way of knowing whether one or the other, or both, are meant. This neutralization of the distinction between conception and perception by truncation is very common in interior monologue. Sentence thirteen resumes direct narration, and fourteen and fifteen, of course, are dialogue, that is, direct tagged speech.

We can see that it takes relatively little in the way of direct free thought to suggest the effect of "interior monologue." And, further, though fragmentary syntax may accompany this style, the only obligatory technique is direct free thought—self-reference by first person pronoun (if used), the present orientation of verb tenses, and the deletion of quotation marks.

What absolutely distinguishes interior monologue from other representations of consciousness is its prohibition of express statements by a narrator that the character is in fact thinking or perceiving. The words purport to be exactly and only those that pass through his or her mind, or their surrogates, if the thoughts are perceptions.

The mixed character of the above extract from "Calypso" is no accident. Critics have noted the difficulty of unrelieved pure interior monologue, of conveying the outer actions and situation of a character if the text is totally locked up in his mind. Inferences can only go so far. Joyce had good reason for switching back and forth between interior monologue and covert narration, at least in the sections devoted to Leopold and Stephen. To show Leopold moving around the city required an objective view. The immersion in a mind can only be complete when the

character's physical situation is absolutely fixed and changes in the ambiance unimportant. Molly's interior monologue can be pure because she is in bed, immobile, in the dark, with only sleep, memories, and speculations on her mind. But in earlier sections, the smoothness with which Joyce passes from inside to outside, from Bloom's internal rumination to the narrator's snapshots of him, a man among others walking the streets of Dublin, is a marvelous piece of artistry. It contrasts strongly with Edouard Dujardin's ineptness in sustaining interior monologue in his *Les Lauriers sont coupés*, when it would perhaps have been better to get outside it from time to time. As Merleau-Ponty pointed out, the result is an undesireable doubling of consciousness. Lines like "Ces gens me regardent entrer . . ." ("These people see me enter") are particularly gauche, since characters only comment on the disposition of their bodies when they feel self-conscious or the like; but self-consciousness is not at issue at this particular moment in the novel.

Stream of Consciousness = Free Association

What of the term "stream of consciousness"? How shall it be defined? Or, to ask a more useful question, since we are interested in a deductive poetics of the narrative: How shall we decide which set of features to assign to it? Shall it be treated as a simple synonym for interior monologue? Or are there sufficient differences to warrant a distinction? My own conclusion is that one can be usefully sustained, though on a basis slightly different from that proposed by previous scholars.

In early discussions, the difference between the two terms was simply etymological. "Interior (or "internal") monologue" was the English adaptation of the French *monologue intérieur* (coined apparently by Dumas *père*), while "stream of consciousness" was a phrase first used in William James's *Principles of Psychology*, later making its way into Anglo-American literary discussions (such as May Sinclair's introduction to Dorothy Richardson's *Pilgrimage*). The terms were first treated as synonyms (and still are by many critics). Later, various distinctions were drawn (a practice common in the historical development of English).

In one of the best studies of the subject, Lawrence Bowling argued that "interior monologue" should be limited to cognitions, to the depiction of thoughts already in verbal form in the character's mind, the direct imitation of one's silent "speaking" to oneself. "Pure sensations and images which the mind does not translate into language" he preferred to call "sense impressions" (my "perceptions"). His example from Dorothy Richardson's *Honeycomb*:

grey buildings rising on either side, falling away into the approaching distance—angles sharp against the sky . . . softened angles of buildings against other buildings . . . high moulded angles soft as crumb, with deep undershadows . . . creepers fraying from balconies . . .

By the convention, Miriam only senses these things, but does not articulate them. She does not pronounce to herself the *words* "grey buildings" and so on. Still, these are her direct impressions, not some narrator's account, in *his* words. The latter Bowling would call, appropriately, "internal analysis." For Bowling, "stream of consciousness" should mean the whole of the "narrative method by which the author attempts to give a *direct quotation of the mind*—not merely of the language area but of the whole consciousness." Thus, in his view, "stream of consciousness" includes not only the record of verbalized thoughts ("interior monologue" proper) but also that of "sense impressions," occurrent but not formulated into words by the character's mind, yet not the product of an internal analysis by a narrator.

Certainly the distinction between "direct quotation" and "internal analysis" should be preserved. But how can we speak of a "direct quotation of perceptions, sense impressions" if they do not involve the character's very words? "Quotation" means the transmission of someone's very words. An answer might be that it is an "as-if" kind of quotation. There really are no words: words are used *faute de mieux*. Since perceptions are nonverbal, the narrative structure requires an expression that is nonverbal. In other media there are such means—the cinema could in fact communicate Miriam's sense impressions purely visually. (This demonstrates once again that narrative discourse is quite inde-

pendent of its medium.) Verbal narratives however cannot go beyond words, so they are used, but something must be done to suggest that they are not words, that the experiences communicated have nothing to do with words. What sort of something? What makes Bowling sure that the passage is a direct quotation of Miriam's sensations and not a narrator's internal analysis? For him it is the truncated syntax—the "brief phrases, separated by three elliptical dots," the use of nouns without verbs if an object is not moving and attached to a participle if it is.[26] Obviously, however, cognitive thinking can be expressed the same way. Perhaps Bowling is not claiming that truncated syntax is a unique property of "sense impressions," only that given such content, it can serve to mark the form as stream of consciousness rather than internal analysis.

But why should we use "stream of consciousness" to account for "sense impression?" Why is not "sense impression" itself quite adequate as a term? We should preserve Bowling's valuable distinctions by reversing them: let "interior monologue" be the class term and two other terms refer to the two subclasses "conceptual" and "perceptual." "Conceptual interior monologue" can label the record of actual words passing through a character's mind, and "perceptual interior monologue," the communication, by conventional verbal transformation, that of the character's unarticulated sense impressions (without a narrator's internal analysis).

"Stream of consciousness" then is freed to mean something else, namely the random ordering of thoughts and impressions. This is appropriate to the implications of "stream." The mind is engaged in that ordinary flow of associations, at the opposite pole from "thinking to some purpose."

26. Truncated syntax is a convention supposed to suggest either that the mind tends to grammatical shortcuts in ordinary musing, or that there exists a phenomenon like "prespeech" or "preverbal" mental activity that does not follow the normal rules of grammar. Linguists would find this view specious, since abbreviated syntax cannot be meaningful without a normal syntax from which to depart. Further, the number of aberrations that stream-of-consciousness writers permit themselves is very limited. Like other conventions, truncated syntax can mean anything that author and audience agree to let it mean. It has become a *sign* of musing or the like, and a sign needs no real or "motivated" connection with its significate.

The attention of the mind may either be brought to bear upon its object deliberately (and this is called "controlled association"), or it may be distracted from one object to another by an unexpected, sudden, or otherwise arresting or striking stimulus (and this is usually called "free association"). It is the process of free association that is especially characteristic of stream-of-consciousness writing, not because controlled association is lacking in it, but rather because the direct presentation of free association is usually lacking in other methods of writing.[27]

Interior monologue is marked by syntax: it ascribes present tense verbs and first person pronoun-reference to the thinking character (or the implication of these where the syntax is truncated). Stream of consciousness, as used here, goes beyond syntax: it constrains the arrangement of semantic elements according to the principle of free association. There is no reason why the two must co-occur (though they usually do). Authors readily combine the free associative principle with the use of the epic preterite, tags, and so on. As Scholes and Kellogg point out, stream of consciousness can be an ordering principle even in dialogue. Or contrarily a sustained interior monologue can show content development of a highly purposive, teleological, "controlled-associative" sort.

It is true, historically, that interior monologue and stream of

27. H. A. Kelly, "Consciousness in the Monologues of 'Ulysses,'" *Modern Language Quarterly*, 24 (1963), 7. Another definition, from Eric Auerbach (*Mimesis*, Princeton, 1953, pp. 473–475): "the flow and the play of consciousness adrift in the current of changing impressions . . . the continuous rumination of consciousness in its natural and purposeless freedom . . . a natural, and even, if you will, a naturalistic rendering of those processes in their peculiar freedom which is neither restrained by a purpose nor directed by a specific subject of thought." A more dubious claim is that "stream of consciousness" is a *genre*—Melvin Friedman, in *Stream of Consciousness: A Study in Literary Method* (New Haven, 1955): "when critics identify the two terms they are confusing a 'genre' —stream of consciousness—with a 'technique'—interior monologue. A stream of consciousness novel should be regarded as one which has as its essential concern the exploitation of a wide area of consciousness, generally the entire area, of one or more characters. . . . Indeed, there is no stream of consciousness technique; one would commit a serious error in critical terminology by speaking of it as such. Stream of consciousness designates a type of novel in the same way as 'ode' or 'sonnet' designates a type of poem." It is hard to conceive any sense in which "genre" would be appropriate in this context. What does "stream of consciousness" usefully have in common with the pastoral, the verse satire, the Gothic novel?

consciousness tend to co-occur in texts. But if we are to keep our analyses clear and sharp, we must not let them become so entangled that we cannot examine each for itself. Without distinctions and the capacity to distinguish, we cannot deal with new configurations, new constellations of features. Robert Humphrey's account of the "stream of consciousness," for example, will tell us nothing about the method of *La Jalousie* and many other avant-garde narratives. And, to say it once again, the capacity to predict new possibilities is precisely what makes literary (and aesthetic) theories interesting and viable.

There has been much discussion of free association but little practical illustration of it, particularly in comparison with controlled association. Perhaps the best way to illustrate free associative passages is to contrast them with depictions of the mind clearly *not* in that mode. *Pride and Prejudice* is a good foil: consider the moment just after Lady Catherine has warned Elizabeth not to anticipate a proposal from Mr. Darcy. Elizabeth mulls over the surprising discussion:

> The discomposure of spirits, which this extraordinary visit threw Elizabeth into, could not be easily overcome; nor could she for many hours, learn to think of it less than incessantly. Lady Catherine it appeared, had actually taken the trouble of this journey from Rosings, for the sole purpose of breaking off her supposed engagement with Mr. Darcy. It was a rational scheme to be sure! but from what the report of their engagement could originate, Elizabeth was at a loss to imagine; till she recollected that *his* being the intimate friend of Bingley, and *her* being the sister of Jane, was enough, at a time when the expectation of one wedding, made everybody eager for another, to supply the idea. She had not herself forgotten to feel that the marriage of her sister must bring them more frequently together. And her neighbours at Lucas lodge, therefore, (for through their communication with the Collinses, the report she concluded had reached Lady Catherine) had only set *that* down, as almost certain and immediate which *she* had looked forward to as possible, at some future time.

One is immediately struck by the purposiveness implied in this representation of the workings of Elizabeth's thinking. Her mind is entered for only one reason, to satisfy the following plot requirement: she must be shown to be agitated, curious, and, in spite of herself, hopeful. She has already rejected

Darcy's offer of marriage and has no particular reason to believe that it will be repeated. Yet she has come to regret her earlier prejudice against him. Suddenly, Lady Catherine descends upon her, speaks of a rumor that the two are engaged, and demands that Elizabeth promise not to marry him. Elizabeth refuses to make such a promise, by reflex of pride more than calculation. After Lady Catherine's departure she feels perplexed, angry, yet strangely hopeful (in a repressed way, as befits her general circumspectness and sense of decorum—even within the privacy of her own mind). The passage tells us, firstly, that she is discomposed; secondly, that she cannot take her mind off a visit extraordinary not only in its substance but in the urgency attached to it by Lady Catherine, who clearly feels that Darcy may indeed act; thirdly, that she wonders how such a rumor could have begun; fourthly, that the fact that Darcy is Bingley's friend and she Jane's sister must have prompted speculation about her prospects too; and finally that the Lucases have already consummated a match which she has begun to contemplate only in the privacy of her own mind.

The selection that is made from Elizabeth's consciousness is almost as severely organized as dialectic itself. First her generalized and still inarticulate discomposure; then her analysis of why the event is upsetting; then her attempt to determine reasons and sources for the rumor; and finally her speculation about what will come of it all. What could be neater and, above all, more pointed in form? And less like free association? What is important for our purposes is not that Elizabeth has a tidy mind (though of course she does), but that the implied author treats mental depiction, like other narrative actions, as simply "what happens next" along the plot line. The plot is strongly teleological: it answers the question "Will Elizabeth and Darcy finally marry?" No digressions from that question are allowed to occur. Free association would obviously mar the straightforward drift of this classical narrative style. Everything in such novels, including the cogitations of characters, is, as Mikhail Bakhtin would say, "plot-pragmatic."[28] Psychologically, the style is

28. Bakhtin, *Dostoevsky's Poetics*, p. 5.

neither more nor less "realistic" than later styles. It simply employs a different notion of realism, presupposing that the process of mental association is subordinate to the thoughts themselves, which in turn are at the strict service of the plot.

Now consider the beginning of "The Lotus-Eaters" section of *Ulysses*:

[1] BY LORRIES ALONG SIR JOHN ROGERSON'S QUAY MR. BLOOM walked soberly, past Windmill lane, Leask's the linseed crusher's, the postal and telegraph office. [2] Could have given that address too. [3] And past the sailor's home. [4] He turned from the morning noises of the quayside and walked through Lime street. [5] By Brady's cottages a boy for the skins lolled, his bucket of offal linked, smoking a chewed fagbutt. [6] A smaller girl with scars of eczema on her forehead eyed him, listlessly holding her battered cask-hoop. [7] Tell him if he smokes he won't grow. [8] O let him! [9] His life isn't such a bed of roses. [10] Waiting outside pubs to bring da home. [11] Come home to ma, da, [*sic*: probably should be a period] [12] Slack hour: won't be many there. [13] He crossed Townsend street, passed the frowning face of Bethel. [14] El, yes: house of Aleph, Beth. [15] And past Nichols' the undertaker's. [16] At eleven it is. [17] Time enough. [18] Daresay Corny Kelleher bagged that job for O'Neill's. [19] Singing with his eyes shut. [20] Corny. [21] Met her once in the park. [22] In the dark. [23] What a lark. [24] Police tout. [25] Her name and address she then told with my tooraloom tooraloom tay. [26] O, surely he begged it. [27] Bury him cheap in a whatyoumaycall. [28] With my tooraloom, tooraloom tooraloom, tooraloom.

This is the representation of a man thinking, but he is not thinking to any particular purpose, his thoughts are not directed or chained—as are Elizabeth's—to some inexorable march of events. The events in *Ulysses*—the funeral, Leopold's idyll with Gertie Macdowell, his meeting with Stephen—do not "go" any-where, in the traditional sense. No state of affairs changes in any important way, as it does in *Pride and Prejudice* (Elizabeth starts out single and ends up married). Whatever artistic losses might be incurred by reversing events—say, having Leopold visit the telegraph office before the funeral rather than after—the narrative logic would remain pretty much the same. Joyce, Woolf, Ingmar Bergman, and other modern artists do not treat plot as an intricate puzzle to be solved. It is not a change in the state of affairs, but simply the state of affairs itself. In this con-

text the rambling stream of consciousness makes its natural home.

Yet this passage is not a mere chaos of impressions. Free association has its own organizational principles, which Freud and others have made clear—principles of generalization, analysis, exemplification, and so on. Along with these occur "less respectable" mental phenomena—puns and other *Klang*-associations, repressions, condensations.

Let us look at a few of these principles, for instance that of *physical contiguity* in sentence two. Bloom's proximity to the postal telegraph office is communicated directly by the narrator. Whence we leap to his mental reaction in interior monologue— "could have given that address too." We infer, by the contiguity principle, that the deictic "that" refers to the latest object named by the narrator. (Only later shall we understand the full meaning: the postal telegraph office would be as good as the post office as a secret address for his surreptitious correspondence with Martha.) Bloom's perception of the post office is not registered but only implied in the blank space between the two sentences. Physical contiguity operates again in sentences five and seven: Bloom sees a boy smoking a cigarette and is prompted to offer paternal advice. So *reconsideration* becomes the organizational principle in eight: Bloom has second thoughts ("O let him"). This in turn has been prompted by *speculation* ("His life isn't such a bed of roses," nine), including the mental *evocation of a scene* in the boy's life ("Waiting outside pubs," ten), including *imagined dialogue* ("'Come home to ma, da'"). The basis of connection with the next sentence is *cotemporality*—the boy taking a break from his job prompts the observation "Slack hour." Between the narrated thirteenth sentence and the monologued fourteenth, there is a *Klang association*—"Bethel. El", and within the fourteenth the Klang combines with *metonymy*— "Bethel—El—Aleph, Beth—" the name of the synogogue followed by the first two letters of the Hebrew alphabet.

We have already learned in the previous episode of the death of Paddy Dignam. The words "At eleven it is" (sixteen) cross Bloom's mind as he passes Nichols' the undertaker's; "it" must mean Dignam's funeral. Contiguity and memory cooperate. Fur-

ther we guess that "O'Neill's" (eighteen) is also a funeral parlor, on the principle of *another example of a class*; therefore, "that job" must be Dignam's funeral, and Corny Kelleher must be a funeral-director's agent. This is a network of surmise, of course, but later events—the whole of the Hades episode—prove it to be correct. The rhymes and nonsense words like *tooraloom tay* (twenty-five, twenty-eight) are associated with Corny by *metonymy*—he is a jokester and singer of light songs—but they also entail a principle of *phonetic obsession* or the like.

The convention of stream of consciousness has it that there is no externally motivated organization of the character's thoughts, nor, of course, a narrator to make a selection among them. The effect is quite different from the constantly purposive account of Elizabeth's thought. The reader knows that extended passages of her thought will tend to rehearse and comment upon past events, even when she is wondering what is to come. Her thinking is inveterately goal-oriented, easily reducible to question-and-answer logic, leading up to a final answer. All the thinking, like all the other action in *Pride and Prejudice*, follows what Barthes calls the "hermeneutic" set of the traditional nineteenth-century novel. References are always clear, and they follow each other in neat order. But Bloom's thoughts are constantly *in medias res*. At any instant an unfamiliar topic can arise. In many cases, explicit resolution—the identification of a deictic pronoun, for example—will only come later, sometimes much later, sometimes never.

Interior Monologue in the Cinema

The cinema uses interior monologue and stream of consciousness infrequently, and it is interesting to consider why. Some theorists suggest the influence of the behaviorist school of modern fiction (for example, Hemingway), in which language is generally depreciated, in particular the language of thinking. More likely, since films *show* everything, offscreen voices in general have come to be thought obtrusive and inartistic, and those speaking in truncated syntax and free-associative patterns particularly so.

Achieving interior monologue in films is easy enough techni-

cally. All that is required is that the voice-over be identifiable as the character's, whose lips do not move. But that combination may evoke other meanings as well. Only the context can tell us whether it is indeed his interior monologue, or a soliloquy, or even a retrospective commentary on the action (as a football player might comment on his performance at a post-game movie). Other features may be used to clarify the situation. A whispering voice-over may suggest the privacy of interior monologue. And of course the text may be fragmented in syntax and free in psychological associations, as in classic interior monologue passages in verbal narrative. But this seems very rare—I can only remember one or two movies, for instance, Hitchcock's *Murder* (1930),[29] in which it occurs. Because of the medium's conventions, it is possible to be fooled. The first several times that I saw Jean-Luc Godard's *Une Femme Mariée*, I assumed that the voice-over whispering in freely associative fragmented syntax represented the wife's interior monologue. The last time I saw it, I changed my mind: it seemed, rather, an abstracted and disembodied commentary on the action, not the wife's voice at all, but a set of clichés, as trivial as the articles in the lady's magazine *Elle* that she and her maid read, or the chatter about their apartment that passes for conversation when she entertains a visitor. The fragmentation in this case does not reflect the immediacy and free-flowing character of the thinking process, but the meaningless sterotypes of advertising and cheap fiction. Unlike the thoughts of Leopold or Stephen, such bits of phraseology as we hear from the unseen lips of the voice-over—"What did he mean?" "I wonder if I can," "I love you" and so on—bear no immediately explicable relation to the heroine's ongoing thinking. They form rather a commentary on the quality of her life, like the snatches of banal popular song that also accompany her actions.

---

29. Hitchcock expressly uses the term "stream of consciousness" (rather than a standard cinematic term like "offscreen voice" or "voice-over") to describe this scene, showing that he had the literary tradition clearly in mind (François Truffaut, *Hitchcock*, New York, 1966, p. 53).

5 DISCOURSE:

Covert versus Overt Narrators

A clear sonorous voice, inaudible
To the vast multitude.
> William Wordsworth,
> *The Excursion*

I was in the Spirit on the Lord's day,
and heard behind me a great voice,
as of a trumpet.
> *The Revelation*

It is less important to categorize types of narrators than to identify the features that mark their degrees of audibility. A quantitative effect applies: the more identifying features, the stronger our sense of a narrator's presence.[1] The "non"- or minimally narrated story is simply one in which no or very few such features occur.

Still, a fundamental distinction can be made between covert and overt narrators, and that is the task of this chapter. Not every feature can be discussed in detail, so the focus is on the salient and particularly the problematic features.

Three matters are of preliminary concern: the nature of indirect discourse, the manipulation of the surface of the text for covert narrative purposes, and the limitation of point of view to a particular character or characters. The first two are very much open topics, as recent research has shown. The complexities of indirect discourse have spawned a large literature that is not yet conclusive. Contemporary linguistics has challenged the traditional formulations and raised some fascinating questions about indirect style. It has also begun to analyze the mecha-

---

1. There is a hierarchy of "degrees of narratorhood" implicit in Wayne Booth's *reductio ad absurdum* of the dogma of "objective" argument in narratives (*Rhetoric of Fiction*, pp. 16–19). But I take the notion of degree of narratorhood seriously.

nisms for placing special emphasis on certain elements in sentences—by which the covert narrator may "surreptitiously" manipulate his sentence structures, thus backgrounding or foregrounding narrative elements of varying degrees of importance. The mechanism of "presupposition" is discussed here by way of example. Closely related to covertness, indeed often confused with it, is the limitation placed by the implied author on the narrator's knowledge.

Shifting to the overt narrator, we consider a spectrum of features, ranging from least to most obtrusive markers: from set descriptions and reports of what characters did *not* say or think, to the various kinds of commentary—interpretation, judgment, generalization. This chapter (and the book) concludes with some observations about the narrator's interlocutor, the narratee.

Covert Narrators

Covert or effaced narration occupies the middle ground between "nonnarration" and conspicuously audible narration. In covert narration we hear a voice speaking of events, characters, and setting, but its owner remains hidden in the discursive shadows. Unlike the "nonnarrated" story, the covertly narrated one can express a character's speech or thoughts in indirect form. Such expression implies an interpretive device or mediator qualitatively different from the simple mindreading stenographer of nonnarrated narratives. Some interpreting person must be converting the characters' thoughts into indirect expression, and we cannot tell whether his own slant does not lurk behind the words: "John said that he would come" may transmit more than "John said 'I will come,'" since there can be no guarantee that John used those exact words. Hence our intuition of a shadowy narrator lurking in the wings.

The terrain of covert narration is bewildering, and it is easy to lose one's bearings. I was disconcerted to hear in a lecture recently that Joyce's "narrators" included most of his major characters—Eveline, Lenehan, Gabriel, Stephen Dedalus, Leopold and Molly Bloom. The impropriety of assigning the term "narrator" to the character's own mental voice in interior

monologue was demonstrated in Chapter 4.[2] The point is even clearer where characters' thoughts are expressed by covert narrators. It is simply a mistake to argue that Lenehan is in any sense the "narrator" of "The Gallants." When he speculates, reminisces, or whatever, he is not telling a story to anybody, not even himself. It is an outside speaker who is reporting ("internally analyzing") his thoughts:

In his imagination he beheld the pair of lovers walking along some dark road; he heard Corley's voice in deep energetic gallantries and saw again the leer of the young woman's mouth. This vision made him feel keenly his own poverty of purse and spirit. He was tired of knocking about, of pulling the devil by the tail, of shifts and intrigues.

Clearly Lenehan's vocabulary does not include "deep energetic gallantries," "his own poverty of purse and spirit," "shifts and intrigues." And since these are not his words, he cannot be the narrator of the story which they recount. The narrator is *imputing* the feeling of "poverty of purse and spirit" to Lenehan, but it is only an imputation, an internal analysis or report by a covert narrator. When words and phrases that could be part of Lenehan's vocabulary appear—"tired of knocking about," "pulling the devil by the tail"—we are conscious of quotation in indirect free form.

Indirect Tagged and Free Style

Any analysis of the complex relations between the speech acts of characters and narrators requires an understanding of the ways of communicating speech (external voice) or thought (in-

2. Dorrit Cohn, "Narrated Monologue: Definition of a Fictional Style," *Comparative Literature*, 18 (1966), 102, ventures an explanation of the reason for this kind of mistake: "The arguments in favor of an internal angle of vision, so forcefully stated by Henry James, Percy Lubbock, and Joseph Warren Beach, have led to the belief that the separate narrator is absent from the dramatized novel, and that therefore the 'central intelligence' is himself the narrator, in the same sense as the 'I' is the narrator of a story told in the first person. Lubbock may have started this misapprehension when he referred to the character in whom the vision rests by such names as 'dramatized author,' 'spokesman for the author,' or 'fresh narrator.' But despite these misleading metaphors, Lubbock himself was fully aware that in all third-person novels the figural psyche is supplemented by 'someone else . . . looking over his shoulder. . . .'"

ternal voice). A basic distinction is that between quotation and report, or in more traditional terms, "direct" and "indirect" forms, a distinction that has been commonplace for centuries. Usually formulated in terms of speech—the difference between "'I have to go,' she said" and "She said that she had to go"—it obviously applies to thinking as well: "'I have to go,' she thought" and "She thought that she had to go."

The surface differences between the two forms are quite clear-cut. In both cases there are two clauses, one optional and the other obligatory. For clarity's sake I shall call the introductory or optional clause the "tag" ("she said") and the second the "reference." The tag clause signals that it is the reference clause which contains what is reported or quoted ("I have to go" or "She had to go"). In English, the differences between direct and indirect style involve (1) the tense of the predicate of the reference clause, (2) the person of the subject of the clause, and (3) the (optional) presence of "that." In indirect style the tense of the reference clause is generally one tense *earlier* than that of its direct counterpart. And the pronoun is changed from first to third person.

The deeper semantic relations of the two forms, however, are more obscure. Until recently, it was thought that they were straightforward variants of each other, that "She said she had to go" meant the same as "She said 'I have to go'". But linguists have shown that important differences discredit that easy assumption.[3] For example, some sentences can only appear in direct form. "Egbert blurted out, 'How I have loved it!'" cannot be transformed to "Egbert blurted out how he had loved it" and still preserve its original meaning. In the first sentence "how" means "how much," while in the second it means "in what manner." Similarly, "Clarissa whispered, 'There!'" cannot occur in indirect form—*"Clarissa whispered that there." Per-

3. See Ann Banfield, "Narrative Style and the Grammar of Direct and Indirect Speech," *Foundations of Language*, 10 (1973), 1–39 (and the literature quoted therein); see also the important study by Roy Pascal, *The Dual Voice* (Totowa, N.J., 1977). The examples are taken from Banfield's article, which I find challenging even as I disagree with it. Asterisks mark un-English forms.

haps the most interesting restriction, from the narrative point of view, is that only direct forms can cite the speaker's exact words; indirect forms give no such guarantee. Thus it is possible to question only the language of indirect report clauses; we can say "Oedipus cried out that he had done something horrible with his mother, but I won't repeat what he actually said," but not *"Oedipus cried out, 'I have done something horrible with my mother,' but I won't repeat what he actually said."

The indirect form in narratives implies a shade more intervention by a narrator, since we cannot be sure that the words in the report clause are precisely those spoken by the quoted speaker. Of course, they may be, as when they differ radically in diction and/or syntax from the established "well-spoken" style of the narrator: for example in "Eveline" the sentence ". . . latterly he [Eveline's father] had begun to threaten her and say what he would do *only* for her dead mother's sake." The context clearly indicates that the italicized portion is the lower-class Irish dialect counterpart of "*if it were not* for her dead mother's sake." But the well-spoken narrator is not speaking in lower-class dialect. There are several other kinds of expressive effects which suggest that the character's speech or thoughts are being directly quoted. For instance, parts of the sentence can be shifted around and elements deleted to give them more prominence, as someone might do in the heat of actual expression: "John shouted out that how Mary could behave so badly was beyond his comprehension." Interjections can be introduced: "Richard protested that Lord! he didn't like it." Or hesitations: "He protested that he, God help him, he could not be held responsible." Or special emphasis: "He protested that *he* could not be held responsible."[4]

On the other hand there may be good evidence that the words are not exactly quoted, as in the Oedipus example cited above. We sense that the "I" has paraphrased Oedipus' original words.

4. Despite Banfield, who asterisks them, these are eminently possible in fiction. But not all expressive elements can occur. Banfield is right in arguing that the indirect counterpart of sentences like "Clarissa exclaimed, 'What a lark!'" is not possible (p. 7).

The "I" may equally summarize, epitomize, interpret, or otherwise alter the exact words of the quoted speaker. And, of course, the "I," the reporter, who must be the narrating subject of such sentences, may not refer to himself, so that the *pronoun* "I" need not actually appear.

In the nineteenth century there arose in most European languages another distinction which crosscuts that between direct and indirect speech and thought, namely that between "tagged" and "free" style (*style indirect libre, erlebte Rede*).[5] Free style deletes the tag. Thus:

	Tagged	Free
Direct:		
Speech	"I have to go," she said	I have to go
Thought	"I have to go," she thought	I have to go
Indirect:		
Speech	She said that she had to go	She had to go
Thought	She thought that she had to go	She had to go

Free speech and thought are expressed identically, and thus ambiguously, unless the context clarifies.

Direct free forms, I have argued, characterize interior monologue. Indirect free forms do not, precisely because a narrator is presupposed by the third person pronouns and the anterior tense. They may, of course, co-occur with direct free forms: examples abound in *Ulysses*. But often, as in Virginia Woolf's major novels, they co-occur only with indirect-tagged forms.

Still, the meaning of the indirect free form is not the simple remainder of indirect tagged form minus the tag. It has a greater degree of autonomy, and though ambiguity may persist, the absence of the tag makes it sound more like the character speaking or thinking than a narrator's report. A sentence like "She felt that John, bless his soul! would provide for the family" could

5. See the bibliography in footnotes to Dorrit Cohn's article and that in Stephen Ullmann's "Reported Speech and Internal Monologue in Flaubert," *Style in the French Novel* (Cambridge, 1957). The first reference to "*style direct libre*" that I know, cited by Derek Bickerton, "Modes of Interior Monologue: A Formal Definition," *Modern Language Notes*, 28 (1976), 233, occurred in L. C. Harmer, *The French Language Today* (Melbourne, 1954), p. 301.

mean that either the character or the narrator, or both, were blessing John's soul. Whereas in context the indirect free counterpart "John, bless his soul, would provide for the family" seems more exclusively the blessing of the character. This is true of a whole host of expressive features: exclamations, questions, expletives, imperatives, repetitions and similar emphases, interruptions, the words "yes" and "no," colloquialisms, and other forms of "unnarrative" diction (for example, pet names, technical jargon, foreign language elements, etc.). A narrator could hardly remain covert if he himself were to use such forms.

Take exclamations, for example. A covert narrator is hard put to use them because they express strong feelings—deprecation, enthusiasm, or whatever. Such expression would call undue attention to those feelings: we would begin to wonder about them and particularly whether "thereby hangs a tale" about *him*. Exclamations do not suit the role of effaced or transparent mediator. The logic of covert narration permits only the character to exclaim. In Joyce's "The Dead":

Gabriel's warm trembling fingers tapped the cold pane of the window. How cool it must be outside! How pleasant it would be to walk out alone, first along by the river and then through the park! The snow would be lying on the branches of the trees and forming a bright cap on the top of the Wellington Monument. How much more pleasant it would be there than at the supper-table!

We assume that the exclamations are exclusively Gabriel's, a direct quotation of his mind's speech. We have no reason to believe that the narrator is exclaiming.[6]

Stylistically, the reference clause can be either identical with or clearly distanced from the surmisable words of the character, indeed, so distanced as to seem only the narrator's paraphrase. I can present indirectly the statement of a fired streetcleaner in language which is or is not evidently his: "He said he was canned and it was the goddamned foreman's fault." Or "He

6. Why exclamations must mark the indirect free discourse of a character is argued in a subtle article by Pierre Guiraud, "Modern Linguistics Looks at Rhetoric: Free Indirect Style," in Joseph Strelka, ed., *Patterns of Literary Style*, Yearbook of Comparative Criticism, Vol. III (University Park, Penn., 1971), p. 83.

said that his resignation was enforced, implying that questions of a distinctly jurisdictional nature had been raised." And either of these can occur in free indirect style. Thus free indirect style divides into subclasses, attributable to character or to narrator. In between, there are statements of varying degrees of ambiguity. For language that is clearly the character's, a suitable label, recently proposed, is *narrated monologue*.[7] "Narrated" accounts for the indirect features—third person and prior tense—while "monologue" conveys the sense of hearing the very words of the character. Narrated monologue is clearly distinguished from narrative report (internal analysis), where the character's thinking or speech is communicated in words that are recognizably the narrator's. Finally, there is the relatively common ambiguous situation, discussed below, where it is difficult to know whose voice speaks.

The kind of indirect mode considered so far is purely verbal, that is, an account of *words* spoken or thought by the character. But there is clearly another kind of report, whose basis is, rather, perceptions. From the end of Chapter IV and the beginning of Chapter V of *Madame Bovary*:

> The old servant appeared, presented her respects, apologized for not having dinner ready and suggested that Madame look over her new house in the meantime.

V

> The brick front of the house was flush with the street, or rather the road. Behind the door hung a coat with a short cape, a bridle and a black leather cap. . . .

And so on through a description of the parlor, the hall, Charles's office, a large room used as a woodshed and storeroom, and the garden. Then

> Emma went up to the bedrooms. The first one was not furnished, but the second one, the conjugal chamber, had a mahogany bed standing in an alcove hung with red draperies. . . .

7. Cohn, "Narrated Monologue," p. 98. Among the many other terms that have been suggested are "substitutionary speech," *verschleierte Rede, erlebte Rede*, "independent form of indirect discourse," *uneigentlich direkte Rede*, "represented speech," "narrative mimicry," *Rede als Tatsache, monologue intérieur*

This is not a mere description of the house at Tostes by an out-side narrator, but a sense of how the place struck Emma on her first view of it. Though no verb refers to Emma's perceptions, they are clearly implied—that is, we infer that the second sentence is really a shortened form of "She saw that the brick front of the house was flush with the street," and so on. This cannot be called "indirect free thought": the full form is not "Emma thought that the brick front of the house was flush with the street'." It is rather a "free indirect perception."[8]

Let me illustrate the distinctions between narrated monologue and internal analysis with two quotations. Here is something of the logic by which I think we decide whose voice it is that we hear in indirect discourse. The opening sentences of "Eveline" again:

(1) "She sat at the window watching the evening invade the avenue." At first we are uncertain that there is a narrator. The discourse may be only an enactment, the narrative equivalent of an actress sitting on-stage by a window painted on the backdrop. "Sitting at the window" could clearly pass as "nonnarrated," but "watching" is ambiguous. A character may be described as watching something from an external vantage, hence no narrator. Or the verb may verbalize her perception, hence a covert narrator.

Then we encounter the phrase "evening invade the avenue." The metaphor clearly presupposes a mind capable of its invention; if it is not Eveline who does so, the speaker can only be the narrator. Later evidence validates this hypothesis (number five below).

(2) "Her head was leaned against the window curtains and in her nostrils was the odor of dusty cretonne." The first part of

indirect. See Paul Hernadi, _Beyond Genre_ (Ithaca, N.Y., 1972), pp. 187–205, and Edward Versluis, "Narrative Mimicry and the Representation of the Mental Processes" (Ph.D. dissertation, University of Chicago, 1972).

8. Or "substitutionary perception," in the phrase of Bernard Fehr, "Substitutionary Narration and Description: A Chapter in Stylistics," _Von Englands geistigen Bestanden_ (Frauenfeld, 1944), pp. 264–279. Fehr notes some interesting features of substitutionary perception, for instance that it is regularly followed by progressive rather than simple verb forms: 'He saw one of the men who had returned with Silva. _He was standing_ in his boat. . . .'

this sentence again might seem to present a simple enactment. But in the jelling context it seems more like a covert narrator's pronouncement, a free indirect perception.

(3) "She was tired." This is ambiguous: either "She felt [that she was] tired," or "My [the narrator's] report is that she was tired," whatever she thought. (Or *both*: the ambiguity of free indirect forms.)

(4) "Few people passed." Ditto: "She saw few people pass" or "On my [the narrator's] authority few people passed." Or both.

(5) "The man out of the last house passed on his way home." Here clearly we distinguish two vocalic styles. "Out of" is a class dialect form of "from." The voice that speaks of the evening "invading" the avenue is clearly not the one that speaks of a man "out of" the last house; clearly the former belongs to an "author"-narrator and the latter to the character. The basic form of the sentence is indirect free perception but the phrase "out of the last house" is a direct quotation, hence narrated monologue.[9] (Corroboration occurs later in the text in usages like "used to" as iterative instead of the more literary "would," "she always had an edge on her," "hunt them in," "not so bad," including forms that indicate that Eveline is still very young: "grownup," "keep nix," and so on.)

Several changes that Joyce made when "Eveline" was republished in *The Dubliners* (it had originally appeared in the *Irish Homestead*, September 10, 1904) are obvious attempts to make her mental voice more prominent. In the revision, she wonders where "all the dust came from"; in the original, her room is said to "secrete" dust. A subjunctive is replaced by a dialectal form: her father's "saying what he would do if it were not for her dead mother's sake," becomes "what he would do to her only for her dead mother's sake." Perhaps the most interesting change is the dropping of the quotation marks that originally

9. Graham Hough has identified the convention of the "well-spoken" narrator and its importance as a norm against which the voices of the characters are placed. He points out that the contrast is characteristic of the novel but not the epic ("Narrative and Dialogue in Jane Austen," *Critical Quarterly*, 12 [1970], 201).

embraced the word "edge" in the sentence about Miss Gavan: "Miss Gavan had an 'edge' on her. . . ." Deleting the quotation marks turns the sentence into narrated monologue. (The quotation marks would mean not direct free thought but a narrator's "Jamesian" self-consciousness about slang.)

So we distinguish the simple colloquial voice of the character Eveline from the voice of a covert narrator of literary ability. The distinction, of course, is supported by the story's content. We have now read enough to sense that her environment is poor (the curtains are dusty because they hang in a decrepit building in a neighborhood where the atmosphere is smoky), that she has lived in that neighborhood since she was a child, playing in empty lots with the other children of the neighborhood (not in the green fields of an exclusive boarding school), and so on. Even without the evidence from diction, these recognitions would make it unlikely that she is "literary," say a would-be author struggling in a loft. Later sentences confirm our judgments about the first two sentences: they are clearly a narrator's report.[10]

This laborious and unnatural way of reading is not, of course, what the reader actually does, but only a suggestion of what his logic of decision must be like. As narratee he *hears* the narrator's report; the snatches of the character's actual verbiage he *over-hears*.

Sometimes it is not possible to decide whether the words in indirect free form are the character's or the narrator's, for example, if both speak in a highly literate manner. This is not a negative characterization, since the merging of the two voices may well be an intended aesthetic effect. The implication is "It doesn't matter who says or thinks this; it is appropriate to both character and narrator." The ambiguity may strengthen the bond between the two, make us trust still more the narrator's authority. Perhaps we should speak of "neutralization" or "unification," rather than ambiguity.

10. Thus the incorrectness of Clive Hart's assumption (in "Eveline," *James Joyce's Dubliners: Critical Essays*, London, 1969, p. 51) that the "invasion" figure of the first sentence is "just the sort of hyperbole that a girl like Eveline might be expected to use."

Thus, the covert narrator can describe from a clear external vantage point, dip down to quote from the character's thoughts in his own or the character's very words, or plant an ambiguity about a locution, indistinguishably telling and showing, narrating and enacting the character's inner life.

Brilliant examples of the "neutralized" indirect free style occur in Virginia Woolf's *Mrs. Dalloway*. The first sentences:

> Mrs. Dalloway said she would buy the flowers herself. For Lucy had her work cut out for her. The doors would be taken off their hinges; Rumplemayer's men were coming.

A "sympathetic" effect arises because there is no reason to assume that Clarissa's idiolect differs significantly from the narrator's. Such statements imply that character and narrator are so close, in such sympathy, that it does not matter to whom we assign the statement. Indifferently "For you see, dear reader, Lucy had her work cut out for her" (that is, "I, the narrator observe that"), or "[Mrs. Dalloway remembered that] Lucy had her work cut out for her." Indeed the ambiguity goes further, since a *speech* could as easily be implied: "[Mrs. Dalloway *said* that] Lucy had her work cut out for her." All three possibilities hover above the sentence. A feeling is established that the narrator possesses not only access to but an unusual affinity or "vibration" with the character's mind. There is the suggestion of a kind of "in"-group psychology: "It was understood by all parties, including 'myself' (the narrator), that Lucy had her work cut out for her." The content of the first sentence prepares us for this consensus: Mrs. Dalloway is reported simply as saying that she would buy the flowers, not saying that to any particular person. It seems more pronouncement than dialogue. There arises a sense of the broader social context: Mrs. Dalloway is accustomed to having a cooperative audience, maids, cooks, and butlers. The same kind of consensus operates at the beginning of Katherine Mansfield's "The Garden Party." "And after all the weather was ideal. They could not have had a more perfect day for a garden-party if they had ordered it": indistinguishably the thought of one or all of the family, or what one of them said to the others, or the narrator's judgment of the situation.

But the indirect free style is by no means committed to sympathy. It may work ironically.[11] In a beautifully conceived passage Flaubert plays the dreams of Charles and Emma Bovary against each other:

When he came home in the middle of the night he did not dare to wake her. . . . Charles looked at his wife and daughter. . . . How pretty she would be later, at fifteen! She would look just like her mother, and they would both wear wide straw hats in summer; from a distance they would look like two sisters . . . they would think about her marriage: they would find her some fine young man with a good position; he would make her happy, and it would last forever.

Emma was not asleep, but only pretending to be; and while he sank into sleep beside her she lay awake, dreaming different dreams.

She and Rodolphe had been traveling for a week, drawn by four galloping horses toward a new country from which they would never return. They went on and on, their arms intertwined, without speaking. Often from the top of a mountain they would suddenly catch sight of some magnificent city, with domes, bridges, ships, forests of lemon trees and white marble cathedrals with storks' nests on their pointed steeples.

The irony lies in the juxtaposition of the indirect free plunges into the two disparate fantasy worlds. The minds are a million miles apart, though the bodies are separated only by inches.

As I have argued, indirect tagged forms go further toward illuminating a narrator's presence. Indeed, the tag may directly interpret the character's thought, feeling or speech: "John concluded that he was right" implies a greater degree of narrator-mediation than "John thought that he was right" precisely because the mental process through which John has achieved his certainty is characterized by the narrator.

Also interpretive are sentences in which the thought or sensation is not couched in a *that*-clause, but in a nominal phrase. This further syntactic move underlines a kind of epitomization,

11. Dorrit Cohn too has noted that the free indirect style "implies two basic possibilities: fusion with the subject, in which the actor identifies with, 'becomes' the person he imitates; or distance from the subject, a mock-identification that leads to caricature. Accordingly there are two divergent directions open to the narrated monologue, depending on which imitative tendency prevails: the lyric and the ironic" (110–111). "Lyric" strikes me as less descriptive of the effect than "sympathetic," in its root sense of the word—"in agreement with another's taste, mood, feeling, disposition, etc."

hence greater narrator audibility. "John concluded the correctness of his position" is more evidently the internal analysis of the situation by a narrator, since it is even less certain that John had in fact uttered to himself the precise words "the correctness of my position."

"Internal analysis" or "narrator's report" is what critics doubtless mean by "limited third person narration," though, as I argue above, "third person" is improperly used. In pure covert narration, the narrator does not refer to himself at all, so there is no real parallelism with "first person narration." In the latter the narrator indeed refers to *himself* through the first person pronoun. But in the former it is the *character* who is referred to by the third person pronoun: the narrator simply does not refer to himself at all. It is no more meaningful to call him "he" than "I" or "you."

The Manipulation of Sentences for Narrative Purposes: Presupposition as an Example

Let us turn to some other linguistic properties of significance to narrative texts. Language is an extremely verstile tool, and clever authors can deploy a wide range of verbal underlinings and concealments, promotions and deceptions. It is only recently that linguistics and philosophy have developed instruments delicate enough to measure these effects. For instance, we can now account for "topicalization," the movement of a sentence element to a more prominent position to highlight it: "That I have to see" or "To visit Hawaii is my dream." Or for the cleft sentence, which emphasizes an element by anticipating it with *what*: "What you need is a good car." Perhaps the most interesting of expressive devices—and one that well illustrates the utility of the others—is that called "presupposition." [12]

The covert narrator must watch what he says lest he reveal

12. The importance of presupposition in narrative was first impressed upon me by Gerald Prince's "On Presupposition and Narrative Strategy," *Centrum*, 1 (1973), 23–31. Prince's sources are given in his first footnote. An early discussion appears in J. L. Austin, *How to Do Things with Words* (New York, 1962), pp. 48–53. Austin distinguishes presupposition from entailment and implication. See also Ducrot and Todorov, *Dictionnaire encyclopédique des sciences du langage* (Paris, 1972), 347–348, which lists a bibliography.

himself, make his presence overt. He must avoid the kind of direct assertion that would show his hand. Presupposition is a handy device for this evasion. A presupposition is a portion of a sentence (the other part an assertion) that is offered as a *datum*, something that "goes without saying," already understood, perforce agreed upon by everyone including the listener. If I say "I'm glad to see that Jack has stopped drinking so heavily," what I have presupposed—not only for myself, but for you, the listener, too—is that Jack has in fact been drinking heavily. The only new assertion is "I am glad to see X." The rest must be presupposed to be true for the sentence to mean anything. A question about the presupposition only affirms its validity: if you ask "Has Jack been drinking heavily?" you are simply acknowledging your own ignorance, since I have already *said*— indirectly, of course, in the presuppositional way—that he has. The legal teaser "When did you stop beating your wife?" is a classic example of invidious presupposition.

Of course, you could say "That's wrong, Jack never did drink heavily," denying the legitimacy of the presupposition. But narratees (or at least narratees who are not also characters) are in no position to question or deny what a narrator tells them. So a covert narrator can always establish something as given without actually asserting it. We must accept the given "fact," helplessly, as the price we pay if we are to follow the discourse at all. Presupposition allows the covert narrator to manipulate us and at the same time to compact his presentation. He establishes without directly stating. Or to put it differently, presupposition facilitates a surreptitious narration behind the direct narration:

'Is it snowing again, Mr. Conroy?' asked Lily.

She had preceded him into the pantry to help him off with his overcoat. Gabriel smiled *at the three syllables she had given his surname*. . . .

I italicize the presupposed portion of the sentence. It possesses absolute authority: we simply cannot doubt that Lily has in fact pronounced his name in three syllables. Her act is presupposed; all that is asserted is that it was one that made Gabriel smile. Note too that Lily is excluded from the association we form with

Gabriel; she does not know that it is more cultivated to use two syllables, nor why Gabriel smiles. In a later sentence,

The *indelicate* clacking of the men's heels and the *shuffling* of their soles reminded him that *their grade of culture differed from his*,

presuppositions confirm a value structure that the narratee cannot help but share. We have no way of questioning whether the clacking was in fact indelicate, whether the soles shuffled, whether "their" grade of culture was in fact different from his. We can only accept the narrator's word for it, which reflects Gabriel's feelings. Now Gabriel may in fact be wrong—the clacking may be delicate, the shuffling stylish, and his own grade of culture not superior to the dancers inside the drawing-room. But then the narrator would have to say so, that is, make a direct assertion (thus becoming overt), or to enter the mind of some other, more believable character with contrary presuppositions. In the latter event, however, we would find ourselves in an ambiguous situation. We would need some external clue as to whose presuppositions were closer to the "truth." The strategy of contradictory points of view has often been utilized in narratives, and presupposition is a powerful device for hinting that the character whose consciousness is presented is deluded, naive, ignorant, self-deceiving, or whatever.

Limitation of Authority in Narrative Transmission

Having considered how properties of verbal narrative can be used to sustain the illusion of covertness, we can turn to a broader question that has preoccupied narrative theorists since Henry James, namely that of limitations placed on what the narrator is given the power to say. This power is frequently referred to as his "authority."

The idea of an implied author limiting his spokesman's knowledge is not difficult to accept. Each art sets its own boundaries, although differences may arise about their nature and extent. Robert Frost, for instance, rejected the free verse form embraced by Whitman, Sandburg, Williams, and others: he compared it to playing tennis without a net. In a similar vein,

Henry James came to deny his narrators access to the minds of every character except the hero.

But the notion of "limitation" is itself not always clearly delimited. One opposition is to "omniscience," Knowing All, where "all" includes the outcome of every event and the nature of every existent. Knowing All, of course, need not mean Telling All. Narrators regularly conceal information: that is a normal selective function of the discourse, and even covert narrators must know How Things Will Turn Out. (The exceptions are letter or journal narrators, as discussed above.)

So in most discussion omniscience is opposed to "limitation" in terms of the capacity to enter characters' consciousnesses.[13] It is terminologically efficacious to restrict "authority" to that function and to use other terms for other powers.

For instance, the question of space: the narrator may be allowed to report only one scene at a time (visually one in which his central consciousness is present). Or he may have the power to shift freely back and forth between scenes in an attempt to convey simultaneous actions (as in the county fair chapter in *Madame Bovary*). Or he may (separately or additionally) assume the power of ignoring individual scenes and spatially summarizing what has happened (sometimes called the "panoramic" function). This capacity to skip from locale A to locale B without the authorization of an on-the-scene central intelligence should be called "omnipresence" rather than "omniscience." Logically there is no necessary connection between the two. Narratives may allow the narrator to be omnipresent but not omniscient, and vice versa.

Another area of privilege concerns time: the narrator may be restricted to the contemporary story moment, retrospectively seen, or he may be allowed to range into past or future, either through specific scenes, or through summaries, speaking of events of long duration or iteration in only a sentence or two, or, contrarily, expanding events in such a way that it takes longer to read about them than it took them to occur. We have considered these matters in Chapter 2; here we note them only

13. Booth, *Rhetoric of Fiction*, p. 160: "The most important single privilege [of the narrator] is that of obtaining an inside view of another character."

insofar as they mark features of the narrator. It is essential to understand that the features are logically independent, even though it frequently happens that they co-occur. But there is no logical necessity for a narrator to be, say, both omniscient and omnipresent (for instance, the narrator of *Mrs. Dalloway* is sometimes omniscient but not omnipresent).

Because the covert narrator has entree into a character's mind does not mean he constantly exercises it. Abrupt silences can achieve striking effects. For instance, Faulkner's critics have noted cunning withdrawals from the inner view at critical moments. A good example from *Light in August*:

> Before [Joe Christmas] tried it he remembered that he had seen no screen in the light windows upstairs. . . . [Then after climbing up] perhaps he thought of that other window which he had used to use and of the rope upon which he had had to rely; perhaps not.

The withdrawal heightens our sense of Joe Christmas' secretiveness—even his narrator does not know the full hardness of his heart. Or the device may be used to suggest Joe's own sense of lack of control: "Something is going to happen to me." *What* is a secret kept even from himself. The use of words like "possibly," "perhaps," "probably," "it is likely that," "as if," "whether because of X or Y" are not mere mannerisms in Faulkner's novels. They insist, rather, on the irrational in human decisions, the unclarity of human motivation.

An even more complex situation arises in narratives where the withdrawal of narrator's authority coincides with withdrawals in the story-content. Cortázar has provided a fascinating example in "The Idol of the Cyclades." Two archaeologists, Somoza and Morand, have discovered the ancient statue of a fertility goddess on a Greek island and have smuggled it back to Paris. Though they own it jointly, Somoza has jealously kept it in his studio. The Now of the narrative is the time of a visit by Morand to Somoza, who has summoned him. Morand, in turn, calls his wife Teresa to join him at Somoza's, on the face of it an inexplicable act because he has kept Teresa away from Somoza ever since he learned that Somoza had fallen in love with her. (Teresa is clearly identified with the fertility goddess. On the island, she had been sunning herself with her bikini top

off. When she heard their shouts of discovery, she rushed up bare-breasted.) Somoza suddenly attacks Morand, under the idol's influence, and Morand kills him, seemingly in self-defense.

[1] Before turning to look at him, Morand vomited in the corner of the loft, all over the dirty rags. [2] He felt emptied, and vomiting made him feel better. [3] He picked the glass up off the floor and drank what was left of the whiskey, thinking Teresa was going to arrive any minute and that he had to do something, call the police, make some explanation. [4] While he was dragging Somoza's body back into the full light of the reflector, he was thinking that it should not be difficult to show that he had acted in self-defense. [5] Somoza's eccentricities, his seclusion from the world, his evident madness. [6] Crouching down, he soaked his hands in the blood running from the face and scalp of the dead man, checking his wrist watch at the same time, twenty of eight. [7] Teresa would not be long now, better to go out and wait for her in the garden or in the street, to spare her the sight of the idol with its face dripping with blood, the tiny red threads that glided past the neck, slipped around the breasts, joined in the delicate triangle of the sex, ran down the thighs. [8] The hatchet was sunk deep into the skull of the sacrifice, and Morand pulled it out, holding it up between his sticky hands. [9] He shoved the corpse a bit more with his foot, leaving it finally up next to the column, sniffed the air and went over to the door. [10] Better open it so that Teresa could come in. [11] Leaning the hatchet up against the door, he began to strip off his clothes, because it was getting hot and smelled stuffy, the caged herd. [12] He was naked already when he heard the noise of the taxi pulling up and Teresa's voice dominating the sound of the flutes; he put the light out and waited, hatchet in hand behind the door, licking the cutting edge of the hatchet lightly and thinking that Teresa was punctuality itself.[14]

By disowning the discourse (so to speak), the narrator shows Morand, our previous norm for rationality as well as the central consciousness, lose himself and become the slave of the idol. What started out as an accident, in self-defense, becomes transformed into a sacrifice, and Morand waits for his next victim, his own wife. The discourse is manipulated first by separating the conceptual point of view of the character from his overt physical actions. It is the body that initially becomes subject to the idol's power. Only later does the mind follow, at which point the con-

14. Translated by Paul Blackburn.

ceptual point of view of the character also separates from the narrator's. But this happens gradually, with some overlapping. In the first five sentences, Morand's actions—vomiting, drinking whiskey, thinking about the police, and so on—seem reasonable responses to the horrendous experience he has gone through. His sanity (and the narrator's association therewith) is underlined by indirect free style in the fifth sentence. But in the sixth he soaks his hands in Somoza's blood: his rationality falters as he performs a ritual act. Yet only his body seems infected; the overt physical action is depicted objectively. Checking his watch *seems* a civilized habit. The first part of the seventh sentence, communicating an inner view in indirect free style, has him still rational, concerned for Teresa's mental state. But in the second part, his preoccupation with the precise trace of the blood strikes an eerie note, and in the eighth sentence there is a subtle withdrawal of a civilized perspective: "The hatchet was sunk deep into the skull of the sacrifice." This description is separated from Morand, up to the last word; one might imagine that the hatchet had found itself in the skull for accidental reasons. But not after we read the word "sacrifice." We can only attribute the change from "accidental victim" to "sacrifice" to a dramatic change in Morand's psyche. What follows confirms the change: pulling the hatchet out of the forehead, shoving the corpse with his foot up to the "column" (which had existed before only in Somoza's imagination), sniffing the air, soaking his hands in "the sacrifice's" blood—these confirm Morand's conversion. So that the import of the tenth sentence, though it is again an inner view in the indirect free mode, is only apparently ambiguous. It derives not from solicitude for Teresa's arrival; on the contrary, he is leaving the door open the better to attack her. That still must be inferred—only in the final sentence, after stripping himself naked, as did Somoza, do we learn that Morand's mind too has become enslaved by the idol.

Shifting Limited versus Omniscient Mental Access

The narrator may shift his mental entry from one character to another and still remain relatively covert. "Shifting limited"

access is different from continuous omniscience, but not because of a shorter duration of entry, or distinctions between showing and telling, detail and summary, mere presentation and explanation, free indirect and tagged indirect discourse, report and interpretation. These are supplementary features that may or may not co-occur.

The chief criterion is the *purpose* for which the move from one mind to another is made. Like stream of consiousness, the shifting limited access expresses no purpose. It does not serve the teleology of plot. It evokes a disparate group of individuals thinking, but not to any common end. Thinking is itself the "plot"; its vagaries in no way subserve an external march of events. "Shifting limited" means a switchover to the next mind without problem-solving or unwinding a causative chain. In such passages, the narrator does not ransack mind after mind (like a bee ransacking flowers) for answers to hermeneutic questions. The mental entries seem matters of chance, reflecting the randomness of ordinary life.

Erich Auerbach finds a subjective impressionism striving for an objective view in the shifting limited style of *To the Lighthouse*, a style that he calls "the multipersonal representation of consciousness":

The essential characteristic of the technique represented by Virginia Woolf is that we are given not merely one person whose consciousness (that is, the impressions it receives) is rendered, but many persons, with frequent shifts from one to the other. . . . The multiplicity of persons suggests that we are here after all confronted with an endeavor to investigate an objective reality, that is, specifically, the "real" Mrs. Ramsay. She is, to be sure, an enigma, and such she basically remains, but she is as it were encircled by the content of all the various consciousnesses directed upon her (including her own); there is an attempt to approach her from many sides as closely as human possibilities of perception and expression can succeed in doing.[15]

This impressionistic search is not the only aesthetic purpose for which the shifting limited technique is valuable. The abrupt transitions suggest that despite close physical proximity and the thinness of characters' skins and membranes, wholly dif-

15. *Mimesis* (Princeton, 1968), p. 536.

ferent mental universes exist only inches apart. In omniscience, contrarily, the sense of an all-knowing narrator's presence reassures us that no matter how different character's minds may be, they fit snugly into a master plot.

Actual examples will help clarify the distinction. In a section of *Mrs. Dalloway*, Peter Walsh sits on a park-bench and laments the loss of Clarissa:

It was awful, he cried, awful, awful!

Still, the sun was hot. Still, one got over things. Still, life had a way of adding day to day. Still, he thought, yawning and beginning to take notice—Regent's Park had changed very little since he was a boy, except for the squirrels—still, presumably there were compensations—when little Elise Mitchell, who had been picking up pebbles to add to the pebble collection which she and her brother were making on the nursery mantelpiece, plumped her handful down on the nurse's knee and scudded off again full tilt into a lady's legs. Peter Walsh laughed out.

But Lucrezia Warren Smith was saying to herself, It's wicked; why should I suffer: she was asking, as she walked down the broad path. . . .

She was close to him now, could see him staring at the sky, muttering, clasping his hands. Yet Dr. Holmes said there was nothing the matter with him. What, then, had happened—why had he gone, then, why when she sat by him, did he start, frown at her, move away, and point at her hand, take her hand, look at it terrified?

Was it that she had taken off her wedding ring? "My hand has grown so thin," she said; "I have put it in my purse," she told him.

He dropped her hand. Their marriage was over, he thought, with agony, with relief. The rope was cut; he mounted; he was free, as it was decreed that he, Septimus, the lord of men, should be free; alone (since his wife had thrown away her wedding ring; since she had left him), he, Septimus, was alone, called forth in advance of the mass of men to hear the truth, to learn the meaning, which now at last, after all the toils of civilization—Greeks, Romans, Shakespeare, Darwin, and now himself—was to be given whole to . . . "To whom?" he asked aloud.

Here we have three points of view (though only one narrative voice, since all the characters' viewpoints are expressed in indirect style): first Peter's, then Lucrezia's, and finally Septimus'. But these shifts do not "add up to" anything plot-wise. They constitute a fortuitous dipping into the thoughts, at a given plot moment, of unrelated characters. There is no immediate

story connection (whatever the ultimate thematic connection) between Peter and the Smiths. The misunderstanding between Lucrezia and Septimus has no other function than to illustrate their different preoccupations. Lucrezia's mind is commonsensical, normal, sad, understandable; Septimus's is distorted, uncomprehending and incomprehensible, deeply immersed in delusions of grandeur. But no kernel, no question about the action of the narrative is resolved, since *Mrs. Dalloway* does not have that kind of plot.

Consider now these sentences from the Third Chapter of *Vanity Fair* which are genuinely omniscient:

When [Becky Sharp] called Sedley a very handsome man, she knew that Amelia would tell her mother, who would probably tell Joseph, or who, at any rate, would be pleased by the compliment paid to her son. . . . Perhaps, too, Joseph Sedley would overhear the compliment—Rebecca spoke loud enough—and he *did* hear, and (thinking in his heart that he was a very fine man) the praise thrilled through every fibre of his big body, and made it tingle with pleasure. Then, however, came a recoil. "Is the girl making fun of me?" he thought. . . . "Does she really think I am handsome?" thought he, "or is she only making game of me?"

Downstairs, then, they went, Joseph very red and blushing, Rebecca very modest, and holding her green eyes downwards. She was dressed in white, with bare shoulders as white as snow—the picture of youth, unprotected innocence, and humble virgin simplicity. "I must be very quiet," thought Rebecca, "and very much interested about India."

Becky gets too much spice in her curry and gasps for water, causing the elder Mr. Sedley to laugh.

The paternal laugh was echoed by Joseph, who thought the joke capital. The ladies only smiled a little. They thought poor Rebecca suffered too much. She would have liked to choke old Sedley, but she swallowed her mortification. . . .

Old Sedley began to laugh, and thought Rebecca was a good-humoured girl. . . .

This is omniscient precisely because it evokes a clear plot movement. Each new consciousness is dipped into for the express purpose of moving events through to the next stage. First, Becky's mind is preoccupied with strategy. Whence we move immediately into Joseph's mind to find out if the strategy is

working. But her plan almost goes awry because of unforseen digestive problems. Old Sedley laughs and we move back into Joseph's mind for his reaction. Then to the ladies' feelings of sympathy for Becky's discomfort. And finally into the thoughts of old Sedley. Clearly, the narrator is given omniscience in order to trace the second-by-second interplay of attitudes as they proceed to the overriding question: Will Becky's campaign succeed? That question alone prescribes the shifts from consciousness to consciousness.

Overt Narration: Set Descriptions

The set description is the weakest mark of the overt narrator, because it is still relatively unprominencing. Descriptions exist even in nonnarrated stories. But there they must seem to arise from the characters' actions alone: "[Nick] looked up the track at the lights of the caboose going out of sight around the curve" (Hemingway's "The Battler"). The curving track and the caboose are not syntactically highlighted; they are not asserted but simply find their way on the scene, obliquely, as things that Nick happens to see. Their syntactic modesty, slipped in to frame the action, keeps them from constituting a narrator's independent scenic evocation, that is, a set description.

But a narrator's overt presence *is* marked by explicit description, direct communications to a narratee about the setting that he needs to know.[16] "The Bottoms consisted of six blocks of miners' dwellings, two rows of three, like the dots on a blank-six domino, and twelve houses in a block"—we read this before we meet the Morels or indeed any character in *Sons and Lovers*. The explicitness of the description is underlined by "consisted" and the metaphor. An overt narrator has made his presence immediately felt.

Syntax may exaggerate the sense that we are being baldly handed a description. Capote's "A Christmas Memory" calls attention to description as artifice in playful "theatrical-scenario"

16. Booth, *Rhetoric of Fiction*, p. 169: "The most obvious task for a commentator is to tell the reader about facts that he could not easily learn otherwise," for example, "description of physical events and details whenever such description cannot spring naturally from a character."

style: "Enter: two relatives. Very angry. Potent with eyes that scold, tongues that scald." "Morning. Frozen rime lusters the grass. . . ." "Home: Queenie slumps by the fire and sleeps till tomorrow, snoring loud as a human."

In most modern fiction the approach is subtler: both narrator and character have some stake in the description:

In front of Martha was grimed glass, its lower part covered with grimed muslin. The open door showed an oblong of browny-grey air swimming with globules of wet. The shop fronts opposite were no particular colour. The lettering on the shops, once black, brown, gold, white, was now shades of dull brown. The lettering on the upper part of the glass of this room said *Joe's Fish and Chips* in reverse, and was flaking like stale chocolate. She sat by a rectangle of pinkish oilcloth where sugar had spilled, and onto it, orange tea, making a gritty smear in which someone had doodled part of a name: Daisy Flet. . . . [Doris Lessing, *The Four Gated City*]

Martha's involvement in these observations is inescapable. The area described is just what appears within the range of her perceptual point of view (outside shop fronts are seen through the open door; the name of the restaurant is reversed). But the vision is doubled. The scene is described, explicitly. The mixed reference keeps the narrator relatively covert. The communication is not as direct as in the passage from *Sons and Lovers*, but a narrator *is* present, since Martha is herself fixed in the scene by an outside voice ("She sat by a rectangle of pinkish oilcloth").

There are interesting differences between the representation of existents in verbal and in cinematic narrative. As Jean Ricardou argues, the film camera cannot be said "to describe" in any meaningful sense.[17] The number and variety of objects filmed is virtually limitless, restrained only by the frame and their distance from the camera. But because all properties of a filmed object—form, color, size, etc.—can be grasped as a whole, in an "immediate synthesis," the object possesses an "intense autonomy." (One must take special steps, through close-ups and editing, to analyze out individual properties and to show them resemblant from one object to another.)

17. Jean Ricardou, *Problèmes du nouveau roman* (Paris, 1967), ch. 2.

Objects described verbally, on the other hand, pass into the reader's consciousness in a slower way. We cannot grasp all their properties at once. They must be spelled out to us. The fuller the description the longer the account must run. More words are needed to fill in more details. Ricardou sees in this extended "differentiated synthesis" a "relative autonomy" of verbally described objects. That is, because the properties are presented sequentially, their separateness is underlined. The naming of one property of a thing may well evoke the memory or sense of it in other things. So, verbally described objects evoke a paradigmatic constellation of similar objects. Indeed, we can go beyond Ricardou, and argue that the very verbal detailing of aspects of an object suggests that the narrator *intends* a description (whereas we can never be sure, for all its closeups, camera-prowls, synthetic editing, and so forth, that the cinema intends a time-arrested description rather than an ongoing narration—indeed, as I argue above, time cannot be arrested in film except in freeze frames).

Identifications follow the same pattern as descriptions. In the covert mode, a character is named upon his first appearance, without further ado. Or the name may be delayed, for several pages, chapters, or even forever. Or when introduced, it may appear obliquely, for instance, in dialogue: only at the end of the fourth page, after having learned the most intimate of "his" thoughts do we learn that "he" is Raskolnikov. In overt forms, however, the name may be qualified immediately, in a way that sounds like a formal introduction ("Emma Woodhouse, handsome, clever, and rich, with a comfortable home and happy disposition . . .").

The proper name, like the definite article, is deictic, establishing individual specificity. Indefinite first mention of characters implies a more conscious need to introduce, and hence a more overt narrator: "On an exceptionally hot evening early in July a young man came out of the garret in which he lodged in S. Place and walked slowly, as though in hesitation, towards K. bridge." So begins the narrator of *Crime and Punishment*. But Hemingway begins "The major sat at a table against the

wall." The implication is that we know "him" already, in fact, as Walker Gibson and Father Ong have suggested, we are comrades, traveling companions, or if the terminology is technical, adepts.[18] Virginia Woolf's novels plunge into definite deixis with their first breath: "Mrs. Dalloway said she would buy the flowers herself," or ". . . they were talking in the big room with the windows open to the garden, about the cesspool." These are the first sentences of *Mrs. Dalloway* and *Between the Acts*. To ask "Which Mrs. Dalloway?" "Which big room?" "Which cesspool?" is, of course, meaningless—it is that Mrs. Dalloway, that cesspool with which the stories are preoccupied. The narrator effaces himself by marking the characters and setting as *faits accomplis*, depriving the reader of the comforts of formal introduction.

Overt Narration: Temporal Summaries

The precise positions along the spectrum of narrator-prominence are not always clear. To label narrators as minimal, covert, or overt is to some extent arbitrary, as it is to argue that a certain feature marks a boundary line between two kinds of narrator. Despite the reality of features, good arguments can always be raised for different borders.

Why argue, for example, that the power to make independent descriptive statements is a weaker or stronger mark of narrator-presence than that of temporal or spatial summary? The validity of our decisions must rest on the deductive arguments that support them and the consequent design of the whole theory. These are subject to revisions when and as superior counter-arguments are offered.

I placed set descriptions at the "weak" or least prominent end of the spectrum of overt features out of deference to the principle of mimesis. Chapter 1 went into *Bestimmtheit*, the question of determinacy or specification of detail, and noted that cinematic narratives display an infinity of visual details (the color of the hero's shirt, the exact contours of the heroine's hairdo, the minutest architectural particulars of the house they enter).

18. Quoted by Walter Ong, "The Writer's Audience Is Always a Fiction," in *Interfaces of the Word* (Ithaca, N.Y., 1977).

Such details can only be evoked by verbal narrative. Further, these words, in block descriptions, may arrest the story-time, which induces a sense of artifice and of a narrator's presence.

But why should this sense be weaker than that arising from time summary passages? Precisely because descriptive statements in verbal narrative compensate for difficulties in expressing sensory detail. The motive for set descriptions seems less to reveal the narrator than to cope with the exigencies of the medium. We generally accept description without considering it an extraneous addition to action by a manipulative presence. The details are not likely to be felt as frills (hence possible self-indulgences of a narrator) but as information for a completer picture or understanding of the kernel events.

Summaries, on the other hand, do raise such questions. Because language copes better with time than with space, there are options to direct summary, for instance, ellipsis. Summary calls attention to itself because it is a positive rather than a negative solution to the problem of spanning a period of story time that is unnecessary to detail. The mimetic temporal norm, the norm that operates regularly in films and drama, is "scenic"; discourse and story time are co-temporal. The absolutely "non-narrated" narrative deploys time in this way. The more a narrative deviates from this norm, the more it highlights time manipulation *as* a process or artifice, and the more loudly a narrator's voice sounds in our ears. Ellipsis just lets the passage of time occur, without comment. Summary implies that someone has felt a "problem of transition" or the like—and who can that "someone" be if not a narrator? Summary presupposes a desire to account for time-passage, to satisfy questions in a narratee's mind about what has happened in the interval. An account cannot but draw attention to the one who felt obliged to make such an account.

The difference may be illustrated by two passages that occur in "The Seance," by Isaac Bashevis Singer. The story concerns the degrading spectacle of an immigrant of obvious intellect, Dr. Kalisher, who spends his time with a fake medium, Mrs. Kopitzky, in hopes of getting some spiritual illumination, but despises both her and himself for this indulgence:

At the round table on which lay a Ouija board, a trumpet, and a with-ered rose, sat Dr. Zorach Kalisher, small, broad-shouldered, bald in front and with sparse tufts of hair in the back, half yellow, half gray. From behind his yellow bushy brows peered a pair of small, piercing eyes. Dr. Kalisher had almost no neck—his head sat directly on his broad shoulders, making him look like a primitive African statue. His nose was crooked, flat at the top, the tip split in two. On his chin sprouted a tiny growth.

A bit later,

There was a time when he had tried to understand all things through his reason, but that period of rationalism had long passed. Since then, he had constructed an anti-rationalistic philosophy, a kind of extreme hedonism which saw in eroticism the *Ding an sich*, and in reason the very lowest stage of being, the entropy which led to absolute death.

Dr. Kalisher's appearance is "dwelt on" simply because there is no way to convey his appearance except through words. A film adaptation might simply make the actor up to let us see these details at a glance. The words are necessary substitutes for the direct visual reproduction afforded by other media, and so we do not hear very strongly the intonations of a narrator's voice. But the second passage does evoke such intonations; someone is explaining to us how Dr. Kalisher got to this time and this place. My point does not concern the aesthetic felicity of this passage, but simply how it amplifies the sound of a narrator's voice telling us about Dr. Kalisher's past.

"Summary" usually refers to temporal abbreviations; Chapter 2 defined it formally as a structure in which story-time lasts considerably longer than discourse-time, in verbal narrative an effect relatively easy to achieve because of the existence of verbs whose meanings are essentially durative (or iterative). But spatial summary is also common. *War and Peace* provides many examples of broad sweeps. So does *The Grapes of Wrath*:

Once California belonged to Mexico and its land to Mexicans; and a horde of tattered feverish Americans poured in. And such was their hunger for land that they took the land—stole Sutter's land, Guerrero's land, took the grants and broke them up and growled and quarreled over them, those frantic hungry men; and they guarded with guns the land they had stolen. They put up houses and barns, they turned the

earth and planted crops. And these things were possession, and possession was ownership.

The Mexicans were weak and fled. They could not resist, because they wanted nothing in the world as frantically as the Americans wanted land.

Space-summarizing also assumes a more gratuitous power than mere description and so marks the narrator's presence more overtly. It is even more gratuitous than time-summarizing, since language lends itself more circumspectly to the summarizing of time, and everyone can accept the actions of memory (whether personal or more broadly historical) without much ado. But when a narrator takes it upon himself to depict panoramas, to evoke from a bird's-eye view vast terrains or the sweeps of hordes of people, he is calling attention to his exalted position.

A third kind of summary epitomizes the quality of an existent or event. Any kind of direct characterization calls attention to a narrator's voice, but to encapsulate a character or setting in a word or brief phrase implies still greater powers, hence greater audibility. "What they were like," dispersed by hints throughout the text, becomes "explicitly what they are like—in a word," a word that the narrator, in synoptic mastery, presumes to apply. The narrator of *Jude the Obscure* is highly disposed to such synopses: "[Jude] was a boy who could not himself bear to hurt anything." "Vilbert was an itinerant quack-doctor, well known to the rustic population, and absolutely unknown to anybody else, as he, indeed, took care to be, to avoid inconvenient investigations." "[Arabella] was a complete and substantial female animal—no more, no less. . . ."

Reports of What Characters Did Not Think or Say

A step further along the scale of narrator prominence: some narrators assume the power to report what a character did *not* in fact think or say. The mention of possible but unconsummated events calls attention more clearly still to the artifice of the narrative process itself. An example from Hawthorne's "Rappaccini's Daughter":

The youth might have taken Baglioni's opinions with many grains of allowance had he known that there was a professional warfare of long continuance between him and Dr. Rappacini.

Giovanni could have discounted Baglioni's opinions, but he did not because he was ignorant of his rivalry with Rappacini. The narrator tells us in so many words what could have happened but did not.

In Lawrence's *Women In Love*, Chapter 16, Birkin asks Gerald whether his sister's death by drowning upset him, and he replies:

"It's a shock. But I don't feel it very much really. I don't feel any different. We've all got to die, and it doesn't seem to make any great difference, anyhow, whether you die or not. I can't feel any grief, you know. It leaves me cold. I can't quite account for it."

"You don't care if you die or not?" asked Birkin. Gerald looked at him with eyes blue as the blue-fibred steel of a weapon. He felt awkward, but indifferent. As a matter of fact, he did care terribly, with a great fear.

The penultimate sentence in the quotation is a report of Gerald's conscious feelings of awkward indifference. But the sentence introduced by "As a matter of fact" establishes an overt narrator's superior knowledge. He knows not only Gerald's conscious but also his unconscious mind. He is saying in effect "Gerald did not really know how he felt; actually he was afraid." Such expressions convey a narrator's announcement of deeper than ordinary plunges into the mind. Where others would leave the conclusion precisely to inference, the Laurentian narrator tells us in so many words what he "finds" there.

Ethos and Commentary

In the first book of the *Rhetoric* (I.1.2), Aristotle writes:

The character [ethos] of the speaker is a cause of persuasion when the speech is so uttered as to make him worthy of belief; for as a rule we trust men of probity more, and more quickly, about things in general, while on points outside the realm of exact knowledge, where opinion is divided, we trust them absolutely. This trust, however, should be created by the speech itself, and not left to depend upon an antecedent impression that the speaker is this or that kind of man. It is not true, as some writers on the art maintain, that the probity of

the speaker contributes nothing to his persuasiveness; on the contrary, we might almost affirm that his character [ethos] is the most potent of all the means to persuasion.[19]

The reference, of course, is to persuasion in the real world—legal (forensic), ceremonial (epideictic), and deliberative (hortatory). Insofar as a narrative is true, that is, history, the narrator seeks by usual rhetorical means to establish the reliability of his ethos. Assurances of veracity may go all the way from the "No kidding" of someone telling a bizarre piece of gossip to the oath "I do solemnly swear . . ." pronounced by a witness in a law court.

Ethos also functions in fictional narrative, except that its standard is not truth but verisimilitude, the semblance of veracity. How best to show this semblance varies by style and era. Hemingway's solution was to minimize the narrator's presence. Verisimilitude in the Hemingway style is a function of laconism—for the narrator as for the characters. Eighteenth-century authors took another view. Their overt narrators were orators of sorts, though they persuaded their readers not to practical action but to accepting the legitimacy of their mimesis. They portrayed characters and scenes consistent with the "ordinary way of the world"; troublesome questions could be answered by explanatory generalizations.

Since a narrative never communicates the direct speech of the implied author, ethos can only apply to a narrator. Verisimilitude is plausibility only with respect to the fiction (although overt narrators often bolster the illusion with generally accepted truths about the outside world, namely, "philosophic generalization"). To put it in other terms, the narrator's rhetorical effort is to prove that his version of the story is "true"; the implied author's rhetorical effort, on the other hand, is to make the whole package, story and discourse, including the narrator's performance, interesting, acceptable, self-consistent, and artful.

The narrator's ethos depends on the kind of verisimilitude he claims. In autobiographical or witness fiction of the *Moll Flanders* or *Great Gatsby* type, ethical veracity relies on the princi-

19. *The Rhetoric of Aristotle*, ed. Lane Cooper (New York, 1960), pp. 8–9.

ple of "I-saw-it-with-my-own-eyes." "I heard it with my own ears," in fiction, as in law, is already weaker; indeed, its weakness can be played with, as Conrad does in *Lord Jim* and similar fictions. Where the narrator pretends to be "author," his ethical basis is quite different. His perception of events is no longer at issue; he tacitly or openly acknowledges that he himself is the source of the events and existents depicted. His suasory power lies in sagacity or worldliness or whatever the audience believes constitutes credibility.

Commentary

Speech acts by a narrator that go beyond narrating, describing, or identifying will resonate with overtones of *propria persona*. Such pronouncements are best labelled *comments* (though they range an entire gamut of speech acts). Commentary, since it is gratuitous, conveys the overt narrator's voice more distinctly than any feature short of explicit self-mention.

Natural language philosophy has compiled no authoritative list of speech acts, nor does that seem its goal. The names or existence of certain illocutions may be disputed. However, since our purpose is to examine commentary as a narrative feature, such a list is not indispensable. The traditional categories fairly well accommodate thickly commentative novels like those of Fielding. Commentary is either implicit (that is, ironic) or explicit. The latter includes interpretation, judgment, generalization, and "self-conscious" narration. Among explicit comments, the first three are upon the story. "Interpretation" (in this special sense) is the open explanation of the gist, relevance, or significance of a story element. "Judgment" expresses moral or other value opinions. "Generalization" makes reference outward from the fictional to the real world, either to "universal truths" or actual historical facts. "Self-conscious" narration is a term recently coined to describe comments on the discourse rather than the story, whether serious or facetious.

Implicit Commentary: Ironic Narrator and Unreliable Narrator

Irony is complex and exhibits a great variety of manifestations. We shall focus on only one sort, namely that in which a

speaker carries on a secret communication with his auditor at variance with the actual words he uses and at the expense of some other person or thing, the victim or "butt."

If the communication is between the narrator and narratee at the expense of a character, we can speak of an ironic narrator. If the communication is between the implied author and the implied reader at the expense of the narrator, we can say that the implied author is ironic and that the narrator is unreliable.

Wayne Booth has usefully distinguished between stable and unstable irony. Stable irony is (a) intended, (b) covert, (c) "reconstructed" by the reader as a more interesting meaning than the one presented to him, (d) fixed (once the reader has established the ironic meaning he is "not then invited to undermine it with further demolitions and reconstructions"), and (e) finite in application (it refers only to statements actually made).[20] Unstable ironies occur where "the author—insofar as we can discover him, and he is often very remote indeed—refuses to declare himself, however subtly, *for* any stable proposition."[21] I shall consider only stable ironies, since the "remote" implied author—despite his profound literary interest—would be too subtle to create an unreliable narrator.

A standard example of narrator's irony against a character is the first sentence of *Pride and Prejudice*. The "universality" of the "truth" that a rich man perforce needs a wife holds only for the social class under ridicule, the self-satisfied provincial English bourgeoisie of the turn of the nineteenth century, to which neither narrator nor narratee belong. The statement is ironic since clearly at odds with wiser, less materialistic values, which the narratee is invited to share with the narrator. Such irony always rests on implicit flattery, enhanced by an earned, "do-it-yourself" quality. We pat ourselves on the back for recognizing that this is *not* a truth, let alone a universal one.

The narrator's voice may turn ironic only for a moment or stretch globally through an entire narrative. Hardy permits himself an occasional, if feeble, irony to lighten his dismal land-

20. *A Rhetoric of Irony* (Chicago, 1974), p. 6.
21. Ibid., p. 240.

scapes. In *Jude the Obscure*, the narrator's comment about Jude's reaction to his first meeting with Arabella:

He had just inhaled a single breath from a new atmosphere, which had evidently been hanging round him everywhere he went, for he knew not how long, but had somehow been divided from his actual breathing as by a sheet of glass. The intentions as to reading, working, and learning, which he had so precisely formulated only a few minutes earlier, were suffering a curious collapse into a corner, he know not how.

Albeit in the narrator's formal, metaphoric words, this reports the adolescent's sensation of "Hey, how long has *this* been going on?" The irony turns on "evidently" and "curious": the "evidence" of the pervasiveness of sex and its "curious" tendency to interfere with more serious pursuits would only occur to one who has not yet experienced them. With the narrator we indulge in feelings of superiority. But as a local irony it in no way changes poor Jude's fate, about which it is not appropriate to feel superior.

In *The Secret Agent*, on the other hand, ironic narration permeates the novel. It is the narrator's regular vocal stance. The sneer always tells us who is talking. From the description of Mr. Verloc's shop-window, we gather such gems as "old copies of obscure newspapers . . . with titles like *The Torch, The Gong*—rousing titles." Rousing, of course, if you go in for that kind of thing. Irony often calls attention to itself by posing irreconcilables: Mr. Verloc is at once "a seller of shady wares" and "a protector of society." Obviously he cannot be both, and the irony emerges as we learn the nature of his real business.

Once we are tuned to the ironic wave length of a narrator's remarks we can hear it even in indirect free forms. At one point, the interest point of view rests with Winnie and her mother, but we surmise that Verloc's nocturnal activity is shady. The irony emerges in the indirect free discourse of sentences like ". . . when he went out he seemed to experience a great difficulty in finding his way back to his temporary home in the Belgravian square." This naive characterization of Verloc's evening divagations rests on the perspective of Winnie and her mother,

since, from some of the narrator's direct characterizations ("his ostensible business," "his steady-eyed impudence, which seemed to hold back the threat of some abominable menace"), it is clear that Verloc is not a man to get lost in the streets.

The narrator speaks of almost all the characters in *The Secret Agent*, regardless of their politics, station in life, or personal qualities, in an ironic way. "Poor Stevie," Winnie's brother, is, in the family terminology, "delicate," an ironic euphemism for "mentally defective" (Ossipan's word is "degenerate"). Though "he never had any fits (which was encouraging)" his lower lip has an unfortunate inclination to droop. Privy Councillor Wurmt, of the hostile Embassy, manages to be "meritorious" though possessed of a "pasty complexion" and "melancholy ugliness." Mr. Vladimir, the new attaché in charge of espionage, finds that his mirror, useful for studying Mr. Verloc, gives him the added advantage "of seeing his own face, clean-shaved and round, rosy about the gills, and with the thin sensitive lips formed exactly for the utterance of those delicate witticisms which had made him such a favourite in the very highest society." And so on. No one comes off scot-free in the trial, conviction, and parole of Michaelis. He has been given a life sentence for participating in an attempt to free some prisoners from a police van, in which a policeman was inadvertently shot. Though all he did was help to open the van-door, he received the life sentence appropriate to a sadistic murderer:

> . . . no burglar would have received such a heavy sentence. The death of the constable had made him miserable at heart, but the failure of the plot also. He did not conceal either of these sentiments from his empanelled countrymen, and that sort of compunction appeared shockingly imperfect to the crammed court. The judge on passing sentence commented feelingly upon the depravity and callousness of the young prisoner.

A man who tells a jury that he is sorry that he killed someone and also sorry that his sedition did not work sounds naively self-destructive. But equally ironic is the jury's vicious clanging of the prison-door, articulated by the narrator in ironic litotes— his behavior was "shockingly imperfect," an epithet equally ap-

propriate to the high price of tea. The "bleeding hearts" who arrange his ticket of leave fare no better, for instance, than Michaelis' lofty patroness:

> The great lady was simple in her own way. [Michaelis'] views and beliefs had nothing in them to shock or startle her, since she judged them from the standpoint of her lofty position. Indeed, her sympathies were easily accessible to a man of that sort. She was not an exploiting capitalist herself; she was, as it were, above the play of economic conditions. And she had a great capacity of pity for the more obvious forms of common human miseries, precisely because she was such a complete stranger to them.

In these two passages, then, the following are ironized:

1. Michaelis' simpleminded inability to adopt a minimal self-preservative reticence about his revolutionary goals before an obviously hostile audience;

2. The disparity between the court's excessive outrage and the words picked to describe it;

3. People who meddle with the law by securing pardons for criminals;

4. A "great lady," whose lofty position allows her to take simplistic attitudes toward causes precisely because she understands them so little, and who has convinced herself that her wealth did not derive from capitalist exploitation. (Knowing what we do of the British Empire, how could that be?)

The quotation about the great lady is preceded by the observation—ostensibly universal and not simply applicable to this fiction—that "A certain simplicity of thought is common to serene souls at both ends of the social scale." The generalization by itself is not ironic and could as easily appear in a quite different context, say an early nineteenth-century novel in which a romantic aristocrat finds he can communicate only with peasants. But in this context it turns ironic: charity, which somehow should be a product of empathy, is found to derive precisely from its lack. Not only are there four distinct butts, but they are attacked by the narrator on rapidly shifting moral grounds: ordinary prudence (Michaelis is *too* honest); excessive self-righteousness (the court is blinded to Michaelis' lesser degree

of culpability and prevented from recognizing that his self-condemning frankness stems from an ultimate innocence of soul); social irresponsibility (which prompts people to become do-gooders in spheres where they know nothing); and great hereditary wealth (which bars those who enjoy it from ordinary reality). Though Michaelis' sentence was excessive in the first instance, the error is not corrected by the parole won for him by meddlers. The narrator's ground-rules shift, and everyone loses.

In "unreliable narration" the narrator's account is at odds with the implied reader's surmises about the story's real intentions. The story undermines the discourse. We conclude, by "reading out," between the lines, that the events and existents could not have been "like that," and so we hold the narrator suspect. Unreliable narration is thus an ironic form.[22] The convention completely satisfies Booth's four properties of stable irony. The implied reader senses a discrepancy between a reasonable reconstruction of the story and the account given by the narrator. Two sets of norms conflict, and the covert set, once recognized, must win. The implied author has established a secret communication with the implied reader. The narrator's unreliability may stem from cupidity (Jason Compson), cretinism (Benjy), gullibility (Dowling, the narrator of *The Good Soldier*), psychological and moral obtuseness (Marcher in "The Beast in the Jungle"), perplexity and lack of information (Marlow in *Lord Jim*), innocence (Huck Finn), or a whole host of other causes, including some "baffling mixtures."[23]

Our diagram of the six parties to the narrative transaction permits a convenient way to indicate the distinctive by-path of unreliable narration:

implied author -→ narrator → narratee -→ implied reader

22. *Rhetoric of Fiction*, pp. 304–309.
23. Ibid., p. 432, lists the titles of many novels including some that are so subtly unreliable as to be "unstably" ironic, that is, we cannot be sure that the narrator really *is* unreliable. In pursuing ironies and unreliabilities, readerly paranoia is an occupational hazard, as Booth amusingly admits.

The solid line indicates direct communication; broken lines indicate indirect or inferential communication. The two paths for the broken lines correspond to whether or not the narrator is reliable. If he is, the narrative act takes place solely down the main central axis. If not, there are two messages (as in any irony), one credible (above) and the other not (below). The implied message is always the credible one, just as a person's tone of voice is always more credible than the words he speaks.

What precisely is the domain of unreliability? It is the discourse, that is, the view of what happens or what the existents are like, not the personality of the narrator. An unsavoury narrator may give a completely reliable account of a story (that is, one which is unexceptionable in terms of our own inferences). The narrator of *Lolita*, Humbert Humbert, whatever his character is, in my view, reliable. For all his sarcasm about characters and events (his two wives, roadtravel in America, and, of course, excruciatingly, himself), we feel that he is doing his best to tell us what in fact happened. Where he discovers his own unreliability in the telling, he is the first to admit it. Humbert has nothing to lose by being reliable and a great deal to gain, namely the opportunity to unburden himself at last. The communication of his torments in the last chapters is particularly affecting, and they cast a sad verity over the book that even his most acerbic remarks cannot undermine.

The butt of unreliable narration is the narrator himself, not the characters, about whom we form our own conclusions. Thus not only is his presence marked indelibly, but so is the presupposition that he bears a character's relation to the story. Otherwise what interest would he have in giving us a distorted account? His motive can by no means be the sheer joy of storytelling. He may be a minor or peripheral character rather than a protagonist, of course, but he cannot be "nobody." His suspicious recitation of events may, of course, jibe with his character as otherwise evoked. We associate Jason Compson's unreliability as a narrator with his bigotry, penny-pinching, and salaciousness as a character.

Unreliability is generally constant throughout a narrative, but sometimes it may fluctuate. In Dostoevsky's "A Gentle Crea-

ture," there is some change of perspective. As he proceeds, the narrator becomes somewhat more reliable. What makes the story interesting is the narrator's preoccupation with his own reliability. At the outset, he asserts it. He expresses self-satisfaction in the power he exerted over the gentle girl. "It wasn't a bad feeling," he tells us, and that, of course, suggests he still feels it, at least imaginatively, in his effort to reconstruct what actually happened. But so great is his "inconscience," his self-interest, that he readily assumes the reader to be as amazed as he at her "bizarre" reactions. "Believe it or not, I was becoming loathsome to her. Oh yes, I know what I am talking about. I observed it carefully. . . ." And he still apparently thinks of himself as "the most generous of men," he who made her live on one ruble a day, who would take her to the theater after previously telling her to forget it, who reaffirmed in a hundred ways his power to give and to take away. That was how he was, and the act of narrating suggests how he is and will become. In transmitting the story, he begins to have misgivings: "There was something I mismanaged badly. . . ." Still, he continues to rationalize: "Be brave, man, and proud. It is not your fault!" Then, at a certain moment, all pretense gives way, the scales tilt, and he comes to understand what really happened and his guilt. (But in another perspective, the "truth" turns out to be the substitution of one neurosis for another. Where before he used her as the object of his need to dominate, later he turns to her for "love," that is, to receive, as a child receives from a mother. But of course she is by this time too weak, too damaged by life, for that. She has resigned herself to living at a distance. That is, his "love" is just his old neurotic need in a new manifestation, and just as demanding.)

Unreliable narration is a lovely effect in films, since a voiceover depicting events and existents in the story may be belied by what we see so clearly for ourselves. A good example occurs in Robert Bresson's version of Bernanos's *Le Journal d'un curé de campagne*. As a critic observes, "[The curé] feels that the Count is a 'friend', whereas we remain sceptical, the Count's face is too cold, we ask ourselves how the priest could possibly think

he is a friend, we sense that the priest is imagining the friend he so badly longs for." [24] The false message "friend" is communicated by the narrating voice of the priest or by the visible words in his journal. But we "read out" of the language of faces the message "cynical bystander." And we trust our own judgment of character over the impressions of the naive priest.

A more sensational example occurs in Alfred Hitchcock's *Stage Fright*. The whole intrigue rests on what is essentially an untruthful account, in flashback, of events that took place before NOW. Jonathan (Richard Todd) tells his friend, Eve (Jane Wyman), how he has been unwittingly implicated in a murder committed by a famous musichall performer, Charlotte (Marlene Dietrich). As he narrates the events, there is a dissolve to the "events themselves"—Charlotte's appearance in a blood-soaked gown, and Jonathan's hurried visit to her apartment to get her a clean dress, stepping over the body of the dead husband as he does so. Then we see him arranging "evidence" to suggest that Charlotte's husband had been killed by a burglar: he breaks the terrace door window, turns the contents of a desk upside down, and so on. Unfortunately, as he makes his exit, he is seen by Charlotte's maid. Later, visited by the police, he bolts, seeks out Eve at her acting school, and persuades her to drive him to her father's seaside home, where he hopes to be hidden aboard the family boat. The film opens with the two speeding down to the coast in her car, and it is during the trip that Jonathan recounts the events presented above. We have no idea that his version of the story is untrue until the very end.

. . . we see everything, inevitably, from the narrator's [i.e. Jonathan's] viewpoint, knowing only what he tells us. . . . We watch the film with a certain complacency, knowing that this nice young man will win through somehow. . . . Then, at the end of the film we suddenly learn that Charlotte hasn't framed him at all: he really *is* the murderer: the ground is cut away from under our feet. The flashback was a deliberate lie (and, whatever [Eric] Rohmer and [Claude] Chabrol may say, the images lie as well as the words, quite indisputably). [25]

24. Raymond Durgnat, in *The Films of Robert Bresson* (New York, 1969), p. 48.
25. Robin Wood, *Hitchcock's Films* (New York, 1969), p. 37. The reference is to Eric Rohmer and Claude Chabrol, *Hitchcock* (Paris, 1957), with whom François Truffaut in his long interview with Hitchcock concurred (*Hitchcock*,

In other words, the camera conspires with an unreliable narrator. But we have spoken of the camera as the instrument of the cinematic implied author; shall we say *he* lies too? Does the cinematic medium differ from the verbal here (since we have argued that only the narrator can be unreliable, but not the implied author)? I would argue not: the logic is that though the actual shots, the visual images, do indeed "lie," they do so at the service of the narrator, Jonathan, not the implied author. The implied author does in fact allow the truth to emerge at last, so he cannot be called unreliable. Jonathan is only allowed to look like "a nice young man" and therefore believable, in the image he projects as in his words. Otherwise all that is involved is the ordinary cinematic convention of dissolving from a character recounting a story to its purely visual rendition. Hitchcock has simply let the camera represent the lie of a narrator-character. It is not his fault that audiences (including sophisticated French critics) should insist that every story shown by the camera be *ipso facto* "true." By allowing the camera to "lie" for the character-narrator, Hitchcock was only challenging the convention of reliable narration, as so many novelists had already done. Visuals are no more sacrosanct than words. The cinema caught up, in 1951, with a fashion established in verbal narratives well before the turn of the century.

Commentary on the Story: Interpretation

"Interpretation" can be seen as the broadest category of overt commentary. In one sense, it includes the others: if an interpretation proper is any explanation, a judgment is an explanation whose basis is moral evaluation, while a generalization is one that compares an event or existent in the story with real ones in the nonfictional universe. But we shall stick to the three-way distinction, limiting "interpretation" to any relatively value-free

New York, 1967). Hitchcock answered with a sly rhetorical question: "In movies, people never object if a man is shown telling a lie. And it's also acceptable, when a character tells a story about the past, for the flashback to show it as if it were taking place in the present. So why is it that we can't tell a lie through a flashback?" Truffaut's negative attitude toward this possibility seems oddly academic, even puritanic for one of the founders of the *nouvelle vague*.

attempt to account for something in terms of the story itself, without going outside it (as do judgment and generalization).

Even within these confines a multitude of statements are possible. Here are some illustrations from *Père Goriot* (Henry Reed's translation). As has been noted, Balzac was anxious to justify or "naturalize" behaviors, appearances, states of affairs, down to the tiniest morsel of Parisian life. For example: Eugène Rastignac learns the shabby ropes of the Parisian *beau monde* by listening intently to the confessions of women. These typically appear in the direct dialogue, then their gist is interpreted by the narrator. Delphine, grateful for Rastignac's successful wagers that save her from financial ruin, relates her dismal history as Nucingen's wife and de Marsay's jilted mistress. To epitomize for us (as for Eugène), the narrator interprets: "This intermingling of the finer feelings that make women so great with the faults that present-day society forces them to acquire completely baffled Eugène." The exact relevance of Delphine's disjointed account is thus pointed up: it illustrates how fashionable women are pressured by society to mix noble love with sordid money-grubbing.[26]

Or, upon meeting Maxime, the lover of Mme. de Restaud, Eugène says to himself, "'This is my rival, and I intend to beat him.'" The narrator bursts out "Rash youth!" and proceeds to interpret: "He was unaware of Comte Maxime de Trailles' habit of provoking an insult, drawing first, and killing his man." Rastignac's general ignorance, indeed, is a convenient device for overt explanations of Parisian mores: "Eugène was unaware of the feverish anxiety that possessed women of a certain class at that time. No one had told him that a banker's wife would go to any lengths to get through a door into the Faubourg Saint-Germain." "Eugène did not know that you must never call on anyone in Paris without previously extracting from friends of the family a detailed history of the husband, the wife, and the children." And so on.

Interpretations may also be predictions: taking the big leap

26. A generalization is embedded within this interpretation, namely: "Society forces women into iniquity." As we shall see, most of our examples are

into society with precious francs borrowed from his family, Eugène stakes his future on new clothes. Fortunately, his tailor

was one who understood the paternal aspect of his trade and regarded himself as a hyphen between a young man's past and future. The grateful Eugène was eventually to make the man's fortune by one of those remarks at which he was in later years to excel: "I know two pairs of his trousers that have each made matches worth twenty thousand francs a year."

The interpreting narrator may invoke the optative mood as well as the future tense, conjecturing about what might have been. If Goriot's wife had lived, she would have exercised

a certain sway over him beyond the sphere of the affections. Perhaps she might have educated that sluggish nature, perhaps have taught it to care for the things of the world and of life.

Direct character depiction may be combined with interpretation:

Like all unimaginative people, Madame Vauquer was in the habit of never looking beyond the small circle of events to discover their causes. She preferred to palm her own faults off onto other people.

The forms of interpretations are as varied as their contents in Balzac. Obvious explanatory words may be used, like the simple causatives—"so," "because," "since," "as a result." Or the narrator's interpretation may repeat a question posed by the narratee. The handsome Portugese finds it difficult to tell Mme. de Beauséant that he is about to drop her. "Why?" asks the narrator, and interpretation provides the answer: "There is probably no harder task than to present a woman with such a *fait accompli.*" A variant formula introduces Poiret's cupidity: "It may surprise the reader that Poiret. . . ." The interpreting narrator may offer a pseudo-quotation, the better to get to the gist of the matter. As Eugène walks home after his first meeting with Delphine:

"If Madame de Nucingen takes me up, I'll teach her how to manage her husband. . . . The husband is in the gold market . . . he could help me to a fortune at one stroke." It was not put as crudely as this, and he

mixed in character—this is the general nature of overt commentary. The *lexies* of *S/Z* are almost always polyvalent.

was not yet sufficiently expert to sum up a situation and calculate its possibilities.

So the interpreting narrator does it for him.

Interpretation may explain that which no character has occasion to explain, because of ignorance, inarticulateness, dramatic impropriety, or whatever. The effect is common in thesis-novels, like Hardy's. Characters are moved by forces that they themselves cannot fathom. Jude is driven into Arabella's arms:

. . . as if materially, a compelling arm of extraordinary muscular power seized hold of him—something which had nothing in common with the spirits and influences which had moved him hitherto . . . moved him along, as a violent schoolboy . . . seized by the collar. . . .

Hardy's ideological axe frequently sharpens itself on such interpretations: "there seemed a finality in their decisions. But other forces and laws than theirs were in operation." Or in metaphorical or contrary-to-fact form: "Had this been a case in the court of an omniscient judge he might have entered on his notes the curious fact that Sue had placed the minor for the major indiscretion." Or a premonition, as when Jude receives the first note from Sue: "one of those documents which, simple and commonplace in themselves, are seen retrospectively to have been pregnant with impassioned consequences."

Even in *The Ambassadors*, where narration is strongly covert, the narrator makes an occasional interpretation. The famous first paragraph of the novel contains one:

The same secret principle . . . that had prompted Strether not absolutely to desire Waymarsh's presence at the dock, that had led him thus to postpone for a few hours his enjoyment of it, now operated to make him feel that he could still wait without disappointment. . . . The principle I have just mentioned as operating had been, with the most newly disembarked of the two men, wholly instinctive. . . .

In the irony of negative understatement so well described by Ian Watt ("postpone his enjoyment," "wait without disappointment"), there is that merger of narrator and character sympathies we spoke of earlier. But the characterization of the "principle" as a "secret" one, that is "wholly instinctive," suggests that the narrator is actually performing an interpretation. After all,

"secret" from whom if not Strether himself? In these sentences the interest point of view remains Strether's; but precisely to the extent that his feeling is "instinctive" and hidden from himself, he cannot very well be articulating it in words. Hence the voice is clearly the narrator's, telling us what Strether was feeling without acknowledging it. The narrator is helping Strether articulate, just as he helps Maisie, that other babe in the woods.

Commentary on the Story: Judgment

Values, norms, beliefs—Wayne Booth's *Rhetoric of Fiction* has dealt with these elements in the novel with such sophistication that any account can only seem a footnote to his work. He is particularly helpful in showing how the implied author "molds beliefs" by discriminating among and emphasizing certain values, whether traditional, as in *Tom Jones, Pride and Prejudice, Barchester Towers, The Egoist*, or unusual, new or "nonexistent," as in *The Mayor of Casterbridge, Nostromo, Tender Is the Night*.[27]

We can, however, look at the formal mechanism by which judgments are communicated. Here again an examination of the details of statements, their grammar and illocutionary status, turn up some useful particulars. Let us consider how overt judgmental voices make themselves heard in two very different novels.

It is no secret that the narrator of *Barchester Towers* would win the prize at narrative judging (Henry James would call it the booby prize). He judges practically every resident of the cathedral city in so many words, through adjectives drawn on conventional moral norms: Dr. Grantly is "proud, wishful, worldly"; the late John Bold is not "worthy of the wife he had won," but his baby is "delightful," and his sister, Mary Bold, "could have been no kinder." Bishop Proudie, though a "good-

---

27. One issue needing no further discussion is the *legitimacy* of judging. Booth's argument more than meets standards of persuasiveness: see particularly the sections "Molding Beliefs" (*Rhetoric of Fiction*, pp. 177–182), "Relating Particulars to the Established Norms" (pp. 182–189), and the examples from *The Old Wives' Tale* (pp. 145–147) and *Emma* (pp. 256–257, 262–264). Booth's argument is given independent support by Robert Alter, *Fielding and the Nature of the Novel* (Cambridge, 1968), who finds Fielding successfully substituting judgment for psychological analysis.

looking man," "spruce" and "dapper," is "henpecked" by the "despotic" Mrs. Proudie. More subtly ". . . in early years [Mr. Slope] added an 'e' to his name, for the sake of euphony, as other great men have done before him." The judgment is ironic: he *is* something of a slop and he is *not* a great man. And so on through the novel's rich treasure of portraits. Some adjectives are directly judgmental, but others are connotative and metonymic: for instance Mr. Slope's excessively moist handshake, or Squire Thorne's propensity to dye his hair.

So preoccupied with moral judgment is the narrator of *Barchester Towers* that he anticipates arguments with narratees who might form "erroneous" opinions. Of Archdeacon Grantley's disappointment in not receiving the call to the bishopric:

Many will think that he was wicked to grieve for the loss of episcopal power, wicked to have coveted it, nay, wicked even to have thought about it. . . . With such censures I cannot profess that I completely agree.

Or a judgment—say, "Doubting himself was Mr. Harding's weakness"—is mitigated by a generalization—"it is not, however, the usual fault of his order." Doubt is turned into a virtue by making the faith of other clergymen seem like dogma. Or a generalization may buttress a negative judgment; of Mr. Slope's letter to Eleanor Bold:

this letter, taken as a whole, and with the consideration that Mr. Slope wished to assume a great degree of intimacy with Eleanor, would not have been bad, but for the mention of the tresses. Gentlemen do not write to ladies about their tresses, unless they are on very intimate terms indeed.

Or (alas) a generalization may validate an action that is highly implausible yet necessary to the plot. Mr. Harding knows in his bones the compromising character of Mr. Slope's letter, yet (incredibly) fails to warn his (incredibly) imperceptive daughter. Trollope needs a solid page to validate this failure, beginning, lamely enough: "How hard it is to judge accurately of the feelings of others."

A very different approach to narrator's judgment meets us in the opening sentences of Hermann Hesse's *Magister Ludi*. At issue is not a character or event but rather a whole way of

thinking, involving the place of individualism in societies of the future. The narrator argues the value of depicting something of the lives of famous masters of the Glass Bead Game, but prevailing attitudes demand an apologia:

We are not unaware that this endeavour [the biography of Joseph Knecht] runs, or seems to run, somewhat counter to the prevailing laws and usages of our intellectual life. For, after all, obliteration of individuality, the maximum integration of the individual into the hierarchy of the educators and scholars, has ever been one of our ruling principles.[28]

The justification is that Joseph Knecht is the exception that proves the rule, or, in the text's generalization, "the more pointedly and logically we formulate a thesis, the more irresistibly it cries out for its antithesis." Because Knecht so beautifully embodied the collective, hierarchical structure of the society, singling him out for biographical attention does not mean succumbing to the "cult of personality" but, contrarily, reasserting the value of the community.

For us, a man is a hero and deserves special interest only if his nature and his education have rendered him able to let his individuality be almost perfectly absorbed in its hierarchic function without at the same time forfeiting the vigorous, fresh, admirable impetus which make for the savor and worth of the individual.

Here the overt narrator's capacity to judge goes far beyond adjectives and descriptive phrases; it invokes a whole epistemology and argues the matter in a discursive, rhetorical way. In so doing, it presupposes a set of norms quite contrary to the one that the implied audience presumably entertains.

Commentary on the Story: Generalization

Critics have long noted the frequent citation in fictions of "general truths," that is, philosophical observations that reach beyond the world of the fictional work into the real universe.[29]

28. Translated by Richard and Clara Winston.
29. Joseph Warren Beach, for example, cites examples from Fielding in *The Twentieth Century Novel* (New York, 1932), p. 28. Booth speaks of generalization as "implanting" or "reinforcing norms." Generalization is the code that Barthes calls "cultural" or "referential" (*S/Z*, p. 20): the commonsense subcode is "gnomic."

Even professional philosophers are concerned with the curious status of such factual assertions:

> Not all sentences in fiction are fictional sentences. Some merely state explicitly logical truths, the connotation of words, empirical generalizations, empirical laws of human nature, regardless whether they are universal or proportional, and assumptions of all sorts that are taken for granted in our world and which we ordinarily have to provide in order to understand the literary work of art. That "7 is a prime number" and that "All men are mortal" is true even if "uttered" by a character in a novel.[30]

But scientific facts form only one sort of generalization. Commoner (at least in nineteenth-century fiction) is a broad "philosophical" kind of observation, one that relates to truth-conditions in a more contingent way. For example, one might accept at one spot in a text, "A man should always tell the truth"; and at another, "A man should never tell the truth to anyone who will suffer as a consequence." Unlike "Seven is a prime number," such assertions are arguable; they inhabit the universe of rhetoric rather than science. For narrative, as for real-life argumentation, their applicability depends upon how they suit the fictional context, not their truth in an absolute sense.

Both factual and rhetorical generalizations serve the same basic functions, for instance, the ornamental, and particularly the verisimilar.[31] We have noted how generalizations and other comments often arise because of the need for plausibility, since in troubled historical periods the codes are not strong enough to establish a seeming reality. Hence the greater prevalence of nonce-created, author-specific verisimilitude. Generalizations become highly arbitrary. There are so many *parce ques* and *cars* in Balzac that they end up calling attention to themselves, underlining (and in some ways undermining) precisely what they were designed to conceal, the arbitrariness of any narrative

30. Laurent Stern, "Fictional Characters, Places and Events," *Philosophy and Phenomenological Research*, 26 (1965), 213.

31. Booth, *Rhetoric of Fiction*, pp. 197–200, discusses "generalizing the significance of the whole work." But what I call generalization is local rather than global in its application. "Making [the entire work] seem to have a universal or at least representative quality beyond the literal facts of the case" is to me a completely different issue, achievable without any overt generalizing comments at all.

decision (an arbitrariness that lighter-hearted and more daring authors like Sterne and Diderot overtly celebrate). Genette has observed that the explanatory Balzacian generalization, the "general law," "supposedly unknown or . . . forgotten by the reader, which the narrator needs to teach or recall to him," the nonce enthymeme (for that is what it is essentially—a rhetorical, not a logical or poetic tool) may be totally reversible. For each proposition a contrary could just as easily be entertained should the plot require it. When necessary, error leads to victory and not defeat, and achievement to disaster, not success. If a parish priest's desires are not satisfied by a large inheritance but require a canonship, it is because "Everyone, even a priest, must have his hobbyhorse" (*Le Curé de Tours*). But if he *is* satisfied, another generalization can accommodate that: "A sot does not have enough spunk in him to be ambitious." This overfacility at finding explanations clearly indicates an uneasy transitional stage in literary history. It marks a style requiring traditional realism but not commanding an adequate consensus about reality upon which to base it. It supplies its own stereotypes to explain actions that otherwise would seem unclear or unreasonable because the traditional codes have been subverted by history. Balzac and Thackeray constructed verisimilitude artificially to compensate for what could no longer be silently preempted from the public domain. The *topoi* were up for grabs. Writers needed generalizations because motivation was not clarified by known codes. And the time had not yet arrived for completely arbitrary narratives that could conspicuously ignore explanation, simply because "Life is just like that."

But let us look at the nature and function of generalizations through specific examples. *Barchester Towers* again will be our source. Most are "philosophical" in a straightforward way. Trollope was no Balzac. His generalizations were not meant to sound *ad hoc* but simple and sensible, comfortable precisely in their commonplaceness. I quote or paraphrase a random selection: "Listening to sermons is a great hardship" (ch. 6). "Students do badly in catechism" (ch. 6). "Ladies are easily duped by flatterers" (ch. 7). "Everyone gossips ill-naturedly about others, and is surprised to hear that others do the same about

him" (ch. 20). "Englishmen know less about their own than about Continental architecture" (ch. 22). "How many shades there are between love and indifference, and how little the graduated scale is understood" (ch. 24). And so on. These are introduced in a rather ornamental way, yet the ornamentality (despite the apparent paradox) is in fact functional. Singularly enough, there was a value in filling out the requisite number of pages "for Mr. Longmans." The leisurely pace so essential to Trollope's art is measured out by such intrusions. And the generalizations frequently contribute to the combination of litotic wit and mock humility characteristic of his style. The generalizations usually appear to justify an action or a characterization. For instance, the generalization about sermons occurs in the context of Mr. Slope's maiden (and only) performance at Barchester Cathedral. It doubles the misery of the congregation, who already, to a man (if not a woman) detest him. The particular insufferability of this sermon is intensified by the general insufferability of any sermon. The generalization about Englishmen's ignorance of their native architecture appropriately accompanies the description of the wonders of the Thornes' super-Saxon residence, Ullathorne. And so on. Generalization, like any comment in the hands of an able craftsman, is an exact tool for effecting economies—and in many cases otherwise unavailable insights.

Although our concern is not primarily the linguistic surface of narrative per se, one syntactic turn fairly leaps to the eye of generalization collectors as supremely typical. It consists of a noun specified by a deictic (often "that" as demonstrative pronoun) followed by a restrictive clause which clarifies the deixis. The locution is so popular with the verisimilarly nervous Balzac that one occurs in the very first sentence of "Sarrasine," the object of Barthes's scrutiny:

I was deep in one of those daydreams that overtake even the shallowest of men, in the midst of the most tumultuous parties.

"One of those daydreams; you know which kind I mean": our shoulder is nudged intimately by the narrator. We are pressured

to accept by the very mold of the syntax. Simply to comprehend one must adopt the presupposition that people do in fact fall into deep reveries at parties. We are not in a posture to question the assertion because it is not made as an assertion; it glides in on irresistible deictic lubrication. One would have to be perverse indeed (or a theoretician, which amounts perhaps to the same thing) to ask *"Which* reveries?" And if we did so in a public reading, the audience would justifiably shout: *"Those* reveries, you idiot!"

Modern films are generally chary of overt comment. A narrating voice-over of any sort is unfashionable, but especially one that moralizes, or interprets. (This is not true, of course, of films that expressly imitate novelistic techniques, especially parodically, like Tony Richardson's *Tom Jones*.) But a few talented directors have managed to communicate the equivalent of a comment by visual means. An example is the conclusion of Michelangelo Antonioni's *Eclipse*. As one critic observes, the final sequence "gathers up the visible fragments of the world of the film into a telling image of paralysis and futility."[32] The effect is achieved by a sequence of shots that are incomprehensible except as a comment on the story that has just concluded— a woman's restless search for meaning in the lives around her, and her difficulties in establishing a genuine relationship with a man. The sequence shows the urban environment through which she has walked, alone, with her mother, friends, and lovers, but now emptied of her or any familiar presence. The bare and barren cityscape is evoked by such shots as:

The shadow of a tree against a white wall.

Two shadows on the asphalt pavement, cast by the rays of a sun that is not very bright.

A panoramic shot of the stadium behind which Piero and Vittoria had often strolled together and which is now vacant. The street is completely empty.

32. Robert Richardson, *Literature and Film* (Bloomington, Ind., 1969), 50–51.

White traffic stripes painted on the asphalt for the benefit of the pedestrians. Footsteps are heard. They are those of a passing stranger.[33]

Commentary on the Discourse

Comments on the discourse by the narrator have been commonplace for centuries. Robert Alter[34] has shown the elaborate sophistication of such commentary already in *Don Quixote*, and doubtless earlier examples could be found.

A basic dichotomy has suggested itself between discourse comments that do or do not undercut the fabric of the fiction. The former have come to be called "self-conscious" narrations.

Some comments on the discourse are simple, straightforward and relatively harmonious with the story. Trollope's narrator writes of the burdens of authorship, modestly disavows artistic competence, speaks freely of the need to push this narrative button, tip that lever, and apply a brake now and then, but it is clear that he is deeply *into* his story, feels dislike or affection for his characters, and would not for the world disturb the reader's illusion that there really is, "somewhere," a Barchester, with its bishop, dean, archdeacon, prebenderies, and, of course, their wives.[35] Though he imitates the prologue of *Henry V* ("O for a muse of fire"), not to speak of Homer or Virgil, by asking "How shall I sing the divine wrath of Mr. Slope . . . ?" the narrator's is very weak mock heroic. Most of the slightly bemused comments have to do with operating the narrative machinery: "they [the Stanhopes] must be introduced to my readers," "There [Mr. Slope] is, however, alone in the garden walk, and we must contrive to bring him out of it," "We need not follow [Bertie] through the whole of his statement," and so on. This squeaky machinery may annoy us if we are overly committed to the smoothly purring Jamesian style, and it hardly inspires a profound contemplation of the nature of narrative artifice. Trollope may expand into literary critical excursus, as

33. L. Brigante, *Screenplays of Antonioni* (New York, 1963), p. 357.

34. This discussion has profited greatly from my friend's work (particularly *Partial Magic* and the last chapter of *Fielding and the Novel*) and from conversations we have had. I am grateful for his sympathetic ear and wise responses.

35. Alter makes the same point about Balzac, Dickens, and Thackeray in *Partial Magic*, ch. 4.

when the narrator takes it upon himself to attack the principle of plot suspense:

. . . here, perhaps, it may be allowed to the novelist to explain his views on a very important point in the art of telling tales. He ventures to reprobate that system which goes so far to violate all proper confidence between the author and his readers, by maintaining nearly to the end of the third volume a mystery as to the fate of their favourite personage.

But he does so to relieve potential reader anxiety about this particular narrative:

. . . let the gentle-hearted reader be under no apprehension whatsoever. It is not destined that Eleanor shall marry Mr. Slope or Bertie Stanhope.

No conflict arises between the tone of the story and the narrator's discoursive request for permission to depict it. The general attitude is homogeneous, marked by kindly decorum, politeness, consideration for the feeling of the narratee. The narrator's tone resembles that of his hero, Mr. Harding: self-effacing and considerate to a fault. Not that this precludes comic overtones, but it is a tolerant kind of comedy. When the Bishop retires to his nuptial chamber, where so many of the critical decisions of his pastoral care are made, the narrator remarks:

Far be it from us to follow him thither. There are some things which no novelist, no historian, should attempt; some few scenes in life's drama which even no poet should dare to paint. Let that which passed between Dr. Proudie and his wife on this night be understood to be among them.

Or, to explain how Mrs. Stanhope always looked so splendidly dressed:

Whether the toil rested partly with her, or wholly with her handmaid, it is not for such a one as the author even to imagine.

In short, commentary on the discourse in *Barchester Towers* generally takes the form of explaining its own limits, and the limits purport to be those of the narrator's competence, knowledge, and sophistication. In no sense is the fictionality of the fiction or the artifice of the art questioned. The narrative is never undercut.

Trollope's discoursive commentary is a long way from Diderot's, whose narrator in *Jacques The Fatalist* glories from the very outset in the absolute arbitrariness of invention, and its effect on the reader:

> You see reader how I am already launched, how, in separating Jacques from his master and putting them through as many hazards as I please, it's all up to me whether I make you follow the story of Jacques' love-affairs for one year, two years, three years.

How easy it is to make stories, to gull you narratees if I wish, to lead you by the nose! Our confidence is about the last thing that this narrator wants. The passage illustrates beautifully the feature of self-conscious narration, which I cannot define better than does Robert Alter:

> A self-conscious novel is one that systematically flaunts its own condition of artifice and that by so doing probes into the problematic relationship between real-seeming artifice and reality. . . . A fully self-conscious novel is one in which from beginning to end, through the style, the handling of narrative viewpoint, the names and words imposed on the characters, the patterning of the narration, the nature of the characters and what befalls them, there is a consistent effort to convey to us a sense of the fictional world as an authorial construct set up against a background of literary tradition and convention.

It is "a testing of the ontological status of the fiction." We are "asked to watch how [the novelist] makes his novel, what is involved technically and theoretically in the making."[36]

Another passage from the first chapter of Diderot's novel is even more outrageous in toying with the narrative contract. Jacques helps a woman accompanying the surgeon to her feet from the awkward and compromising position in which she finds herself after falling from her horse. The narrator's comment underscores the arbitrariness of his or any narrative. He not only refuses the story that he could have written, but accuses the narratee of trying to get him off the track, just (so to speak) for the cheap *present* thrill. He stalwartly refuses to be distracted from his path (though he has already told us that any path is random), in order to spoil his narratee's titillated vision of the woman with her skirts and petticoats over her head. The

36. Ibid., pp. x–xiii.

first person plural—"let us put the peasant back on the horse behind her rider, permit them to go and return to our two voyagers"—is not the royal *we*, but precisely the narrator rubbing the narratee's nose in the arbitrary convention. It says: "You and I, dear fellow, must keep our minds on our business if we are ever to hear the story I've decided to tell; and you—by the contract that you willingly signed in picking up this book—must agree to get this provocatively distracting woman back on her way."

Such toying with the basic narrative conventions is ironic in the sense of "Romantic irony." But some self-conscious narration goes even farther, seemingly bent on destroying, not merely playing with them. Passages like the following, from Samuel Beckett's *Watt*, are literally destructive, or "deconstructive" (in the Brechtian sense):

And then to pass on to the next generation there was Tom's boy young Simon aged twenty, whose it is painful to relate

?

and his young cousin wife his uncle Sam's girl Ann, aged nineteen . . . and Sam's other married daughter Kate aged twenty-one years, a fine girl but a bleeder (1), and her young cousin husband. . . .

At the bottom of the page is a footnote that reads:

(1) Haemophilia is, like enlargement of the prostate, an exclusively male disorder. But not in this work.[37]

Were it not for the footnote, we could write the narration off as unreliable (the narrator simply does not know anything about medicine). But since the footnote repeats, indeed asserts the anomaly, we conclude that a gratuitous monkey wrench is being thrown into the works out of sheer antinarrative spite. The footnote says something like "All these stories are bores and lies and I wouldn't put any stock in them if I were you. For you see how I can make you swallow the most patent absurdities just by telling you to. 'Not in this work,' indeed!"

In the cinema, commentary on the discourse is rare but not unknown. In a delicious sequence, Buster Keaton, playing a

37. Quoted by Richard Ohmann in an essay in *Literary Style: A Symposium*, ed. Seymour Chatman (New York, 1971), 44–45.

movie projectionist in *Sherlock Jr.* (1924), falls asleep in the booth. The movie he is projecting becomes his dream; oneirically he strides down the aisle and crawls up into the screen. At first he remains a foreign object, the background changing behind him as he struggles to "catch up" with it: "Diving off a high rock to save a blonde heroine struggling in the waves, he land[s] on desert sand under the astonished gaze of a lion." [38]

A much more profound and sustained example of self-conscious cinema is Dziga Vertov's *The Man with the Movie Camera* (1928). Ostensibly a survey of the City, from morning to evening, from life to death, the real purpose of the film is to demystify the art and artifice of making a film. This goal is achieved in a number of ways. The film begins by showing an empty movie theater preparing itself to see a film, the seats lowering themselves, and so on. At the end the camera "takes a bow" after recapitulating (like the musical finale of an opera) bits of the action it has recorded. It achieves the equivalent of a narrator's self-reference by filming shots of the cameraman filming the shots that moments before and after we take to be the subject of the "main" film. ("One sees, emerging from a mine shaft, a worker steering a coal wagon, shot at a tilt. He passes, and one sees the cameraman prone on the ground, filming him." [39]) Or by reversing the film, in what has been called the cinematic equivalent of the rhetorical figure *hysteron proteron*: the act of buying a piece of beef can be turned backwards, and the meat "literally" returned to a "resurrected" cow. Or intercutting with one sequence another that is nothing less than the editor cutting the object-sequence that is the final product. By these devices occurs "a subversion *through* consciousness [that is, by raising the audience's consciousness] of cinematic illusionism." [40] It is clear that Vertov was attempting to achieve in his medium what

38. René Clair, as quoted in Georges Sadoul, *Dictionary of Films*, trans. P. Morris (Berkeley, 1972), p. 339.

39. Annette Michelson, "'The Man with the Movie Camera' from Magician to Epistemologist," in *Artforum*, 10 (March 1972), 61–71.

40. Ibid., p. 69. Some other techniques for achieving this effect cited by Michelson are animation, sudden changes in projection speed not motivated by the story, including freeze-frame (a continual reminder that the screen is flat and not deep), split-screen, and other optical illusions.

Cervantes, Sterne, Diderot, and later Beckett, Nabokov, and Fowles have done in theirs.

The Narratee

Having considered various properties of the covert and overt narrators, we can turn, finally, to his interlocutor, the narratee. He is much less well-known; indeed, his very existence has only recently been recognized. Studies of the narratee raise several interesting questions: Who precisely is he? How do we identify him? What narrative tasks does he perform? Gerald Prince has begun to answer these questions:

A narrator may ostensibly direct his narration to himself, as in Butor's *La Modification* or Philippe Sollers' *Drame*. He may direct it to a receiver or receivers represented as characters (*Arabian Nights, L'Immoraliste, Heart of Darkness*). The character-receiver may be a listener (Dr. Spielvogel in *Portnoy's Complaint*, the Caliph in *Arabian Nights*) or a reader (Mme de Merteuil, Valmont, or Cecile in *Les Liaisons dangereuses*, Isa or Robert in *Le Noeud de vipères*); he may himself play an important part in the events narrated to him (*La Modification, Les Liaisons dangereuses*) or, on the contrary, no part at all (*Portnoy's Complaint*); he may be influenced by what he reads or listens to (*L'Emploi du temps*) and then again he may not (*Heart of Darkness*). Sometimes, the narrator may have one receiver in mind, then another one, then still another one (*Le Noeud de vipères*). Sometimes, his narration may be intended for one receiver and fall into another receiver's hands: in *Les Faux-Monnayeurs*, Edouard keeps a diary for himself but Bernard happens to read it. Often, a narrator addresses his narration to a receiver who is not represented as a character, a potential real-life receiver (*Doctor Faustus, Eugen Onegin, Billion Dollar Brain*). This receiver may be referred to directly (*Doctor Faustus*) or not (*Billion Dollar Brain*). He may be a listener (oral narrative) or a reader (written narrative); and so on and so forth.[41]

41. "On Readers and Listeners in Narrative," *Neophilologus*, 55 (1971), 117–122. Prince has also published "Notes towards a Categorization of Fictional 'Narratees,'" *Genre*, 4 (1971), 100–105, and his best essay on the subject, "Introduction à l'étude du narrataire," *Poétique*, 14 (1973) 178–196, upon which most of my own account is based. My disagreements are minor but should perhaps be mentioned. Prince tends to proliferate discursive entities beyond the needs of the situation. He suggests that there exists not only a *lecteur réel* and a *lecteur virtuel* (our "implied reader") but also a "*lecteur idéal* . . . he who would perfectly understand and entirely approve the least of [the author's] words, the subtlest of his intentions" ("Introduction," p. 180). It seems to me that these qualities are already contained in the virtual or implied reader; at least I cannot see why they should not be. What theoretical good is there in

The degree to which a narratee is evoked is also a matter of interest. Does the overt/covert distinction also apply to narratees? Prince thinks so: he contrasts "those narratives which contain no reference to a narratee" with "those which, on the contrary, define him as a specific individual." We can also recognize a more basic dichotomy between intradiegetic and extradiegetic narratees, that is, between those in a frame-story, and those external to stories. These distinctions can be illustrated by the following diagrams:

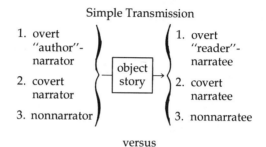

Simple Transmission

1. overt "author"-narrator
2. covert narrator
3. nonnarrator

object story →

1. overt "reader"-narratee
2. covert narratee
3. nonnarratee

versus

Frame Transmission

overt narrator as character in frame story

object story →

overt narratee as character in frame story

---

presupposing an intermediary, a "reader *manqué*," who does *not* understand perfectly and approve the narrator's words and intentions? Why posit less-gifted souls, since these entities exist only for the sake of theory in the first place, and theory requires the simplest explanation possible? Nor do I see the need for another entity which he argues, the "narratee degree zero"—who knows only the denotations, not the connotations of words. If narratives are second-order systems (that is, ones that already presuppose competence in an enabling medium), I cannot think of a good reason for theoretically constructing beings deficient in the first-order powers. Since connotations are in the language at large (or at least in the *text*, that is, the language-as-discoursed), what purpose is served in imagining a reader who comes to a narrative without these competences?

In general, a given type of narrator tends to evoke a parallel type of narratee: overt narrators evoke overt narratees, and so on. But this is not inevitably true: a first person narrator may be addressing a "nonnarratee," that is, "no one," as in Camus' *L'Etranger*.

No matter how minimal or extensive the frame story may be— whether Marlow talking to his cronies or Scheherazade elaborately struggling to save her life—it forms a narrative in its own right, with its own laws of events and existents, discourse and so on. But it has additionally mobilized the important power of self-embedding. Self-embedding is a familiar concept to linguists and occurs in other semiotic systems as well. Narrative self-embedding does not inhere at the mere surface of a medium (for example, verbs of report, like "John told them that once he found himself in the Congo and . . ."), but in the narrative structure itself. A variety of devices have been utilized in the cinema, for example, to inform audiences that what they are about to see is a story-within-the-story they have been watching—dissolves, "rippling pool" optical effects, and so on.

Theoretically, self-embedding can be as extensive as the capacity of memory itself. At its climactic point, John Barth's story "Menelaid" goes seven deep in an orgy of punctuation. Menelaus is the narrator: his disembodied voice (MV) tells a story in which Menelaus as character (M^1, first quotation mark) recalls a prophecy of Proteus' that some day, while drinking with Peisistratus and Telemachus, he would tell them (PT, second quotation mark) what he told Helen aboard ship on the way home from Troy (H^1, third quotation mark) about what Proteus advised him to do (P, fourth quotation mark). But Proteus would only do that after he heard how Menelaus had learned to catch him; Menelaus had been taught by Proteus' daughter Eidothea, but only after he told her (E, fifth quotation mark) what he and Helen had discussed (H^2, sixth quotation mark) after he captured her in Deiphobus' bed *in flagrante delicto* at the fall of Troy, namely the story of their original honeymoon and his gulling by Paris (M^2 and H^3, seventh quotation mark). The critical question of that ultimate conversation was: "Why did Helen agree to marry Menelaus when she could have chosen

among so many superior men?" Menelaus *had* to know; that was his downfall. At the climax of the story we are confronted by the following barrage of quotation marks:

"'''''"""Speak!" Menelaus cried to Helen on the bridal bed,' I reminded Helen in her Trojan bedroom," I confessed to Eidothea on the beach,' I declared to Proteus in the cavemouth," I vouchsafed to Helen on the ship,' I told Peisistratus at least in my Spartan hall," I say to whoever and where I am. And Helen answered:

$$
\begin{array}{c}
\text{"} \quad \text{'} \quad \text{"} \quad \text{'} \quad \text{"} \quad \text{'} \quad \text{"Love!"} \quad \text{'} \quad \text{"} \quad \text{'} \quad \text{"} \quad \text{'} \quad \text{"} \\
\uparrow \qquad \uparrow \ \uparrow \ \uparrow \ \uparrow \ \uparrow \ \uparrow \ \uparrow \qquad \uparrow \ \uparrow \ \uparrow \ \uparrow \ \uparrow \ \uparrow \ \uparrow \qquad \uparrow \\
\text{MV} \quad \text{M}^1\text{M}^2\text{H}^1\text{P E H}^2\text{H}^3 \qquad \text{H}^3\text{H}^2\text{E P H}^1\text{M}^2\text{M}^1 \quad \text{MV}
\end{array}
$$

Or, in diagram form:

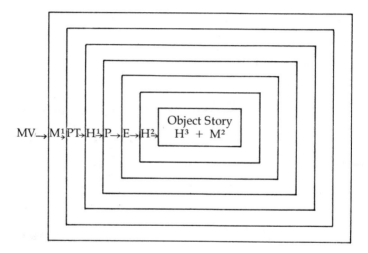

The explicit citation of narratees parallels that of narrators. The narratee may be referred to simply by the second person pronoun, as the narrator refers to himself by the first. Or some familiar epithet may be applied: "your author" easily evokes a corresponding "my (or) dear reader." The use of the first person plural is a little more complex, because in English at least it has both inclusive and exclusive functions. "We" may simply refer "royally" to the narrator. Or it may mean, exclusively, "you, the narratee" and "I, the narrator." Or, inclusively, "Not only

we two, but every other like-minded (that is, "reasonable") person in the world." In the latter case, we are not so much concerned with narratee structures as with narrative "generalizations" of the sort discussed earlier.

The invocation of the narratee by implication is a more delicate matter. Any portion of narrative text that is not strict dialogue or a bare account of actions, and especially those that seem to be explaining something, performs this function. Just as explanatory passages presuppose an explainer, they also presuppose an explainee. Passages in which elements are directly characterized are introduced for the benefit of a narratee. For instance, from *Sons and Lovers*: "There was always this feeling of jangle and discord in the Leivers family"; "Miriam was her mother's daughter"; "Miriam and her brother were naturally antagonistic, Edgar was a rationalist who was curious, and had a sort of scientific interest in life." Lawrence's decision that information about Miriam and Edgar should be communicated in this summary and direct way necessarily presupposes a someone who is listening to the someone who is telling.

More direct forms of communication occur between the narrator and narratee. These stay short of outright naming of the narratee, but they clearly sound like bits from the narrator's half of a dialogue going on between the two.

Sometimes the context signals a dialoguic gap, a hole in continuity during which the narratee must have addressed a remark to the narrator. Less secure authors mark such ellipses with dots; more sophisticated ones do not. On the second page of Camus' *La Chute*, after the narrator has offered to order a glass of gin for the narratee because the bartender, a "gorilla" who speaks only Dutch, will not be able to understand a request in French (thus establishing that the narratee is at least *francophone*), he says:

But let me leave you, Monsieur, happy to have obliged. I thank you, and I would accept if I were sure of not being a bother. I'll move my glass next to yours.

The narrator first offers to go back to his original place; but then he joins the narratee. The latter's voice is not reported, but we

can "hear" it in the space between *obliged* and *I*. The narrator would have no reason for thanking the narratee unless he had done or said something in the interim to elicit thanks—little imagination is required to guess that he has in fact extended an invitation. Though a gap occurs at the surface level, the narrative context supplies strong clues. The matter is clinched by the final sentence, where the future tense signals directly that a conventional gesture of friendship has been made (the placing of one's glass next to another's as "read out of" a "bar-behavior code").

It has been noted that the narratee, like the narrator, may change during the course of the narrative—either develop as an individual or be replaced by another individual. It may even happen (*Père Goriot* is an example) that the narrator loses track of his narratee, has difficulty in deciding at any given moment who exactly he is. Perhaps the most interesting case is where narrator and narratee are identified, or where they exchange functions. In *La Nausée*, Roquentin, like other diarist-novelists, is his own narratee. In *The Canterbury Tales* and *The Decameron*, narratees become, each in turn, narrators, since the frame story consists of a playful contract that each contribute as well as listen to the common entertainment. In *L'Immoraliste*, one of Michel's narratees becomes the narrator, by means of a letter, of Michel's story to Michel's brother, the new narratee.

What are the narrative tasks performed by the narratee? Following our basic dichotomy, I separate intra- from extradiegetic functions. Intradiegetically, within a frame story, he performs as audience for the narrator, an audience upon whom the various artifices of narrative rhetoric may be practiced. Recalling that rhetoric in fiction has to do with verisimilitude rather than arguable "truth," the acquiescing narratee can show that the narrator's efforts to convince, to win acceptance of his version are in fact successful. In *A Thousand and One Nights*, the caliph keeps listening; therefore Scheherazade lives. In the simplest case, where there is no reason to question it, the narratee's acceptance is warrant for the narrator's reliability. If, on the other hand, we suspect the narratee's gullibility, our decision is more

difficult. Are both narrator and narratee unreliable? Or is the narrator reliable despite our misgivings about his narratee?

The narrator-narratee relation can parallel or confirm in some way the themes of the object story. Prince gives two good examples of how inner and outer relationships intertwine:

In *Père Goriot*, the narrator maintains power relations with his narratee. From the beginning, he struggles to anticipate the latter's objections in order to dominate and convince him. He tries everything—cajolery, prayer, mockery, menace—and, we surmise, he ends by persuading him. . . . This kind of war, this thirst for power is also found at the level of the characters [in the object-story]. On the level of events as on that of narration, the same combat has taken place.

In *La Chute*, the relationship of narrator to narratee not only corresponds to the events in the story, but provides the only real key to its central question, that is, whether or not Clamence's self-vindication is valid:

In *La Chute* . . . it is uniquely by studying the reactions of Clamence's narratee that one can know if, according to the text, the arguments of the protagonist are so powerful that they cannot be denied, or if, on the contrary, they are only special pleading, clever but ultimately unconvincing. Of course, throughout the novel, the narratee does not speak a single word. . . . Whatever the identity of the narratee, all that counts is the degree of his acceptance of the hero's arguments. Now the narrator's discourse gives evidence of a growingly fierce resistance on the part of his narratee. Clamence's tone becomes more and more pressing, his sentences more and more embarrassed as his story proceeds and his auditor escapes him. Several times during the final part of the novel, he seems seriously shaken.[42]

Since the narrator mediates between the narratee and the world of the work, particularly its characters, questions of distance arise. If we posit two basic degrees of distance among these three personages, "close" and "far," we can recognize five different kinds of relations. Narrator and narratee may be close to each other but far from the character (the case of irony for example); narrator may be far, and has placed narratee and character in close contact (see the example from *The Secret Agent* immediately below); narrator and character are close, and far

42. Prince, "Introduction," pp. 195–196.

from narratee (as in unreliable or naive first-person narration); all three are close (a sense of general sympathy prevails, as in "The Garden Party"); all three are far (an unsympathetic narrator writes of unsympathetic characters, as in Céline).

An example of one of the rarer types (the second above) is the following passage from Conrad's *The Secret Agent*. Mr. Verloc has just had an unpleasant interview with Mr. Vladimir and is standing at his dingy parlor window over the dark street.

[He] felt the latent unfriendliness of all out of doors with a force approaching to positive bodily anguish. There is no occupation that fails a man more completely than that of a secret agent of the police. It's like your horse suddenly falling dead under you in the midst of an uninhabited and thirsty plain. The comparison occurred to Mr. Verloc because he had sat astride various army horses in his time.

The sentence beginning "There is no occupation . . ." first strikes us as a narrator's generalization, and *your* is interpreted accordingly—"anyone who finds himself in that predicament" —perhaps "your," rather than "one's," to suggest a more intimate reference to a narratee. The final sentence, however, reveals that these were in fact Verloc's thoughts in indirect free form. Despite that, "your" seems to retain something of its original force: Mr. Verloc can be imagined to be addressing an interlocutor in his own imagination (the only place where he can permit himself such confidences). The narratee is *his* version of the narratee, hence also an object ironized by the narrator, since the real narratee is in on the joke.

Another complex irony may be established, that between the narratee and the implied reader. Just as the narrator may be unreliable, so may the narratee. The clearest evocation I have so far seen is quoted by Prince from *Tom Jones*. The narrator instructs his narratee: "To treat of the effects of love to you must be as absurd as to discourse on colours to a man born blind . . . love probably may, in your opinion, very greatly resemble a dish of soup or a sirloin of roastbeef." This only works to the extent that the implied reader does not agree with the presumptive narratee's opinion that love does in fact resemble soup or beefsteak. The implied reader invoked by the implied author

(at odds with the narratee evoked by the narrator) is precisely one who takes a more serious attitude toward love.

Such cases highlight the narratee's mediation because of his distance from the implied reader. But mediation also operates in reliable situations: direct judgments or interpretations uttered by a narrator may be strengthened by the acquiescence (even tacit) of a narratee. Indeed, an otherwise vocal narratee's failure to question or object to a narrator's statement endorses its credibility. If the narratee should say "Yes, I understand," the case is strengthened even further. The implied reader who questions such solidarity must prove that the narratee is an easy dupe, or in league with the narrator. If evidence is lacking, he must accept the endorsement. Such direct communication of values and opinions between narrator and narratee is the most economical and clearest way of communicating to the implied reader the attitudes required by the text. Many modernist texts that consider ambiguity an aesthetic good therefore avoid direct address.

Another function that the narratee may perform is that of defining more clearly the narrator himself. It is through his interaction with the narratee that the narrator of *Tom Jones* strikes us as "very sure of himself, but justifiably, since he is infinitely superior to his narratee, both in knowledge and wisdom; a bit tyrannical since he does not hesitate to bully, even brutally, anyone not in agreement with him; but withal a good sort and always ready to make up."[43]

By the same token, the *absence* of such definition may itself be a marker of some kind: Merseault, in *L'Etranger*, lives at such a distance from everyone that, despite his first-person address, he does not evoke a narratee. He might just as well be talking to himself. The effect is all the more poignant since he is not in touch with himself either.

Chaim Perelman, the famous legal rhetorician, has noted the interesting fact that any speaker may "by a kind of fiction, in-

43. Ibid., p. 193.

sert his audience into a series of different audiences." (The example he gives concerns characters rather than narrators and narratees, but the principle would clearly hold for the latter as well.) He quotes from *Tristram Shandy*:

> He [Tristram's father] . . . placed his arguments in all lights; argued the matter with her like a Christian, like a heathen, like a husband, like a father, like a patriot, like a man. My mother answered everything only like a woman, which was a little hard upon her, for, as she could not assume and fight it out behind such a variety of characters, 'twas no fair match: 'twas seven to one.[44]

Surely this is the epitome of audience-definition, and a parody of it. The speaker dazzles his audience into acquiescence by tailor-making an argument to suit every conceivable objection. In so doing, he theoretically destroys the audience's independence. It is not at all that rhetorical maneuver which utilizes a multiplicity of arguments to satisfy an audience composed of individuals from different walks of life—butcher, baker, candlestickmaker, Tory, Whig, Communist, hippy. The latter multiplicity is not a normal goal in narrative structures. I cannot think of a single good instance, though doubtless some exist. The rarity seems to be a function of the need that most narratives have for the intimacy and specific focus of an actually named or indicated narrator.

44. Quoted in Chaim Perelman and Lucie Olbrechts-Tyteca, *The New Rhetoric: A Treatise on Argumentation* (Notre Dame, 1969), p. 22.

CONCLUSION

I have done; you all have heard; you
have the facts; give your judgment.
                    Aristotle,
                    The Rhetoric

Theory makes heavy reading, and the theorist owes his audience a special obligation to summarize and take stock. Rather than a body of facts about the text we call narrative, I have sought a way of looking at it, to account for features that critics have traditionally found important—plot, character, setting, point of view, narrative voice, interior monologue, stream of consciousness—along with others that have only recently emerged in critical discussion, like the narratee. I have examined these labels afresh, to see how we could make them more self- and inter-consistent. Definitions have been proposed but not definitiveness.

Perhaps I can best summarize by acknowledging some open questions. To begin at the beginning, how useful is the distinction between story, the content element of narrative, and discourse, its formal element? The distinction is not new, but it is not often so starkly argued. Within story, a vital question involves the basis for the connection of events. Contemporary texts seriously challenge traditional notions of narrative causality. Some new principle of organization must be posited: the adequacy of "contingency" remains to be seen. Further, the borders between narrative and other temporal genres need to be examined. There are many marginal texts that are not yet explained. Modernist narratives in particular should be scrutinized to see whether Genette's distinctions among order, duration, and frequency are powerful enough. The codes of verisimilitude require detailed articulation by literary historians so that we can better understand the powerful *un*spoken cultural messages subsumed by most narratives. Much work remains to be done on character, whatever the basis for its analysis: in particular,

the conventions relating to traits (or whatever they shall be called) need the same close historical examination as do those relating to event-sequences. In both instances, the broader semantic implications will have to be worked out, as well as subclassifications of kinds of plots and characters. Setting is practically terra incognita; my brief pages hardly do justice to the subject, particularly its relation to that vague notion called "atmosphere." I hope that recognizing the consubstantial relation between character and setting, as I have done, may prompt a more serious interest in the latter kind of existent.

Further, we need to investigate the complex relations between the media and the abstract discoursive structure. For verbal narrative in particular, we may well ask if "degree of narrator-hood" is the best way to analyze the narrator's voice. Can still other kinds of point of view distinctions be made besides the ones I have proposed? The narrative function of indirect discourse, especially in its free form, calls for systematic reformulation, once linguists and linguistic philosophers have agreed on how best to explain it. Is it useful to distinguish between interior monologue and stream of consciousness, or does that lead to conceptual snags that I have not foreseen? Besides presupposition, what can other new insights into linguistic prominencing tell us about the subtleties of verbal narrative art? And what can we do with recent views of pronominal structure and the whole subject of deixis (for example, what is the semantic status of the narrator in second person narratives like *La Modification*?). Assuming a more complete account of irony, what more could be said about the ironic narrator, particularly in the murky "unstable" realms that narrative artists since Dostoevsky have chosen to populate? And surely the subject of self-conscious narration, despite excellent formulations like Alter's, is not exhausted. Finally, the narratee (like Stanley Fish's "reader") is a fascinating new personage on the aesthetic horizon. I am sure we shall hear much more about that personage.

These are the kinds of questions I hope I have stimulated. For better or worse, my own account rests on a sense of "well-formedness," rather than on the authority of tradition and accepted opinion. Well-formedness is a logical property of sys-

tems, not an æsthetic one. As such it is open to challenge and crossexamination; I not only acknowledge that but welcome it. And I pay my respects in advance to the person who will build the better model.

But of that person I would ask the following:

1. A method: a clear statement of methodological presuppositions, for example, whether evidence shall be gathered to support a formulation (deduction) or to form one (induction).

2. A model: if the dualist and formalist model that I propose is inadequate, what makes it so? If the four sectors created by the intersection of form and substance, expression and content are too many or too little, how many should there be? And why?

3. Taxonomies: in addition (and in contrast) to economy and simplicity, the test of a theory is its capacity to accommodate all exemplars of the structure it claims to handle, and to distinguish interestingly among these. When mine proves inadequate, what are the distinctions that prove it so, and how are these better accommodated by your theory?

4. Timeliness: what sort of texts have appeared that need to be accounted for? By what criteria can they in fact be demonstrated to be new?

For all its recourse to logic, any theory depends heavily on rhetoric. To me that is not a bad word. It is commonplace, and just, to say that the only truly bad rhetoric is unconscious rhetoric. I am fully conscious of *arguing* a set of cases, the dualism of discourse and story, the distinction between interior monologue and stream of consciousness, and so on. Argument seems to be the correct way to proceed. The success of any argument depends on its persuasiveness to an audience, which judges it, appropriately, on its coherence, the power of its explanatory capacity, whether it provides a sufficient diversity of examples to test itself, whether it readily provokes discussion of its methods, conclusions, analyses, and, in particular, whether it anticipates and invites counterargument. At the same time, I believe that persuasiveness itself is a profoundly conventional notion, a reflection of cultural and historical attitudes. "Each

kind of rhetoric has its own appropriate style": Aristotle was thinking of the difference between speech and writing, oratory and composition. But if we equate the word "style" with something like Foucault's *epistème*—the manner of thinking characteristic of a given era—the dictum takes on a powerful new resonance. Saussure, Jakobson, and Chomsky have created a new *epistème* for our generation. Their manner of thinking has provoked upheavals in many disciplines impinging on literature and the arts. The literary critical establishment in America and England—with some notable exceptions—has not entirely welcomed these efforts. Ignoring them will not make them go away. But serious challenges will help deflate their less justifiable pretensions and will sophisticate *everyone's* way of looking at literature. Only good can come of theoretical debate, if the debate is honest, tolerant and objective. No man can read, see, hear all the narratives ever composed, so in a directly practical sense theory depends on the experience of a community of scholars, critics as well as theorists. When critics provide me with interesting examples that my theory does not accommodate, I can only feel grateful for the chance to improve it. In return, I would hope to provide terms that will meet their requirements, terms that have been hardened on the anvil of theoretical debate, so that they can genuinely trust them for their proper work, the elucidation and evaluation of texts.

DIAGRAM OF NARRATIVE STRUCTURE

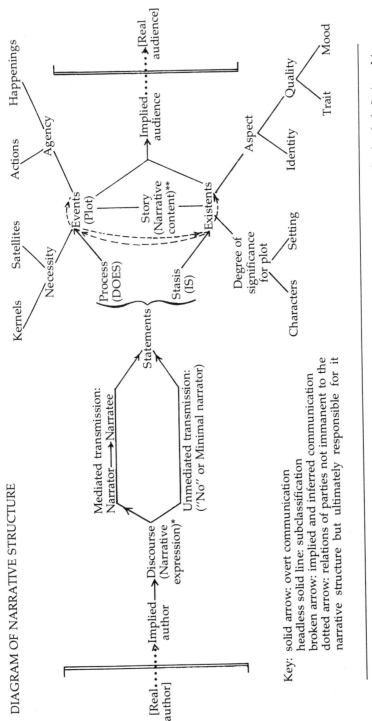

Key: solid arrow: overt communication
headless solid line: subclassification
broken arrow: implied and inferred communication
dotted arrow: relations of parties not immanent to the
narrative structure but ultimately responsible for it

*This is the form of narrative expression; its *substance* or manifestation appears in various media (verbal: fiction, his-tory; visual: paintings, comic strips; audio-visual: cinema, etc.).
**This is the form of the content not its substance.

INDEX

Author and Title

INDEX

Subject

STORY AND DISCOURSE

Designed by Elizabeth Leah Anderson

Composed by G & S Typesetters, Inc., in 10 point VIP Palatino,
2 points leaded, with display lines in Palatino.

Printed offset by Thomson-Shore, Inc.
on Warren's No. 66 Antique Offset text, 50 lb. basis.

Bound by John H. Dekker & Sons, Inc., in Joanna book cloth
and stamped in All Purpose foil.

ALSO BY SEYMOUR CHATMAN

A Theory of Meter
Essays on the Language of Literature (edited with Samuel Levin)
Literary Style: A Symposium (edited and translated)
The Later Style of Henry James

STORY AND DISCOURSE

*Narrative Structure
in Fiction and Film*

W9-CDB-717